News Parody and Political Satire Across the Globe

Edited by
Geoffrey Baym and Jeffrey P. Jones

Routledge
Taylor & Francis Group

LONDON AND NEW YORK

First published 2013
by Routledge
2 Park Square, Milton Park, Abingdon, Oxon, OX14 4RN

Simultaneously published in the USA and Canada
by Routledge
711 Third Avenue, New York, NY 10017

First issued in paperback 2017

Routledge is an imprint of the Taylor & Francis Group, an informa business

This book is a reproduction of *Popular Communication*, volume 10, issues 1-2. The Publisher requests to those authors who may be citing this book to state, also, the bibliographical details of the special issue on which the book was based.

British Library Cataloguing in Publication Data
A catalogue record for this book is available from the British Library

Typeset in Times New Roman
by Taylor & Francis Books

Publisher's Note
The publisher would like to make readers aware that the chapters in this book may be referred to as articles as they are identical to the articles published in the special issue. The publisher accepts responsibility for any inconsistencies that may have arisen in the course of preparing this volume for print.

ISBN 13: 978-1-138-10937-7 (pbk)
ISBN 13: 978-0-415-69293-9 (hbk)

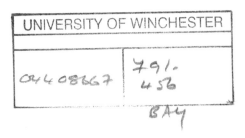

News Parody and Political Satire Across the Globe

In recent years, the US fake news program *The Daily Show with Jon Stewart* has become a surprisingly important source of information, conversation, and commentary about public affairs. Perhaps more surprisingly, so-called 'fake news' is now a truly global phenomenon, with various forms of news parody and political satire programming appearing throughout the world.

This collection of innovative chapters takes a close and critical look at global news parody from a wide range of countries including the USA and the UK, Italy and France, Hungary and Romania, Israel and Palestine, Iran and India, Australia, Germany, and Denmark. Traversing a range of national cultures, political systems, and programming forms, *News Parody and Political Satire Across the Globe* offers insight into the central and perhaps controversial role that news parody has come to play in the world, and explores the multiple forces that enable and constrain its performance. It will help readers to better understand the intersections of journalism, politics, and comedy as they take shape across the globe in a variety of political and media systems.

This book was originally published as a special issue of the journal *Popular Communication*.

Geoffrey Baym is Associate Professor of Media Studies at the University of North Carolina-Greensboro, USA. He is the author of *From Cronkite to Colbert: The Evolution of Broadcast News* (2010) and numerous articles and book chapters on the changing nature of news media and political discourse.

Jeffrey P. Jones is Director of the Institute of Humanities at Old Dominion University, USA. The author of *Entertaining Politics: Satiric Television and Political Engagement, 2nd edition* (2010), he is also co-editor of *Satire TV: Politics and Comedy in the Post-Network Era* (2009) and *The Essential HBO Reader* (2008).

Contents

CONTENTS

Citation Information

The chapters in this book were all originally published in the journal *Popular Communication*, volume 10, issues 1-2 (February 2012). When citing this material, please use the original page numbering for each article, as follows:

Chapter 1
News Parody in Global Perspective: Politics, Power, and Resistance
Geoffrey Baym and Jeffrey P. Jones
Popular Communication, volume 10, issues 1-2 (February 2012)
pp. 2-13

Chapter 2
"Find Out Exactly What to Think—Next!": Chris Morris, *Brass Eye,* and Journalistic Authority
Graham Meikle
Popular Communication, volume 10, issues 1-2 (February 2012)
pp. 14-26

Chapter 3
From the "Little Aussie Bleeder" to *Newstopia*: (Really) Fake News in Australia
Stephen Harrington
Popular Communication, volume 10, issues 1-2 (February 2012)
pp. 27-39

Chapter 4
No Strings Attached? *Les Guignols de l'info* and French Television
Waddick Doyle
Popular Communication, volume 10, issues 1-2 (February 2012)
pp. 40-51

Chapter 5
The Comical Inquisition: *Striscia la Notizia* and the Politics of Fake News on Italian Television
Gabriele Cosentino
Popular Communication, volume 10, issues 1-2 (February 2012)
pp. 52-65

Hanne Bruun
Popular Communication, volume 10, issues 1-2 (February 2012)
pp. 158-169

Chapter 14
Live From New York, It's the Fake News! *Saturday Night Live* and the (Non)Politics of Parody
Amber Day and Ethan Thompson
Popular Communication, volume 10, issues 1-2 (February 2012)
pp. 170-182

Notes on Contributors

Alice Bardan is Assistant Lecturer in the Department of English at the University of Southern California, USA.

Geoffrey Baym is Associate Professor of Media Studies at the University of North Carolina-Greensboro, USA.

Hanne Bruun is Associate Professor in the Department of Information and Media Studies at the University of Aarhus, Denmark.

Gabriele Cosentino is Assistant Professor of Communications and Media Studies at John Cabot University, Italy.

Amber Day is Assistant Professor in the English and Cultural Studies Department at Bryant University, USA.

Waddick Doyle is Associate Professor of Communications at the American University of Paris, France.

Stephen Harrington is Lecturer and Subject Area Coordinator in Media and Communication in the Creative Industries Faculty at Queensland University of Technology, Australia.

Anikó Imre is Associate Professor and Director of Graduate Studies at the University of Southern California, USA.

Jeffrey P. Jones is Director of the Institute of Humanities at Old Dominion University, USA.

Guido Keel is Lecturer and Senior Researcher in the Institute of Applied Media Studies at Zurich University of Applied Sciences, Switzerland.

Katharina Kleinen-von Königslöw is Senior Research Assistant in the Department of Communication at the University of Vienna, Austria.

Sangeet Kumar is Assistant Professor in the Communication Department at Denison University, USA.

Graham Meikle is Senior Lecturer in the Department of Communications, Media and Culture at the University of Stirling, UK.

Mehdi Semati is Associate Professor in the Department of Communication at Northern Illinois University, USA.

Limor Shifman is a Lecturer in the Department of Communication and Journalism at the Hebrew University of Jerusalem, Israel.

Matt Sienkiewicz is Assistant Professor of Communication and International Studies at Boston College, USA.

Ethan Thompson is Associate Professor of Communication at Texas A&M University – Corpus Christi, USA.

News Parody in Global Perspective: Politics, Power, and Resistance

Geoffrey Baym

Jeffrey P. Jones

As scholarly examinations of the US news parody programs *The Daily Show* and *The Colbert Report* multiply, we must recognize that American satirists claim no monopoly on the genre. Upon closer inspection, news parody appears as a truly universal phenomenon; in any culture where television is used as a means of disseminating authoritative information about the real, parody—what some have labeled, or mislabeled "fake news"—plays an increasingly important discursive function. In this article, we provide an overview of international forms of news parody and political satire as they take shape across continents and cultures. We consider the global flow of parody formats, and the multiple ways in which news parody adapts to differing political, economic, and regulatory contexts. Further, we explore the semiotic labor that parody performs in deconstructing broadcast news and wider discourses of authority. Finally, we discuss the political significance of global news parody and the role the genre plays as a popular response to power.

In the midst of the UK phone-hacking scandal that consumed international attention in the summer of 2011, an interesting issue arose on the globally popular US news parody program *The Daily Show with Jon Stewart*. In late July, when British Prime Minister David Cameron was called before a testy House of Commons to defend his relationship with agents of Rupert Murdoch's News Corporation, *The Daily Show* ran a montage of Cameron facing a barrage of heated comments, to which Stewart gleefully proclaimed, "England is *awesome!*" Despite the satirical praise, viewers in the United Kingdom who tuned in to the weekly global edition of the program usually broadcast on Channel 4 were not able to see that particular segment—a point Stewart himself incredulously discussed on his show a couple of weeks later. Then, he explained that although the global edition of *TDS* is aired in 85 countries around the world, "including," Stewart noted, "such free speech havens as, I don't know, Chad, Somalia, Saudi Arabia, Syria, and Yemen"—"I'm huge in Yemen," he jested—British rules prevented a UK audience from seeing his friendly, although satirical, treatment of Parliament.

The reason, partially explained by Stewart, is that although Parliament agreed in 1989 to allow television cameras into its chambers, it explicitly forbade the use of that footage "in any light entertainment program or in a program of political satire." Hoping to preserve the dignity of political power, the "rules of coverage" concede that Parliamentary footage may be used "in broadcast 'magazine' programs which also contain music or humorous features, provided that the different types of item are kept separate."[1] On *TDS*, a puzzled Stewart insisted that he had seen "parliamentary footage used on satirical shows in Britain before," a claim supported by a clip of a grotesque (and quite rubbery) "Margaret Thatcher" scolding a room full of equally grotesque (and rubbery) British lawmakers. That clip, of course, was from the long running and globally influential satire show *Spitting Image*, which for eight years skewered British politicians with its now-iconic puppetry.

Along with his homage to *Spitting Image*, Stewart's brief discussion of his own global reach and the British rules governing satire raise a number of points that the contributions to this collection explore. At the least, the reference to *Spitting Image* reminds us that *TDS* did not invent political TV satire, or as we will see, news parody. Indeed, most efforts to trace the origins of the genre wind back to the United Kingdom, whose creative comedic minds have over the years helped pioneer the blurring of news and entertainment and the use of television comedy to poke at, if not outright undermine, the conventions and pretensions of so much of what passes on television as "news." At the same time, Stewart's reference to the 85 countries that broadcast *The Daily Show's Global Edition* makes the point that news parody, even a program aimed so clearly at an American audience, resonates around the world. Even in countries as nondemocratic and, one might suspect, as humorless as, say, Somalia, one can find a comedian making serious fun of politicians and the news media that cover them. Indeed, as some of the authors in this collection suggest, it may be particularly in countries lacking healthy democratic debate where news parody plays its most vital role.

Third, Stewart's abbreviated discussion of the British rules governing the use of Parliamentary footage make it clear that even in one of the world's oldest democracies and in the culture that has historically made a primary contribution to the genre of television parody, satirists must always work within the political, legal, and regulatory context that both enables and often constrains what they can do. As we will see, producers of parody must negotiate a myriad of contextual frameworks—legal but also economic and cultural—that encourage some kinds of parody while dissuading others. Finally, the Stewart-Parliament incident demonstrates that beyond decorum and the belief that the serious work of governance demands a "discourse of sobriety" (Nichols, 1991), the British rules of coverage implicitly recognize the power of the popular and the underlying danger that parody can pose for the status quo.

This collection takes up these issues. We begin from the fundamental point that "the news"—as perhaps the most ubiquitous form of television programming found throughout the world—is also one of the most parodied television genres as well. What is more, such parodic and satirical response is truly a global phenomenon. Despite the considerable amount of scholarly attention paid to North American programs such as *The Daily Show*, little attention has been paid to news parody across national and regional contexts. We have little understanding of the number and

---

[1] See http://www.parliament.the-stationery-office.co.uk/pa/cm200203/cmselect/cmbroad/786/78608.htm. For consistency, the British spelling of "programme" has been changed to American style.

range of parody programs one can find on televisions around the world, let alone of the similarities and differences among various global approaches. We have yet to consider what gives rise to such programming in countries with radically different media systems, political arrangements, and cultural contexts or why, broadly defined, the genre itself has become universally popular. Nor have we explored the multiple ways that such programs offer critiques and negotiate power. Through case studies of news parody in countries as diverse as the United Kingdom, Hungary, Italy, Palestine, India, and Iran, this project seeks to enhance our understanding of the intersections of news, comedy, and politics, as well as the power and possibilities of parody.

From a definitional perspective, we intentionally cast a wide net, recognizing that news parody is and can comprise many textual forms, from faux news anchors who posture authoritatively at pretend news desks, to puppet shows, sketch comedies, and panel discussions. As editors, one of our initial challenges was learning to see beyond our own assumptions of what constitutes parody and recognize the ways in which our own political, economic, and cultural context has shaped those assumptions. Thus we have not found it useful to categorize at the micro-level the varying types of programming that formalists might want to identify as say, satire or parody, social or political satire, and "fake news" or humorous discussions of the news. Instead, the key ingredient for us is that the programming we examine here uses humor to engage with, and offer critiques of, contemporary political life and current events. Hence "news parody" becomes an umbrella term for what at times can vary quite significantly in practice. While many programs discussed here do, in fact, employ a fake news style (similar to *The Daily Show*) in direct parody of the television news form, others use quite different methods (puppets, for example) in pursuit of similar goals.

Similarly, the programs covered here vary in the nature of their critique, ranging from the banal to the brutal. For instance, even within the context of US media, we see such extremes when comparing *Saturday Night Live's* "Weekend Update" and *The Colbert Report*. The former is longer running and much more familiar to popular audiences, yet the latter would be far more valued if one were strictly interested in *political* significance. In short, our operative mode in this project is expansive, rather than restrictive. We include forms of parody and satire that are *meaningful to audiences* within respective countries and satirical traditions; we do not attempt to impose narrow formalistic definitions to satisfy academic yearnings for clean typologies.

PARODY MATTERS

In our efforts to make sense of the wide and long-standing appeal of news parody and political satire across the globe, we begin from the fundamental assumption that parody is a serious matter, that it is, to quote Robert Hariman (2008), "essential for an engaged, sustainable, democratic public culture" (p. 248). Mikhail Bakhtin (1981) also reminds us that laughter is a form of resistance to power, and parody a critical means of confronting and deconstructing discourses of authority. We find it sensible, then, that *news* parody would resonate across a vast range of national and regional contexts. Itself a ubiquitous form of programming worldwide, television news constitutes a core aspect of public life—a central discursive locale for the circulation of information and argument fundamental to democratic (or, as some of the chapters in this collection suggest, *democratizing*) practice. At the same time, however, news is also a product of power. It always asserts the epistemological privilege of claiming "the way it is," and offers those in positions of power, both political and economic, an authoritative platform for the shaping of public perceptions.

For the many manifestations of news and public affairs parody one can find around the world, the basic assumption that a democratic populace needs what James Madison once called a "source of popular information" (quoted in Alger, 1998, p. 4) serves as the launching point for critique of the actual sources of popular information, an examination, in varying degrees of acuity, of news practices in a variety of settings. In his contribution to this collection, for example, Graham Meikle explores the critique offered by the British comedian Chris Morris, one of the sharpest interlocutors of "the news." Meikle argues that in his remarkable series *Brass Eye* (and before that *The Day Today*), Morris quite insightfully exposes the conventions of overly sensationalized and often breathless television news: its dramatic music, its thrilling if not always meaningful graphics, and its mode of address—its often explicit claim that, as an institution nominally committed to the public good, it is looking out for *you*. *Brass Eye*, Meikle suggests, "is a sustained exposure of the machinery" of broadcast news, exaggerating the conventions of news and current affairs programming until their "constructed nature becomes both apparent and absurd."

One sees something similar in a remarkable range of cultural contexts, from the work of the Danish comedian Mikael Bertelsen, whose show *De Uaktuelle Nyheder* translates roughly to "News of No Current Interest," to the recently launched German version of *The Daily Show*, to any number of Australian "fake news" programs, which as Stephen Harrington explains in this issue, have long functioned to expose the "vanity and phoniness" of Australian broadcast news, its mistaking of production quality for informational value. The central thrust of news parody, therefore, and perhaps the meat of its popular appeal is its work in deconstructing the artifice of news—the naturalistic illusion that news is (or could be) an unmediated window on the world ("Give us 30 minutes," the US CNN Headline News once insisted, "and we'll give you the world"). Even on the "Weekend Update" segment on the long-running US program *Saturday Night Live*, which as we have already suggested counts among the more banal forms of news parody, its hosts have reveled in revealing their own artifice ("I'm Chevy Chase and you're not"), a comment on the undeniable, if often elided fact, that they, along with the real TV journalists, are always performing for the camera. Amber Day and Ethan Thompson argue here that on "Weekend Update" the intention has been less a parody of the news for the sake of political critique, but instead a vehicle to achieve other comedic, programming, and franchise branding strategies. In Italy, however, as Gabriele Cosentino explains in his contribution to this special issue, the popular program *Striscia la Notizia* ("The News is Creeping") was created specifically to expose the artifice of news, and to undermine its ideological underpinnings. "You'd be watching the newscasts, thinking to simply receive news," the show's creator, Antonio Ricci, has written, "instead they're selling you a political idea, and a car too."

With several of the parodic programs considered in this collection, the focus shifts from the form of news to its content, from the *ways* in which news speaks, to that which it *speaks of*. News parody offers critical examination of both the information provided by the real news and the agendas that lie behind or beneath it. As regular viewers of *The Daily Show* in the United States have come to recognize, news parody not only exposes the machinery of news but in its more piercing forms also can confront the broader machinery of public discourse. We find several examples of parody interrogating the efforts by those in positions of power to shape popular understanding of the political sphere. We see this at its sharpest in the Iranian program

Parazit (arriving via satellite and avenues of social media), which, as Mehdi Semati explains here, routinely confronts the explicit efforts of Iran's theocratic regime to control public information.

Even in its least acute forms, where parody is less explicitly engaged in the semiotic struggle over public influence, it routinely provides opportunities simply for citizens to laugh at those who populate the narratives of news. As we see in discussions of programs in countries as diverse as France, Israel, and India, news parody is a comedic response to the ubiquity of images and the celebration of celebrity—entertainment and political stars alike—and the power both hold as foci of societal discourse. The shows present an opportunity for comeuppance, a means though which audiences are invited to reinterpret, ridicule, and challenge the characters that populate citizens' public imaginations.

In addition to its deconstructive function—its efforts to unpack the form and content of news—news parody at times performs a constructive role, providing the citizenry with discursive resources often absent in "real" news. Jon Stewart, of course, has been ranked among the most trusted "journalists" in the United States. In Italy, that honor remarkably has gone to the giant red puppet Gabibbo, the star of the show *Striscia,* who actively solicits tips for potential news stories. Public opinion polls in Italy find that people more readily communicate their concerns to Gabibbo than they do to the country's real journalists. In turn, the show has, over the years, been credited with breaking several important national stories. So, too, following the model of Jon Stewart's interviews on *The Daily Show*, are increasing numbers of parodic programs offering real conversations with serious political figures. In such a discursively integrated landscape, it becomes increasingly difficult to identify the boundaries between real news and fake news, between parody and its referent.

News parody, therefore, ultimately functions as a kind of epistemological leveling—a challenge, if not inversion, of what Michel Foucault (1980) called "regimes of truth." The various comedians, actors, and puppets around the world who use parody to interrogate the news are at the same time both constitutive and constituent of wider cultural transformations in the nature of public trust and the allocation of authority. Parody rejects the verticality and linearity of news—the built-in assumption that *they*, from positions of privilege, speak (down) to *us*, and that we, in turn, have little role in the process but as passive receivers of their truths. Parody becomes a public response, sometimes through the "talking back" it provides and sometimes simply as a means of "talking to" and "talking with." Whichever way, news parody is a practice that invites a communal challenge to both the form and substance of an authorized discourse so central to power. The possibilities for humor within that context seem limitless.

A BRIEF OVERVIEW

Perhaps the seminal program in the genre was the early 1960s BBC program *That Was The Week That Was*. Although it only ran from 1962 to 1963, *TW3* (as the program was popularly known) introduced a radically new way of talking about politics on television—a hybrid blend of news, political conversation, and comedy that challenged the serious, formal, and hierarchical approach to news and political talk characteristic of the time. Presented by David Frost, whose own career has repeatedly crossed the boundaries between journalism and entertainment, *TW3* would spur numerous international imitations or interpretations. Frost himself contributed to an American version of the show, which ran on US television from 1964 to 1965 and featured, among many others, comedians Buck Henry, Alan Alda, and Henry Morgan. At the same time, a variation on *TW3* called *This Hour Has Seven Days* had a brief run on Canadian television.

TW3 would lay the groundwork for further innovations in the emerging genres of parody news and televisual political satire, both in England and abroad. In the mid-1970s, the US sketch comedy program *Saturday Night Live* first offered its parody segment "Weekend Update," which still today remains a central element of the show. A few years later, the BBC would produce a harder-edged version of *TW3*, this time called *Not the Nine O'Clock News*. That program also was imported to the United States in the much more banal form of HBO's *Not Necessarily the News*. More recently, the satirist Chris Morris has stood at the cutting edge of British news parody with his 1990s programs *The Day Today* and *Brass Eye*. In the United States, of course, Jon Stewart and Stephen Colbert continue to build on the tradition, while in Canada the comedian Rick Mercer hosts the self-titled *Rick Mercer Report*, a program that bares many similarities to *The Daily Show*. Mercer rose to fame for his role on the other Canadian mock news program *This Hour Has 22 Minutes*, itself a reinvention of the 1960s satirical program *This Hour Has Seven Days* (Day, 2011; Tinic, 2009). Australia equally has a lengthy tradition of news parody, embodied most recently in the experimental program *NEWStopia*, which aired from 2007 to 2008.

Television producers in the United Kingdom also developed a quite different but equally significant model of parodic TV with the 1980s program *Spitting Image*. During its eight-year run, the show used surrealistic puppets to caricature and critique politicians and public figures. Despite, or perhaps because of its controversial nature, it attracted weekly audiences as large as 12 million people and won an International Emmy award for "Outstanding Popular Arts." As with other versions of British satire, the program also spawned numerous international versions in countries as disparate as the United States, Russia, and Israel. In the late 1980s, French television producers would launch their own version of a satirical puppet show with *Les Guignols*, a program that remains on air today. As with *Spitting Image*, *Les Guignols* has been recreated in a range of other countries, some as close as next-door Spain, others as far away (both geographically and culturally) as Cameroon and India.

As these examples make clear, news parody hardly has been an English-only phenomenon. Something similar can be found in Italy, for example, with the already mentioned program *Striscia* and its star, the puppet Gabibbo. In Mexico, an edgy and at times subversive clown named "Brozo" has been a mainstay on television over the past 20 years. For a decade, Brozo— whose name is a play both on the American television clown "Bozo" and on the Mexican concept of "la Broza" or the lower class—hosted the morning talk show *El Mañanero* (slang for quick morning sex) in which he offered a bawdy and rambunctious interrogation of politics and current events. More recently, Brozo has appeared on a weekly prime-time news parody program entitled *El Notifiero*, which translates roughly into "The News on Fire" (Ruggiero, 2007). In South America, one can find a number of versions of the program known on Brazilian television as *Custe o que Custar* ("No Matter the Cost"). Drawing on the original Argentinean version, the show features a number of studio anchors and "reporters" who together cover the news, critique politics, and interview public figures. In just a few years, the show has become highly viewed, and its format exported around the world. In addition to Argentina and Brazil, variations appear in Chile, Italy, France, and Spain, and the production company has sold the rights to an as-of-yet undeveloped US version.

We also find news parody in what we thought would be unlikely places. Several of the young democracies of Eastern Europe, for example, have their own versions of parody and political satire programming. On the Hungarian commercial television program *Heti Hetes* ("The Witty Seven"), a panel of seven well-known Hungarian celebrities, whose public personae date back to the country's socialist past, dissect the news. That program bears similarity to Bill Maher's work in the United States but more directly can be traced to the program *7 Tage – 7 Köpfe* ("7 Days – 7 Heads"), which aired on the German television network RTL. Similarly, in Romania, the program *Cronica Carcotasilor* ("The Nagger's Chronicles") draws on the Italian program *Striscia* to criticize Romanian politics, media, and popular culture.

So too has news parody become a staple on television across the non- or emerging democratic nations in the Middle East. These include the war-torn country of Afghanistan, where the show *Zang-e-Khatar* ("Danger Bell") has been called Afghanistan's answer to *The Daily Show*, and is pushing the boundaries of public political criticism. In Iraq, the private Al-Sharqiya network, the country's first privately owned television operation, likes to call itself "the voice of the people," largely for its blend of objective news, cultural criticism, and political satire. The Palestinian Authority uneasily celebrated *Watan Ala Watar* ("Country Hanging by a Thread") as a symbol of its political opening but then shuttered the program when the authorities found the commentary threatening to its relations with other Arab nations. Quite differently, the Iranian program *Parazit* (which translates alternately as "static" or "jamming"—as in signal, or *culture* jamming) is produced in the United States by expatriate Iranians and transmitted via satellite into Iran (in opposition to Iranian law), with financial and technological assistance from the United States government.

GLOBAL FLOWS/LOCAL CULTURES

The story of transnational news parody is thus necessarily a story of global programming flows. Historically, the British *TW3* inspired versions across the English-speaking world. Both the British puppet show *Spitting Image* and the French program *Les Guingols* also have moved around the world—the latter quite intentionally, as its production company has formal agreements (including the providing of training in building and maintaining the cast of puppets) with counterparts in several countries. Currently, *The Daily Show* is being imitated and reproduced with varying degrees of resemblance. In German, as Katharina Kleinen-von Königslöw and Guido Keel explain in their article in this special issue, the *heute show*, which translates literally to "The Daily Show," is remarkably similar in form and content to the original. On a regional level, as noted above, Hungarian producers have reworked a format from Germany; Romania one from Italy.

In each instance, part of the power of news parody seems to lie in its portability, its ability to cross national, cultural, and linguistic boundaries. In each instance of global format transfer, the original is reinterpreted within older national-cultural artistic and performative traditions. Thus parody programs in Germany, Denmark, and Hungary draw on those countries' tradition of political cabaret. Parody in India speaks to that country's historical, anti-colonial oppositional press. Indian parody also draws, as does parody in Romania and Palestine, on far older satirical literary traditions. Particularly in postcolonial and postsocialist countries, the producers of parody meld global forms with local traditions particularly to address and mediate national fissures.

7

In India, as Sangeet Kumar discusses in this issue, competing news parody programs negotiate the linguistic and cultural divides of postcolonial Indian life, including splits in language (English versus Hindi), geography (urban versus rural), and politics (foreign versus domestic). In Hungary and Romania (as Anikó Imre and Alice Bardan argue, respectively), satiric programming produces a form of national intimacy, a play and usage of language as a means of contesting and negotiating challenges to national identity presented by postsocialist life. In Israel, parody programs have played an important role in helping the populace negotiate its national identity and its relationship to the surrounding Arab world. In sum, what the contributions to this special issue help us understand is that news parodies play a broader role in mediating and negotiating cultural issues both within and beyond the formal political field.

POLITICAL ECONOMIES

As parody flows across national identities and cultural traditions, it equally transcends political-economic systems, from advanced capitalist democracies, to postcolonial and postsocialist countries, to emerging democracies, and, with financing from other nations and the use of technological means to transcend geographic boundaries, even to authoritarian regimes. The contributions to this special issue demonstrate how and why such usages address differing needs and operate within different political-economic constraints.

In countries where monopolistic public service broadcasting channels began facing competition from private commercial networks, for example, news parody often became central to those competitive battles. Whereas political and entertainment programming historically had been clearly segregated in the public systems, commercial channels attempted to demonstrate their distinctiveness by blending the two through parodic news programming. In the process, they also sought to attract younger audiences who had tired of the well-worn discourse of authoritative state lecturing through public channel news and documentary. Because the still-dominant location for news was on the state channels, the emphasis on news parody became a not-so-subtle means of questioning the authority not just of the news but also of the state control of broadcasting more broadly, achieved in part by directly counterprogramming parody against the public channel's news hour. Yet by offering political content, however entertaining, private channels could also demonstrate that they provided audiences with some degree of politically relevant programming and were not (as previously feared) just purveyors of mindless entertainment. This was especially true in France, as Waddick Doyle explains in this issue, where cultural legitimization was as important as the legal authority to broadcast.

One sees the same thing in Italy, although there, parodic news on the commercial channel also served the interests of Silvio Berlusconi, who not coincidentally owned the private commercial competitor, by undermining the voices of his critics on public broadcasting. In Israel, as Limor Shifman discusses in this issue, the types of satire airing on commercial and public systems differed, depending on how the programming served the broader needs of the channel. The satiric content on the public channel tended to refer back intertextually to other popular cultural figures who appeared on the channel, serving a quasi-promotional function. On the private channel, satire has tended toward the fantastic and the fictional, thereby helping the channel elide partisan criticisms entirely. In the United States, *The Daily Show* has helped solidify the economic position of Comedy Central (and in turn, enhanced the value of the parent company Viacom). "Weekend Update" long helped *Saturday Night Live* and the NBC television network achieve a variety of commercial goals. Finally, in India, as Kumar notes, the parodic news programs actually appear *on* the 24-hour news channels themselves, further effacing distinctions between informing citizens and entertaining consumers. In sum, beyond the value of political critique, news parody often has played an important economic function, including its role in branding, attracting particularly profitable demographics, competing against public broadcasting, and securing the cultural legitimacy of its producers.

This discussion also emphasizes the interweaving of technology—in particular satellite television distribution—in the conditions of economic competition and struggles over cultural legitimacy. In Europe, public systems often have been resistant to strong political satire programming (as has been the case with Germany and Denmark). However, as technologically enabled competition encouraged private channels to offer parody, public channels in turn often felt pressure to invigorate their approaches to public affairs. In Palestine, technology and political autonomy present an even more interesting dialectic. As Matt Sienkiewicz notes in his contribution to this special issue, the Palestinian Authority (PA) attempted to demonstrate its openness as a liberal democracy by allowing satirical programming that was quite critical of the government. Yet when such criticisms extended to regional rulers during the Arab Spring, the PA shut down the program. But digital technologies—in particular social media outlets—have proven difficult for the PA to control and contain, and thus the programming lives on (at least in re-runs) outside its borders. Similarly, the program *Parazit* is not only transmitted into Iran via satellite but also is accessible to tech-savvy Iranian audiences through Facebook, YouTube, and bootleg DVDs. As such, the program exists as a contemporary form of *samizdat*, but one where the funders—the US government, through the Voice of America—invite dissent not through the old methods of polemics or information, but rather, through mockery. Such an approach has the additional benefit of crafting popular cultural appeal; as Mehdi Semati notes, young Iranians have taken to imitating the clothing and expressions of the show's hosts as a means of exchanging dissent. In short, technology has been a driving force in the development and dissemination of news parody, irrespective of government approval.

POLITICAL ENGAGEMENT

As we traverse the wide range of parody programs produced in and for differing governmental structures and media systems, it becomes clear that parody has also become an increasingly central mechanism for public engagement with the state, and the formal realm of legislative and electoral politics. In the United States, for example, where Jon Stewart regularly interviews national politicians and power brokers, scholarly speculation abounds that *The Daily Show* is influencing what people know about politics and the degree to which citizens—especially, but not only, the young ones—are interested in the political process (Holbert, Lambe, Dudo, & Carlton, 2007; Xenos & Becker, 2009). Although arguments diverge as to whether that influence is positive or negative, it seems a clear point of agreement that, as the US public service journalist Bill Moyers once said, "You simply can't understand American politics in the new millennium without *The Daily Show*" (PBS, 2003). The articles in this special issue make it equally clear that the political relevance of news parody is a global condition.

The role of news parody in serving as an intermediary between publics and their states in turn raises two interrelated issues. On one hand, it highlights the extent to which parody facilitates public involvement in electoral politics and legislative processes in ways the "real" news might not. In Germany, for example, broadcasters and politicians alike have begun to think carefully about the *heute show*—the German adaptation of *The Daily Show*. As Katharina Kleinen-von Königslöw and Guido Keel explain in this issue, the public broadcaster ZDF has embraced the show, hoping it might have the ability to re-energize political engagement among young Germans, who like their counterparts in many advanced democratic states, have increasingly tuned out from the traditional public sphere.

On the other hand, this asks us to seriously consider the role news parody plays in actually influencing elections and legislation. In the United States, Jon Stewart has long argued that his show has no political influence, an assertion some suggest is a form of political cover to ensure the program maintains its comedic freedom (Baym, 2005). The comedian Chevy Chase, who first hosted *Saturday Night Live's* "Weekend Update," denied that his fake news could have any real effect, although, as Day and Thompson tell us here, he also speculated that his relentless parody of then-President Gerald Ford led to the incumbent's loss in the 1976 election. In Israel, meanwhile, as Shifman tells us, the puppet show *Hartzufim* was credited with ruining the public image of one powerful Israeli politician, but improving public sentiment toward Yasser Arafat. Similarly, Doyle explains that 15% of French voters said the puppet show *Les Guignols* influenced their choice in that country's 2002 presidential election. Perhaps for these reasons, German politicians at least are weary of the fake news. There, for instance, a member of parliament warned the country's finance minister to be careful in his speech on nuclear energy because it inevitably would be examined "line-by-line" on the *heute show*.

Of course, politicians the world over understand that as popular entertainment shows, news parodies also offer unique opportunities for them to brandish their public image and influence the national conversation among demographic groups other than those traditionally attendant to news. Thus, in Denmark, as Hanne Bruun tells us, politicians both right and left and even the country's prime minister played along with surreal studio interviews with the comedian Mikael Bertelsen, whose interview style seems similar to Stephen Colbert's approach in his bizarre "Better Know a District" segments (Baym, 2007). Perhaps more bizarre, as Kumar notes, Indian politicians regularly appear on the Hindi-language puppet program *Gustakhi Maaf*, where they talk to themselves, or at least themselves in latex form (viewers of *The Daily Show* might remember something similar when the former Republican National Committee chairman Michael Steele appeared alongside the Muppet-style puppet the program had created in his image). In the United States, politicians have for several years seen *Saturday Night Live* as a safe kind of playground, even when their comedic doppelganger has stood right beside them (e.g., with Tina Fey mocking Sarah Palin, and Amy Poehler impersonating Hillary Clinton).

Palin's appearance on *SNL* seems remarkable given the fact that both Fey and Poehler had earlier used the show to endorse Hillary Clinton. That point in turn raises the core question of whether news parody has a political agenda of its own. Jon Stewart consistently rejects efforts to label him as "liberal," although his policy preferences (discernible from the serious arguments he makes) lean progressive. In France, the agenda has been far more transparent—the writers of *Les Guignols* have used the show actively to work against right-wing parties and candidates. In Italy, however, while the program *Striscia* postures as neutral, spreading its ridicule across the political spectrum, it has been remarkably tame in criticizing former Prime Minister Berlusconi, who owns the channel on which it airs. Constentino explains here that the show's creator has sought to promote a market logic toward political power, an agenda that undoubtedly has served the interests of Berlusconi's media and political empire. Yet among the programs considered in this collection, the most explicit political agenda is located in the US-produced and financed Iranian program *Parazit*. Explicitly crafted as a 21st century form of political propaganda, it uses humor instead of polemics to (as the show itself asserts in its opening) "tickle the foundation of power" and "install a government with the help of the people."

CONCLUSION: PARODY, POWER, RESISTANCE

Although specific functions differ from country to country, nearly all of the manifestations of news parody we encounter here sit in necessary relation with—both as reaction to and creation of—shifting parameters of trust toward representational institutions. Amid what Bakhtin (1981) might have called a *centrifugal* age, marked by the cultural and discursive forces of decentralization, parody focuses what Imre calls a "posttrust lens" on the political domain. It encapsulates a search for truth and meaning in a time when populations have grown increasingly suspicious that traditional discourses no longer suffice. In many of the examples explored here, news parody can be seen as a means for addressing the delegitimized role of news media as de facto public proxies—a core aspect of broader representational crises common across many national and cultural boundaries. News parody thus often serves a watchdog function by monitoring and exposing media excess and artifice, strategically aiming its sights on the machinery of news and current affairs programming that routinely make claims on the real. So, too, does parody quite often use the form of news to take aim at its discourse—at the rhetoric of officialdom that is regularly circulated and amplified by television news.

Of course, not all parody is necessarily acute. Much is trite, seeking little more than a laugh, or an audience share. Other forms have served the interests of economic power, functioning as a means to help undermine cultural trust in traditional public systems. At its sharpest, however, parody is an increasingly significant form of cultural and political resistance. The power of parody lies in its ability to turn hegemonic discourses upon themselves (see Baym, 2010; Day, 2011; Jones, 2010). Citing the work of Boyer and Yurchack (2010), Imre and Bardan both argue that mediated western political discourse has become increasingly similar to that found in late-socialist countries, where official language (of politicians, but also news media) has become hypernormalized, ideologically rigid, performative, and largely devoid of meaning. Under such conditions, a strategy of resistance used in late-socialist society was parody that did its work by *inhabiting* the norm itself, that is, overidentifying with the subject or discourse as a way of breaking traditional interpretive frames. The author Marcel Proust once wrote (as is popularly translated), "The real voyage of discovery consists not in seeking new landscapes but in having new eyes." Thus the parodist inhabits a familiar landscape, but through ridicule, offers new ways of seeing the form of that landscape and the language that inhabits it.

If one can draw connections between parody in late-socialist Eastern Europe and that in the contemporary advanced capitalist democracies of the west, the contributions here further demonstrate that news parody has become what Harrington refers to as a "global television language," or a central textual form in what Semati describes as "global intertextuality." Not only are news parodies one of the more popular transnationally circulated texts, but they also comprise a way in which people across various political, cultural, and social systems have come to talk about, comment upon, and at times take action against the discourses that shape their lives. Indeed, in the popular uprisings across the Arab world, which took root as this collection developed, mockery through prevalent cultural forms has been central to discourses of rebellion (see Kristof, 2011; Wright, 2011). Although in the Arab Spring of 2011, this occurred less through television (for reasons Semati and Sienkiewicz make clear here) than through poetry, music, and comedy, this special issue demonstrates that television increasingly has become the stage for a globally resonant kind of popular resistance in the textual form of news parody. And as the anecdote about Jon Stewart and the British parliament that opened this introduction reminds us, governments rarely need to be reminded that laughter may be the most dangerous forms of "speech" its citizens can employ.

REFERENCES

Alger, D. (1998). *Megamedia: How giant corporations dominate mass media, distort competition, and endanger democracy*. New York, NY: Rowman & Littlefield.

Bakhtin, M. (1981). *The dialogic imagination* (C. Emerson & M. Holquist, Trans.; M. Holquist, Ed.). Austin, TX: University of Texas Press.

Baym, G. (2005). *The Daily Show*: Discursive integration and the reinvention of political journalism. *Political Communication, 22*(3), 259–276.

Baym, G. (2007). Representation and the politics of play: Stephen Colbert's *Better Know a District*. *Political Communication, 24*(4), 359–376.

Baym, G. (2010). *From Cronkite to Colbert: The evolution of broadcast news*. Boulder, CO: Paradigm Publishers.

Boyer, D., & Yurchak, A. (2010). American Stiob: Or, what late –Socialist aesthetics of parody reveal about contemporary political culture in the West. *Cultural Anthropology, 25*(2), 179–221.

Day, A. (2011). *Satire and dissent: Interventions in contemporary political debate*. Bloomington, IN: Indiana University Press.

Foucault, M. (1980). *Power/knowledge: Selected interviews and other writings 1972–1977* (C. Gordon, L. Marshall, J. Mepham, & K. Soper, Trans.). New York, NY: Pantheon Books.

Hariman, R. (2008). Political parody and public culture. *Quarterly Journal of Speech, 94*(3), 247–272.

Holbert, R. L., Lambe, J. L., Dudo, A. D., & Carlton, K. A. (2007). Primacy effects of *The Daily Show* and national TV news viewing: Young viewers, political gratifications, and internal political self-efficacy. *Journal of Broadcasting & Electronic Media, 51*(1), 20–38.

Jones, J. P. (2010). *Entertaining politics: Satiric television and political engagement* (2nd ed.). Lanham, MD: Rowman and Littlefield Publishers.

Kristof, N. D. (2011, April 16). The power of mockery. *New York Times*. Retrieved from http://www.nytimes.com/2011/04/17/opinion/17kristof.html

Nichols, B. (1991). *Representing reality: Issues and concepts in documentary*. Bloomington, IN: Indiana University Press.

PBS. (2003, July 11). *NOW with Bill Moyers*. Retrieved from http://www.pbs.org/now/transcript/transcript_stewart.html

Ruggiero, T. E. (2007). Televisa's Brozo: The jester as subversive humorist. *The Journal of Latino-Latin American Studies, 2*(3), 1–15.

Tinic, S. (2009). Speaking "truth" to power? Television satire, *Rick Mercer Report*, and the politics of place and space. In J. Gray, J. P. Jones, & E. Thompson (Eds.), *Satire TV: Politics and comedy in the post-network era* (pp. 167–186). New York, NY: NYU Press.

Wright, R. (2011). *Rock the Casbah: Rage and rebellion across the Islamic world*. New York, NY: Simon and Schuster.

Xenos, M. A., & Becker, A. B. (2009). Moments of Zen: Effects of *The Daily Show* on information seeking and political learning. *Political Communication, 26*(3), 317–332.

"Find Out Exactly What to Think—Next!": Chris Morris, *Brass Eye,* and Journalistic Authority

Graham Meikle

This article discusses Chris Morris's fake news TV series *Brass Eye* (1997, 2001). It concentrates on the ways in which *Brass Eye* exposed and undermined not only the textual conventions of TV news and current affairs but also the ways in which the program deployed those textual conventions to highlight and sabotage the cultural authority of public figures who appeared on it. The article first introduces Morris and *Brass Eye,* before identifying some of the key textual strategies of broadcast news that are satirized in the program, including its mode of address, its music, and its visuals and graphics. It then examines how the program's use of those strategies enables it to exercise the authority of broadcast news to expose the accessed voices of public figures within the show.

NEWS AND FAKE NEWS

News is the organized daily production, distribution, and uses of nonfiction drama. News is an industrial product, shaped and marketed by news organizations, but it is also a cultural product, drawing upon and contributing to our understandings of narrative and drama, of shared time and space, of our senses of ourselves and our communities. And news is also a representation of social and cultural authority, in which authorized storytellers present the pronouncements and activities of other authorities. News is a textual system that encapsulates who gets to speak and what they get to speak about: "News represents *who* are the authorized knowers and *what* are their authoritative versions of reality" (Ericson, Baranek, & Chan, 1989, p. 3, emphasis in original).

Such a system of textual authority, built around claims to define reality by defining what counts as true and important, is a clear target for satire—understood here as *art on the attack,* to include both its aesthetic and its critical dimensions. Satirical fake news is where these authorized knowers and their authoritative versions of reality are called into question. Fake news is where fictional and nonfictional drama combine, blur, or merge; where nonfictional events and people— actual news footage, actual public figures—are brought within a fictional frame, highlighting the constructed aspects of the "real" (Day, 2009). Fake news is an important part of a television landscape in transition, as producers and viewers respond to the possibilities of increased choice and control (Lotz, 2007); to new technological possibilities for production, distribution, and reception (Meikle & Redden, 2011); and to shifting contexts of popular culture, in which contending claims on authority, identity, and attention compete with those of formerly accredited experts (Jones, 2010). Fake news is an important part of a complex televisual environment in which questions of real and fake are in ongoing tension, and in which all forms of factual programming depend on increasing degrees of artifice in the pursuit of the real (Kilborn, 2003; Roscoe & Hight, 2001).

The concept of satirical fake news has attracted growing attention in recent years (Baym, 2010; Boler & Turpin, 2008; Gray, Jones, & Thompson, 2009; Jones, 2010), even meriting an entry in a major published glossary of keywords in news and journalism for students (Zelizer & Allan, 2010, p. 41). Gray et al. (2009) offer a range of reasons for the importance of such satirical TV—its sheer popularity, its viral circulation and implication with the emergence of new technological apparatus for television, its complex relationships with conceptions of humor, its practitioners' willingness to take on a Fourth Estate role that real journalists all too often relinquish, and its capacity to energize public discussion (p. 4). A central claim of much discussion of fake news is that in highlighting the artifices and textual strategies of TV news and political programming, the "fake" highlights the workings of the "real," drawing attention to the ways in which reality is constructed and represented (e.g., Druick, 2009).

This article discusses a landmark fake news TV series from the United Kingdom, Chris Morris's *Brass Eye* (1997, 2001). It concentrates on the ways in which *Brass Eye* exposed and undermined not only the textual conventions of TV news and current affairs, but also the ways in which the program deployed those textual conventions to highlight and sabotage the cultural authority of public figures who appeared on it. It thus showed its viewers the limits and the often questionable foundations upon which such claims to authority are built. This article first introduces Morris and *Brass Eye* before identifying some of the key textual strategies of broadcast news that are satirized in the program, including its mode of address, its music, and its visuals and graphics. It then examines how the program's use of those strategies enables it to exercise the authority of broadcast news to undermine the voices of public figures within the show, enabling *Brass Eye* to point to larger questions of social and cultural authority.

CHRIS MORRIS AND *BRASS EYE*

Chris Morris has worked across a broad spectrum of media since beginning his career in the late 1980s on BBC radio. He has broadcast on both local and national BBC radio stations, including the flagship national youth-oriented network Radio 1. His TV work includes the *Jam* version of his disturbing *Blue Jam* radio series, and co-writing the 2005 Channel 4 sitcom *Nathan Barley*— about a London hipster and "self-facilitating media node"—with columnist and TV presenter Charlie Brooker; Morris has also acted in the sitcom *The IT Crowd*. In 1999, Morris wrote a series of spoof newspaper columns for the *Observer* UK Sunday newspaper as Richard Geefe, in which the columnist narrated his preparations for his own upcoming suicide and the book deal that would accompany this ("*Time to Go* will be published by 4th Estate in December, two weeks after Richard Geefe has killed himself"). Most recently, his first feature film as director *Four Lions* (2010), a comedy-drama about clueless British suicide bombers, won the 2011 BAFTA award for Outstanding Debut.

His reputation still largely rests, however, on three fake news series from the 1990s. In 1991–1992, Morris co-wrote and presented *On the Hour,* a satirical radio news program that also launched the careers of Armando Iannucci (*The Thick of It, In the Loop*) and Steve Coogan (*I'm Alan Partridge, The Trip*). *On the Hour* introduced many of Morris's key concerns and strategies—a blend of pitch-perfect parody of the textual features of broadcast news with surrealist language and tropes; a mastery of subversive editing; and a focus on the authority of the presenter ("hello, peasants"). The critical and popular response to *On the Hour* led to the same team transferring to a BBC TV version of the same concept, renamed *The Day Today,* and broadcast in early 1994.

In January–March 1997, UK broadcaster Channel 4 (a commercially funded terrestrial channel with a public-service remit) transmitted six half-hour episodes of Morris's project *Brass Eye,* which he wrote and produced himself, also playing many of the parts within the series. As well as playing the scary anchor with his own name, Morris also appeared as many correspondents: gruff veteran Ted Maul, nerdy Austen Tasseltine, toothy Alabaster Codify, and the various debate show hosts all called David (David Jatt, David Sanction, and David Compression, among them). *Brass Eye* presents itself as a news magazine program, with each episode focusing on a single broad theme: animals, drugs, science, sex, crime, and decline. *Brass Eye* returned for a one-off special, broadcast on Channel 4 on July 26, 2001, responding to an ongoing moral panic in the UK media about pedophilia. This episode itself ignited a moral panic in the press about broadcasting standards—"Unspeakably Sick" said the *Daily Mail*—contributing to what was at the time the largest number of complaints to broadcasting authorities ever generated by a single program (Lockyer & Attwood, 2009). All seven episodes have been released on a collected DVD and since October 2009 have also been available on an official Channel 4 YouTube channel (http://www.youtube.com/show/brasseye), although access to this may be subject to geographical variation.

Brass Eye is a sustained exposure of the machinery of the *authority* of broadcast news. Each episode of *Brass Eye* takes conventions of TV news and current affairs programming and extends them to the point where their constructed nature becomes both apparent and absurd. It highlights the technical and textual elements that combine to make up the news—"the tricks of textuality" (Hartley, 2009, p. 313). It exposes the mechanisms of authoritative pronouncements in broadcast news by persuading a range of public figures, from senior politicians to writers and broadcasters, to say bizarre, absurd, and nonsensical things on television *because* they are on television. In submitting to Morris's authority as anchor of what they believe to be a current affairs program, these figures undermine their own cultural or social authority by demonstrating that they are prepared to talk—often confidently and fluently—about subjects on which they know nothing, or are prepared to lend their image and voice to absurd public awareness campaigns about nonexistent and often surreal social problems or threats. These threats included the dangers of "heavy electricity" caused by "sodomized electrons," or of "Cake," described to MP David Amess as "a made-up drug," although this did not inhibit Amess from going on to ask a question in the UK Parliament about the government's strategy for dealing with cake.

BRASS EYE AND THE STRATEGIES OF TELEVISION NEWS

The hoaxing of these public figures is enabled by *Brass Eye*'s exact understanding of the textual strategies of television news. Morris deploys the authority of the anchor and the interviewer, but undercuts this at the same time by making it visible. He exposes the strategies that broadcasters use by setting them in fresh contexts. He takes the formal textual elements of daily broadcast news and distorts them—music that lasts too long, graphics that are overelaborate, visual aids that do not aid so much as call attention to themselves, a claim for authority based on technological prowess. This section highlights three areas in which *Brass Eye* satirizes the textual strategies of TV news—mode of address, visuals and graphics, and music.

Mode of Address

"Should we revive our ailing culture?" asks Morris as anchor in the "Decline" episode, staring directly into the camera. "Or should we just put it out of its misery? Or should we bring it back to life and then shoot it for letting us down so badly? You haven't got a clue, have you? But you will do, if you watch for 30 minutes." We are all accustomed to experiencing broadcast media messages as though speaking to us directly. Although addressed to nobody in particular, TV news messages address us as *someone*:

> I find, when I turn on the news, that I am spoken to while knowing that millions of others are watching at exactly the same time and seeing and hearing exactly the same things. In each case the experience is the same. In each case it is "for me." [. . .] The news is, in each case, appropriated by me as an aspect of my experience and yet at the same time this experience is shared by countless others. (Scannell, 2000, p. 11)

This is a key feature of the characteristic mode of address of television news. The newsreader or anchor addresses multiple, dispersed listeners as though directly but is in fact addressing no one in particular. They look straight into the camera, outwards towards an implied other—"you." It is this combination of a way of talking and a way of looking, argues Scannell, that helps to create "a public, shared and sociable world-in-common between human beings" (2000, p. 12), or what Benedict Anderson calls an "imagined community" (1991). Peters describes how such strategies were devised by early broadcasters to compensate for the perceived lack of real human content—direct address, conversational tone, a cultivated sense of intimate connection:

> Media culture is a lush jungle of fictional worlds where "everyone knows your name," celebrities and politicians address audiences by first names, and conversational formats proliferate. The conventional concept of "mass communication" captures only the abstract potential for alienation in large-scale message systems, not the multiple tactics of interpersonal appeal that have evolved to counter it. (Peters, 1999, p. 217)

The mode of address of TV news, then, is a stylized construction, yet one which has become taken for granted. *Brass Eye* highlights this again and again, addressing the viewer with derision and sarcastic contempt. Morris leads into the commercial break in the "Animals" episode with the words: "Find out exactly what to think—next." Toward the end of the "Decline" episode, Morris as anchor sums up the evening's talkback calls from viewers: "Your phone calls tonight have been described variously as rabid, pig-ignorant, and stultifyingly ill-informed. Thanks for those."

Visuals and Graphics

Biographer Lucian Randall describes how Morris and Iannucci prepared for *The Day Today* by taking a short BBC news-editing training course. They were given two hours to prepare a two-minute item on the war in Bosnia using available footage, and were given four main pieces of information to include. But they found that one of their key points had to be left out as there were no matching visuals (Randall, 2010, p. 87). This understanding of the relationship between news stories and their visual content underpins many of *Brass Eye*'s most distinctive satirical moments. In the "Crime" episode, Morris points at a monitor and says "the situation is clearly grave enough to merit a black-and-white freeze-frame." Such overliteral visuals are a key device in *Brass Eye*: a real elephant with the words "Mike Fox" painted on its side is used to segue into an item about a character of that name. In the "Crime" episode, Morris as reporter Ted Maul introduces a feature about the town of Cowsick: "Is *alarm* justified? Is *time running out* for Cowsick? Or is this the start of a *new day*—the first day of *spring*?" The italicized words are emphasized by Morris in turn holding up an alarm clock, by sand running out of the clock, by the scene cutting instantly from night to day, and by Morris turning the clock around to point at a spring in its workings.

As well as these overliteral visuals, *Brass Eye* makes extensive use of the digital graphics now central to TV news. As Crisell (2006) describes these: "Moving diagrams and distinctive script may appear on the screen: the color tones of the images may be altered and the images themselves twisted, stretched, rotated, shattered and peeled away like the pages of a book" (p. 57). *Brass Eye* takes these further than the actual news has time to do, exposing the ways in which graphics are simultaneously used to impose visual order on the chaos of events and to augment the authority of the broadcaster through their display of technological resource. The *Brass Eye* title sequence and links between segments, for example, feature a vertiginous CGI landscape of precipices and scrolling horizons. The graphics team, who won a BAFTA for their work on *The Day Today* in visualising such items as the financial news "currency cat," was the same team that worked on ITN news (Randall, 2010). The key difference was that they had months to achieve their effects for Morris's fake news, rather than the daily deadlines of TV news, so were able to create some hyperreal graphics and visual counterpoints to the nonsensical texts, such as the complex CGI graph that accompanies the following sequence in the "Animals" episode:

> Morris (in voiceover): If you plot "number of animals abused" against "what makes people cruel" versus "intelligence of either party," the pattern is so unreadable you might as well draw in a chain of fox heads on sticks. And if you do that, an interesting thing happens—the word "cruel" starts flashing.

Music

The music for both *The Day Today* and *Brass Eye* was composed by Jonathan Whitehead and Morris himself. They analyzed the themes of real news shows, such as the BBC's *Newsnight* program, composed by Oscar-nominated George Fenton, in search of the right degree of gravitas (Randall, 2010). The basic theme was then exaggerated and distorted, using unexpected time signatures and extending musical cues for longer than a real news show would, in order to accentuate the program's projected sense of gravity and portent. The music is crashing, self-important, overextended, with the final chords in each link lingering just that little bit too long. In this way, formal elements of the program draw attention to the uses of such music that normally pass unnoticed.

In one of few discussions of the music of broadcast news, Neil Postman (1985) once argued that the very fact that TV news broadcasts had theme music implicated them within what he saw as a news discourse that was disproportionately weighted toward entertaining the viewer at the expense of informing her:

> As long as the music is there as a frame for the programme, the viewer is comforted to believe that there is nothing to be greatly alarmed about; that, in fact, the events that are reported have as much relation to reality as do scenes in a play. (p. 105)

In contrast, Allan (2010), in analyzing the opening sequences of BBC and ITN news broadcasts on UK TV, points to the use of music as a strategy of *interruption*:

> The opening sequence, usually composed of a 15- to 20-second segment of brightly colored computer-animated graphics, rapidly unfolds to a sharply ascending piece of theme music (the use of trumpets is typical). Its appearance announces the interruption of the flow of entertainment programming by signalling the imminent threat of potentially distressing information. (p. 114)

Allan sees this strategy of interruption as one of five central elements of TV news discourse. He points also to liveness, and the ways in which the opening music and graphics create a sense of urgency and immediacy which in turn contribute to the broadcast's authority; to particular uses and constructions of time and space; to an emphasis on the construction of a particular "us" and "them" formulation of implied audience as imagined community; and to a strategy of professionalism manifest in pristine, hard surfaces throughout the mise-en-scene of the news (pp. 114–115).

The strategy of liveness here is also key to *Brass Eye*. Even though each episode was entirely pre-recorded, each presents the illusion of liveness (Bourdon, 2000; Day, 2009; Marriott, 2007), with its corresponding claim on our attention, its exercise of authority over the viewer. The "Crime" episode opens with Morris as anchor joining a police stakeout—a caption reads "Christopher Morris crouching with police"—before running around in the dark yelling "crime is confusing." This parody of crime-based reality programming and current affairs shows such as *Crimewatch* derives much of its impact from its appropriation of the illusion that they are live and hence more important.

The "Decline" episode, although prerecorded like all of *Brass Eye*, presents itself as coming live from "the nerve-center of tonight's program" as Morris strides up and down before a bank of TV monitors to show "a true picture of the state of Britain." Introducing a cross to reporter Austen Tasseltine (also played by Morris), who is live on the scene at a garage "which is raided every 35 minutes," the anchor says "we have live surveillance cameras—one of them has a reporter stuck on the front." This is a basic Morris move: calling attention to the normalized conventions of TV presenting by the carefully-placed incongruous or inappropriate word or phrase ("*stuck on the front*").

It is *Brass Eye*'s detailed attention to such formal elements of the textuality of TV news that enables Morris to draw public figures into the show's narrative, as discussed in the next section.

PUBLIC FIGURES AND CULTURAL AUTHORITY

A key element of some of the most popular, respected, controversial, and widely discussed fake news programs, from *The Daily Show* to *Brass Eye,* is the appearance of public figures, incorporated into the show's narrative and textual strategies. Politicians, for example, are often keen to reach the demographics most likely to be regular Jon Stewart viewers—Baym (2010) notes that candidates in the 2008 US presidential election appeared on entertainment talk shows such as those hosted by Stewart and Colbert 110 times during the campaign (p. 18). They will submit to the comedic frame of an interview on the show in a process that comes with the risks of what Meyrowitz (1985) describes as "lowering the political hero to our level" (p. 268).

Jones (2010) argues that journalism's claim to cultural and social authority has been challenged from the late 1990s on, as nonjournalist media producers (such as Chris Morris) exposed its machinery and artifices, as audiences took up the possibilities offered by new and contending channels for information and discussion, and as governments and politicians privileged punditry and demagoguery, such as that practiced through Fox News in the United States, through conservative talkback radio in Australia, or through much of the tabloid press in the United Kingdom. One key strategy through which Morris has contributed to this challenging of the authority of the news is through his use of unwitting participants in his programs.

In *Understanding News,* Hartley (1982) distinguishes between different kinds of voice in broadcast news—the "institutional voices" of the anchor and other presenters and correspondents, and the "accessed voices" of interviewees. The primary voices are, of course, the institutional ones, who address the viewer directly. Accessed voices are presented in different ways from the institutional voices of the anchor. "They are all subordinate," Hartley argues, "to the overall structure of a story as presented by the professional broadcasters" (p. 109). A TV news interview is a complex relationship of authority, in which the institutional voice of the interviewer draws the accessed voice of the interviewee into the frame of the broadcast, with both sides aiming to draw further authority from the process of the interview. In a vox pop, the program draws cultural authority from its engagement with ordinary people, through demonstrating its connection to their concerns and opinions. In an adversarial interview of the type practiced by the figures Morris's *Brass Eye* persona often most resembles, such as BBC *Newsnight* anchor Jeremy Paxman, the institutional voice may seek to assert authority over the accessed voice, by exposing them to the risk of contradiction or gaffe. In an interview with an expert on some topic, the institutional voice may seek to draw authority for the broadcast itself through sharing in the authority of their expertise.

Chris Morris's fake news programs used accessed voices in three key ways: in vox pops, in interviews with celebrities and politicians, and in securing the participation of public figures in hoax public awareness campaigns. In *On the Hour* and *The Day Today,* the shows included surreal vox pops with passers-by in the street, who were asked to comment on ludicrous propositions. *Brass Eye* extended this dramatically by persuading dozens of public figures to participate in the program, either by taking part in spoof debate shows or interviews that the celebrity believed to be real, or by agreeing to support fictitious public awareness campaigns that they were led to believe were authentic. This section considers examples of each of these three devices in turn.

Vox Pops

In a precursor to the celebrity ambushes of *Brass Eye, The Day Today* included vox pop segments with ordinary people in the street called "Speak Your Brains." The physical authority of Morris's persona, his delivery and demeanor, his camera and microphone, combine to command responses to even bizarre and silly questions and statements, as in this sequence from episode one:

Morris: Tightening up the law. Is it required today?

Man: I think so, yes.

Morris: In what areas?

Man: Certainly we have to do something about drug peddling.

Morris: If they ran into the new tightened-up law would it smack them up sharp or would it catch them gradually?

Man: I think it needs to smack them up sharp.

Morris: Jerk their heads back?

Man: Oh sure. Certainly, yeah.

Morris: Let's see if we can nail this down. In terms of this elastic band here [*he demonstrates stretching an elastic band*], would you like to see the law tightened up to this tightness: tightness number one, tightness number two, or tightness number three?

Man: I think tightness number three.

Morris: Tightness number three, like this? [*stretches his elastic band*]

Man: I think we've really got to hammer these guys.

Morris: So that tightness being an average Post Office band extended over about eight inches?

Man: Perhaps, yeah. Yeah, I think so.

At this stage of his career, Morris was not using public figures. In a rare press interview for the *Guardian* in July 1994, he explained:

> Part of the point is the sheer randomness of those people—from vicars to builders. You're undermining any talking head on TV, by showing them talking bollocks with apparent authority. In everything I do there are enough clues, you're challenging the situation to collapse by getting stupider and stupider. (Morris interviewed in Dugdale, 1994)

The fact that Morris does, as he says here, provide more than enough clues to these interviewees is important in the following sections, which discuss his escalation of this strategy in its use on public figures.

Interviews

For *Brass Eye,* the idea that any random individual would serve this end was replaced with an emphasis on authentic public figures. In the "Crime" episode, first broadcast on February 26, 1997, Morris, in the guise of *Zeitguest* host David Compression, interviews former Conservative cabinet minister and prominent educationalist Sir Rhodes Boyson about his views on crime and punishment:

Morris: Do you feel that vigilantism is actually going to help in the long run?

Boyson: I think it will arise in an area where something has gone wrong.

Morris: I mean, in Gotham City in the United States they call up a specialist vigilante agent when they're in times of real trouble, by projecting a huge luminous emergency bat sign into the sky, and he comes rushing in and so far that has worked. Is that something that should be encouraged?

Boyson: I'd have to see it, I [. . .]

Morris: Well, it *looks* good.

Boyson:	It would have to be a very—individual with great magnetism.
Morris:	I think that's what it is. It's his special sign.
Boyson:	They're one-offs, that sort of thing. And it's very nice in school-mastering when you have people who are one-offs who can actually do it in a way that nobody else can do it. But don't try and get other people doing it.
Morris:	But when he, you know, Bruce Wayne goes, then it's all going to collapse.
Boyson:	Yeah, well, it's done. It's happened throughout history.

What is striking about this exchange is not that a cabinet minister is unfamiliar with Batman, but rather Boyson's willingness to pronounce authoritative opinions on this fantastic nonsense. He hesitates briefly (*"I'd have to see it"*) but with the slightest reassurance from Morris (*"it looks good"*), Boyson immediately and effortlessly incorporates the Gotham City vigilante of whom he knows nothing into first his own area of professional expertise (comparing Bruce Wayne with teachers from his own experience) and second his wider cultural authority: *"It's happened throughout history."* Morris's authoritative performance and his appropriation of the role as television interviewer enable him to exercise symbolic power—the power to define, to name, to endorse, to persuade (Bourdieu, 1991; Thompson, 1995)—over a senior politician, drawing Boyson into complicity with whatever he tells him. The viewer is left to wonder under what other circumstances Boyson is speaking from such a position of ignorance and to what extent other senior politicians would respond in a similar way.

Campaigns

A live exchange of this kind, on which Boyson presumably had not been briefed in advance, which might have given him the opportunity to ask around about this Bruce Wayne of Gotham City, is different from the public service announcements central to each episode of *Brass Eye,* in which a range of journalists and broadcasters, politicians and pop stars, actors, celebrities, and presenters were persuaded to lend their image, voice, and cultural status to supporting absurd social campaigns. The kinds of deception to which these public figures were subject put *Brass Eye* in a potentially vulnerable position. Channel 4 at that time was obliged to operate under the Programme Code of the Independent Television Commission (ITC), in turn governed by the Broadcast Act of 1990, which offered only limited provision for such deception in the case of investigative journalism, not comedy programs. Interviewers were obliged to make the nature of their program clear to the interviewee, as well as the ways in which the interview material was intended to be used. According to his biographer, Morris saw a public interest defence here, in that exposing the willingness of celebrities and politicians to appear on television endorsing the most preposterous campaigns and causes that he could devise, was a serious project, and that a comedy program could invoke the same rationale as could investigative journalists (Randall, 2010). A complaint to the Broadcasting Standards Commission by Labour MP Barbara Follett about her use in the 2001 pedophilia episode of *Brass Eye* was rejected, with the Commission finding that:

> The means deployed to deceive Ms Follett were justified in the context of the serious issues raised by the programme, in particular the dangers of people in the public eye speaking with apparent authority about matters they do not understand. (Broadcasting Standards Commission, 2001)

The celebrity participants were given as many clues as possible that what they were being asked to say was a hoax. For some of these campaigns, *Brass Eye* created elaborate fronts, with dedicated office space, phone lines, and letterhead, to foster a sense of authenticity, but these were invariably given ludicrous names and logos—the anti-pedophilia campaign "Nonce Sense"; the drugs awareness coalition F.U.K.D. and B.O.M.B.D.; the animal rights campaigners A.A.A.A.A.A.Z. (Against Animal Anger And Autocausal Abuse Atrocities in Zoos).

In the "Animals" episode, actor Britt Ekland is persuaded to promote the work of Morris's fictitious animal rights organization, despite the manifest silliness of what she is asked to say:

> Ekland: Last year, they stopped penguins catapulting each other through the glass roof at Sydney Zoo. Last month, they stopped a pig throwing itself out of a tree onto a python in a two-way death-pact in Chester. Now they want to help Karla, an East German elephant who has got her trunk jammed up her own guts.

In the "Crime" episode, several celebrities, including broadcaster Tommy Vance, cricketer Geoff Boycott, and film director and columnist Michael Winner, are persuaded to read some advice to new offenders which they will be shown on arriving in prison. Broadcaster Vanessa Feltz delivers this message, which she is told will be screened to murderers when they arrive in jail:

> Feltz: Hello, you think you don't know me, don't you? Yes, but you do because I'm the shopkeeper you shot in a mindless hold-up—you blew out my guts, remember? I'm the old lady whose head you stove in with a loose wardrobe in the middle of the night, remember? I'm the little boy whose face you stabbed off in panic when I found you robbing my house, remember? I'm Marvin Gaye, shot by my own father. Oh yes, you know me, alright. Look at my eyes, murderer. You killed *me*. What the *hell* did you *do* that for? Look at me—feel proud, do you? Do you even know what a feeling is? I do, but I can't have any more now, because of you. You? You get out after 25 years. But me? I'm here forever. I *hate* you.

The language is typical Morris, undermining the discourse with the unlikely phrase (*"loose wardrobe," "stabbed off"*) or jarring cultural reference (*"I'm Marvin Gaye"*). As Gray (2009) notes, the hoax campaigns "launch a satiric attack on the abuses of celebrity and public image, mocking the frequency with which those in the public eye will lend their voice and image to political or humanitarian causes, regardless of how little research they have conducted into the issue" (p. 148).

This question of the public figures' lack of research into the campaigns they are endorsing is crucial in the public awareness sequences of *Brass Eye*, as these campaigns illustrate the ways in which public figures are drawn into processes of social and cultural exclusion in the news media. Each of these campaigns mobilizes celebrity participation against a cultural threat of some kind. The news, as Hartley (1992) observes, "is organized around strategies of inclusion and exclusion from 'our' community" (p. 207). In this sense, the news media work to generate and sustain our sense of collective identity, through stories that represent events, values, or people as "us" or "them." The moral panic (Cohen, 2002; Critcher, 2003; Goode & Ben-Yahuda, 1994) is where these processes of inclusion and exclusion are brought into the public sphere, as the news media become the forum for a specific debate about the nature of "us" and the nature of "them."

The 2001 *Brass Eye* pedophilia special contains a sequence about the dangers of new technologies which demonstrates the dynamics of moral panic. Online games are introduced as "the latest menace to require urgent warnings from expert communicators," and ITN reporter Nicholas

Owen, Labour MPs Barbara Follett and Syd Rapson, and broadcasters Philippa Forrester, Kate Thornton, and Richard Blackwood all contribute to a public awareness campaign about an online children's game featuring the fictitious character Pantu the dog. Broadcaster Kate Thornton explains that it's a HOECS game (pronounced "hoax"), standing for Hidden Online Entrapment Control System. Some extracts from what follows:

Owen:	Singapore police have sent us these pictures. This man has plugged his groin into his computer to get sexual pleasure from the actions of a child playing with Pantu.
Thornton:	We even have footage which would be too alarming to show you of a little boy being interfered with by a penis-shaped sound wave generated by an online pedophile.
Rapson:	We believe that pedophiles are using an area of the internet the size of Ireland, and through this they can control keyboards.
Blackwood:	Online pedophiles can actually make your keyboard release toxic vapors that make you suggestible [*he sniffs the keyboard*]. You know, I must say I actually feel more suggestible and that was just from one sniff.
Thornton:	HOECS games can cause serious damage. One child was trapped online for a whole night and, according to a psychiatric report, came away with the jaded, listless sexual appetite of a 60-year-old colonel.
Blackwood:	Now, here are the warning signs to show that your child might be in trouble. Are they upset? Do they smell odd? Weird question, but HOECS games actually make your child smell like hammers.
Thornton:	So come on, experts. Why is no one telling us about this stuff? There's a kid in Canada who's gone almost completely 2D and no one's doing anything about it.
Forrester:	Please—sit your kids down tonight and tell them about HOECS games. Let's strangle Pantu.
Owen:	Let's put a bomb under Pantu's chin and stamp on his throat. Let's rip this dog's brains out.

Again, the absurdist language (*"the jaded, listless sexual appetite of a 60-year-old colonel," "gone almost completely 2D," "smell like hammers"*) goes apparently unremarked by the participants, as do the nonsensical claims about the nature of the technology (*"penis-shaped sound wave," "an area of the internet the size of Ireland"*). And yet, as the introduction to the segment notes, these are "expert communicators," two of whom as members of parliament would be required to make laws on such issues, one of whom was a presenter of the BBC's leading science program *Tomorrow's World,* and another of whom, a senior ITN journalist, was happy to add the words "let's rip this dog's brains out" to a public awareness campaign. Moreover, as Gray (2009) has pointed out, the social threats identified in each of *Brass Eye*'s moral panic campaigns involve foreign elements—the dangerous Czech drug "Cake," the Sri Lankan government's complicity in "heavy electricity," the Libyan festivals in which cows are shot out of cannons, and in this example HOECS pedophile activity in Singapore—which adds an extra dimension of Otherness to the moral panics that Morris conjures throughout the series.

As Jones (2010) points out, political discussion on television has tended to assume informed, authoritative speaking positions: "The assumption by television producers has been that 'expertise' should be the defining characteristic of who gets to speak [. . .] The assumption is built on the belief that such speech is designed primarily to inform or educate, not fulfil other functions of political communication" (p. 43). The accessed voices in *Brass Eye* work above all to expose the dubious foundations of expertise upon which such normative assumptions may be built. Moreover, *Brass Eye* appeared at a time when the assumptions of the network era were being challenged by the rise of new technologies of media production, delivery, and reception; by the corresponding fragmentation of audiences; and by a shifting context of popular culture in which contending claims on authority, identity, and attention now competed with those of the formerly accredited experts.

CONCLUSION

The surreal and aggressive nature of *Brass Eye* sets Morris apart from a figure such as Jon Stewart, who is able to function as a trusted voice on the issues within the news, representative of what Baym (2010) describes as "an emergent paradigm of hybrid media that blends news and entertainment in unprecedented ways" (p. 5). *Brass Eye* is satirical fake news, but it does not *blend* news and entertainment. Instead, the achievement of Morris's work is to expose the textual and cultural machinery of news and current affairs. Morris does not fill a role as a trusted journalistic voice or as someone who can actually take on the mantle of Fourth Estate, as Stewart can in his often very serious and probing interviews with real public figures. As Jones (2010) argues, Jon Stewart's *The Daily Show* is fake "only in that it refuses to make claims to authority and authenticity, as opposed to those claims repeatedly asserted through the techniques and conventions used by news media" (p. 18). *Brass Eye,* in contrast, is fake news that *does* make those very claims to authority and authenticity, through the force of its satire staking out an alternative position from which to critique authority. Morris appropriates and exaggerates the textual conventions of news and current affairs, and deploys these to expose the limitations of the genre's accessed voices.

As Baym (2010) argues (p. 106), *The Daily Show* draws paradoxical power and authority by claiming to be fake, which allows it to go to places that other news shows cannot go; *Brass Eye,* in contrast, claims to be real, and draws public figures into its surreal artifice through the careful maintenance of this pretense. Where *The Daily Show,* in Baym's analysis, operates through a "discourse of inquiry" (p. 111), attempting to penetrate an obfuscatory political culture, *Brass Eye* operates instead through a discourse of exposure, revealing the strategies of broadcast news and current affairs, and the mutual complicity of broadcasters and the public figures whose voices they access.

Why does this matter? News—as a textual system, as a set of cultural practices, as a social forum, and as an industrial product—operates through claims to the real built upon claims to authority. It accesses and authorizes the voices that define and delimit the contours of public debate, and it draws these voices into its own strategies of symbolic power. The achievement of *Brass Eye* is to bring these taken-for-granted processes and strategies to the forefront of its viewers' attention.

REFERENCES

Allan, S. (2010). *News culture* (3rd ed.). Maidenhead, England: Open University Press.
Anderson, B. (1991). *Imagined communities* (rev. ed.). London, England: Verso.
Baym, G. (2010). *From Cronkite to Colbert: The evolution of broadcast news*. Boulder, CO: Paradigm.

Boler, M., with Turpin, S. (2008). *The Daily Show* and *Crossfire:* Satire and sincerity as truth to power. In M. Boler (Ed.), *Digital media and democracy: Tactics in hard times* (pp. 383–403). Cambridge, MA: MIT Press.

Bourdieu, P. (1991). *Language and symbolic power*. Cambridge, England: Polity.

Bourdon, J. (2000). Live television is still alive: On television as an unfulfilled promise. *Media, Culture and Society*, *22*(5), 531–556.

Broadcasting Standards Commission [UK]. (2001). Adjudication: Complaint about unjust or unfair treatment by Ms Barbara Follett MP, submitted on 11 September 2001, about *Brass Eye Special*, broadcast on Channel 4 on 26 July 2001. *Broadcasting Standards Commission* [now replaced by Ofcom]. Retrieved from http://www.ofcom.org.uk/static/archive/bsc/pdfs/fairadj/follett.htm

Cohen, S. (2002 [1972]). *Folk devils and moral panics* (3rd ed.). London, England: Routledge.

Crisell, A. (2006). *A study of modern television: Thinking inside the box*. Basingstoke, England: Palgrave Macmillan.

Critcher, C. (2003). *Moral panics and the media*. Buckingham, England: Open University Press.

Day, A. (2009). And now . . . the news? Mimesis and the real in *The Daily Show*. In J. Gray, J. P. Jones, & E. Thompson (Eds.), *Satire TV: Politics and comedy in the post-network era* (pp. 85–103). New York, NY: New York University Press.

Druick, Z. (2009). TV news parody as a critique of genre. *Television & New Media*, *10*(3), 294–308.

Dugdale, J. (1994, July 25). Taped up for Auntie. *Guardian*, p. 16.

Ericson, R. V., Baranek, P. M., & Chan, J. B. L. (1989). *Negotiating control: A study of news sources*. Milton Keynes, England: Open University Press.

Goode, E., & Ben-Yehuda, N. (1994). *Moral panics: The social construction of deviance*. Oxford, England: Blackwell.

Gray, J. (2009). Throwing out the welcome mat: Public figures as guests and victims in TV satire. In J. Gray, J. P. Jones, & E. Thompson (Eds.), *Satire TV: Politics and comedy in the post-network era* (pp. 147–166). New York, NY: New York University Press.

Gray, J., Jones, J. P., & Thompson, E. (Eds.). (2009). *Satire TV: Politics and comedy in the post-network era*. New York, NY: New York University Press.

Hartley, J. (1982). *Understanding news*. London, England: Methuen.

Hartley, J. (1992). *The politics of pictures*. London, England: Routledge.

Hartley, J. (2009). Journalism and popular culture. In K. Wahl-Jorgensen & T. Hanitzsch (Eds.), *The handbook of journalism studies* (pp. 310–324). London, England: Routledge.

Jones, J. P. (2010). *Entertaining politics: Satiric television and political engagement* (2nd ed.). Lanham, MD: Rowman & Littlefield.

Kilborn, R. (2003). *Staging the real: Factual TV programming in the age of Big Brother*. Manchester, England: Manchester University Press.

Lockyer, S., & Attwood F. (2009). "The sickest television show ever": Paedogeddon and the British press. *Popular Communication*, *7*(1), 49–60.

Lotz, A. D. (2007). *The television will be revolutionized*. New York, NY: New York University Press.

Marriott, S. (2007). *Live television: Time, space and the broadcast event*. London, England: Sage.

Meikle, G., & Redden, G. (Eds.). (2011). *News online: Transformations and continuities*. Basingstoke, England: Palgrave Macmillan.

Meyrowitz, J. (1985). *No sense of place*. New York, NY: Oxford University Press.

Peters, J. D. (1999). *Speaking into the air: A history of the idea of communication*. Chicago, IL: University of Chicago Press.

Postman, N. (1985). *Amusing ourselves to death*. London, England: Methuen.

Randall, L. (2010). *Disgusting bliss: The brass eye of Chris Morris*. London, England: Simon & Schuster.

Roscoe, J., & Hight, C. (2001). *Faking it: Mock-documentary and the subversion of factuality*. Manchester, England: Manchester University Press.

Scannell, P. (2000). For-anyone-as-someone structures. *Media, Culture & Society*, *22*(1), 5–24.

Thompson, J. B. (1995). *The media and modernity*. Cambridge, England: Polity.

Zelizer, B., & Allan, S. (2010). *Keywords in news & journalism studies*. Maidenhead, England: Open University Press.

From the "Little Aussie Bleeder" to *Newstopia*: (Really) Fake News in Australia

Stephen Harrington

This article offers an overview of the key characteristics of "fake" news in the Australian national context. Focusing on two television shows, *The Norman Gunston Show* and *Newstopia*, it historicizes "fake" news within Australian television culture, situating it as part of a broader tradition of what Turner (1989) calls "Transgressive TV." After analyzing the core comedic themes, styles, and intertextual relationships of both shows, the article concludes that, although news parody in Australia has tended to be highly fictionalized, it may nevertheless play a vital role in helping viewers better understand generic devices that frame and govern "real" television news.

In the late afternoon of November 11, 1975, an angry crowd gathered outside Australia's Parliament House in Canberra after hearing reports earlier in the day that Governor-General Sir John Kerr had dismissed the Labor Prime Minister Gough Whitlam and installed Opposition Leader Malcolm Fraser as caretaker Prime Minister. The constitutional crisis had essentially come about after Fraser's Liberal-Country Coalition had used its fortuitous narrow majority in the Senate to block Commonwealth supply bills, thereby forcing Kerr into remedial action that would restore the functionality of the federal government. The Governor-General's secretary walked onto the front steps of Parliament House and formally announced the decision—to loud jeers from the overwhelmingly pro-Labor crowd—ending his statement, as one did, with the phrase "God save the Queen." The vanquished Whitlam then took his place, and responded with what is now seen as one of the most famous sentences in Australia's political history: "Well may we say 'God save the Queen,' because nothing will save the Governor-General."

While this event was, of course, highly significant from a political perspective, what is perhaps most interesting when looking back at "The Dismissal" (as it is now colloquially known) as a moment in the history of popular culture is the fact that, among the dozens of journalists reporting on the event with great seriousness, was Norman Gunston: a fictional television personality played by comedic actor Garry McDonald. Gunston was standing almost directly in front of Whitlam when he emerged from Parliament House and injected some levity into the situation by visibly acting as though the crowd was in fact there to applaud him, and not the deposed Prime Minister. As it happens, he was not far off in playing to the crowd in this way because some (who had previously been yelling "We want Gough!") started chanting "Gunston for Governor General!": a sign that both he and his television show that had begun earlier in 1975 were growing rapidly in popularity.

That a comedian—whose core premise was to parody the conventions of television (and the personalities who frequently appear on it)—was not only present at but also played an active role in such a momentous event in Australian political history reveals just how deeply intertwined satire and politics have been in Australia for nearly four decades.

In this article, I briefly examine Australian news parody, or what some would call "fake" news, through a historical lens in order to sketch some of the common traits that have been shared among the many manifestations of the genre in this country. I focus in some detail on the satirical styles of two television programs in particular: one—*The Norman Gunston Show*—that I argue should be seen as the genesis of Australian television news parody, and another—*Newstopia*—that marks the most recent phase of the genre's nearly four decades-long evolution. Rather than examine Australian news parody as though it exists in a vacuum, I argue that the much-celebrated "fake" news *ethos* is in fact deeply embedded in our national television culture, by highlighting its place within Australia's broader and more widely acknowledged national tradition of what Turner (1989) has called "transgressive TV" (cf. Sternberg, 1995). I then conclude by arguing that a defining characteristic of Australian "fake" news is its very high degree of "fake-ness": that we as a culture generally appear to be rather comfortable with the deliberate and sustained transgression of the semiotic, generic, and authoritative boundaries of television news.

"FAKE" NEWS AS "TRANSGRESSIVE TV"

In Melbourne Tonight (*IMT*) was a night-time variety show which ran nationally—with some extended breaks and variations of name—on Channel 9 in Australia from 1951 to 1975 (McKee, 2001). While it was by no means a news parody, it remains an important starting point for any discussion of Australian "fake" news (let alone any form of Australia light entertainment TV for that matter) because it strongly set the tone for what was to come after it. Understanding it allows us to better understand and contextualize the "fake" news programs we see today (in a show such as *Newstopia*, for example, which will be discussed later in this article), by appreciating from where their subversive tendencies stem.

Hosted by the late Graham Kennedy, who is remembered widely as "The King" of Australian television, *IMT* was renowned for the antics of its hosts and their refusal to conform to the expectations of "normal" television presenters. Turner (1989) has argued that the show is emblematic of the early days of Australian television. In an age where most of the formats were imported, principally from the United States, *IMT*, like other shows of the time, refused to take "the format seriously" and instead used it as "a set of conventions to attack and transgress" (p. 32). Rather than treating their roles earnestly, they often mocked the very show they were hosting, and regularly broke the façade of professionalism that characterizes nearly all television personae worldwide. McKee (2001) has therefore suggested that *In Melbourne Tonight* was "an important part of Australia's public archive of television" and central to the show was "the concept of subversiveness, and its relation to television as a medium" (p. 18). It was, put simply, a text that helped to define what television in Australia *is*.

Turner (1989) has labeled this slightly anarchic style "Transgressive TV" and rightly points out that "one could construct a history of Australian Television from such shows" (p. 30). Indeed, an abridged version of this history, with an emphasis on programs that engaged in "mischievous disruption" (p. 81) of the *real* news of the day, might include:

The Norman Gunston Show (ABC, 1975–1976; Seven, 1978–1979, 1993)

Graham Kennedy's News Show/Coast to Coast (Nine, 1989) (see Turner, 1996)

Clive Robertson's Newsworld (see Turner, 1996)

Good News Week (ABC, 1996–1998; Ten, 1999–2000, 2008–present) (see Stockbridge, 2000, p. 192)

The Fat (ABC, 2000–2003)

The Glass House (ABC, 2001–2006)

The Panel (Ten, 1998–2004) (see Harrington, 2005)

The Chaser's War on Everything (ABC, 2006–2007, 2009) (see Harrington, 2012)

Yes We Canberra (ABC, 2010)

The 7PM Project (Ten, 2009–present)

Hungry Beast (ABC, 2009–present)

While these shows are not "fake" news *per se*, they fit into the category of "transgressive TV" because of their tendency to "not quite [obey] the rules" of television news (McKee, 2001, p. 30). And, importantly, this culture of transgression has proven to be fertile ground for a range of other shows that have more directly produced comedy out of the generic form of news broadcasts. These have transgressed the conventions of the news, particularly the many tropes that underpin the news' self-importance, and the self-importance of the political actors who are the core interest of this type of television programming. Some key examples here include:

The Gillies Report (ABC, 1984–1985)/*The Gillies Republic* (ABC, 1986)/*Gillies and Company* (ABC, 1992)

The Late Show[1] (ABC, 1992–1993)

The sketches of John Clarke and Bryan Dawe ([*A Current Affair*] Nine, 1989–1997; [*7:30 Report/7:30*] ABC, 1997–present)

The Election Chaser (ABC, 2001)/*CNNNN* (2002–2003)/*The Chaser Decides* (2004, 2007)

Real Stories (Ten, 2006)

Newstopia (SBS, 2007–2008)

At this point it is also appropriate to note the (fictional) "behind the scenes" perspective of *Frontline* (ABC, 1994–1995, 1997) (see McKee, 2001; Turner, 1996), which mercilessly satirized the spurious production practices that flourished on a fictional tabloid current affairs program of the same name. McKee has even suggested that "Frontline may have bequeathed a genre to Australian television: the comedy that uses parody in order to discuss current affairs— not necessarily satire, but more a mixture of current affairs and entertainment" (McKee, 2001, p. 294).

---

[1] Although *The Late Show* was a fairly generic sketch comedy/variety show, it did feature a weekly news segment in which Tom Gleisner (playing the role of news "anchor") mocked or parodied recent news footage. This segment also commonly featured "fake" interviews with Rob Sitch, who would impersonate celebrities or newsworthy figures.

While it is far from a *uniquely* Australian phenomenon (as the other contributions in this collection attest to), it is obvious that news satire (and "fake" news) has been a strong feature of Australia's national television culture for more than 30 years. And, while it is impossible here to undertake a detailed analysis of the entire history of the genre in this country, I do wish to flesh out some key moments in this history in the pages that follow. In order to do so, I consider a seminal text as well as the most recent iteration of the genre in order to see both the roots of Australian fake news and its current condition.

ROOTS: *THE NORMAN GUNSTON SHOW*

Norman Gunston was a fictional character played by Garry McDonald. Originally conceived as part of the *The Aunty Jack Show* in the early 1970s, the character became particularly well known from his title role on *The Norman Gunston Show*, which aired on the ABC—Australia's public broadcaster—over three series in 1975 and 1976. At the core of the character is a small-town man with neither the looks nor the talent that would be required of a genuine television star. His dress sense was terrible (wearing either very dull or very garish colors, and pants that were too short), his face was always made up to an almost unhealthily pale shade, he sported a terrible comb-over, and he was colloquially known as the "little Aussie bleeder" (a play on the friendly term "little Aussie battler") due to the ever-present pieces of tissue paper drying the perpetually numerous shaving cuts on his face.

Appearance aside, Gunston's other main trait was that he was truly terrible in front of a camera. He was always visibly nervous, unsure of himself, in many cases visibly overawed by the people he was interviewing, and regularly offered prolonged, awkward smiles directly to the camera between questions. In spite of his lack of ability, Gunston retained a massively over-inflated sense of his own talent, celebrity status, and importance at all times.[2] In true "transgressive" tradition, he violated the unwritten rules of professionalism in television. Cox (2006, p. 12) has summed up the show neatly as "TV sending up its own conventions, its obsession with ratings and awards, its vanity and phoniness."

This approach would not be entirely unfamiliar to anyone who has encountered the work of Sacha Baron Cohen, for example. Like Cohen's Ali G, Borat, or Bruno, Norman Gunston is a carefully constructed character; a ruse to unsettle and surprise the interviewee, and therefore allow a more direct and uncompromising interview. In the same way that Borat Sagdiyev's extreme anti-Semitic antics "lets people lower their guard and expose their own prejudice" (Strauss, 2006), Gunston's weak, "pathetic," and feeble pretenses were used as "camouflage, enabling the satirist it obscured to humiliate and expose" (Turner, 1989, p. 33). Just as the guise of "fake news" allows *The Daily Show*, for example, the freedom to pursue a "distinctly subjective" approach to the news (Baym, 2005, p. 267), and Stephen Colbert's character affords some interviewees a perilous level of comfort, Norman Gunston's incompetence gave his celebrity or political guests (or, more precisely, "targets") a false sense of security, which could then be exploited by a distinctly subversive undertone in the line of questioning that followed.

---

[2] As noted later in this article, Gunston described himself as "sort of Australia's Johnny Carson" (ABC, 1992) when interviewing film star Warren Beatty.

While we might marvel at the litany of political heavyweights that have now been guests on *The Daily Show with Jon Stewart* and suggest that whatever walls that once existed between politics and entertainment have now disappeared, this dissolution of boundaries has been in train for quite a while in Australia. For example, former Prime Minister Sir John Gorton was a guest on *The Norman Gunston Show* in 1975. Why exactly the ex-PM would subject himself unnecessarily to this level of potential humiliation remains a mystery, but it reveals a great deal about an ingrained culture of polite disrespect. When Gorton arrived on the set of his show, Norman Gunston first offered the former Prime Minister a hot beverage and a pineapple doughnut (for "supper"), and then sat him down to ask the first question: "Was there an underhand plot, do you think, to get rid of you in Parliament, or do you think that everyone at the same time sort of came to the conclusion that you were a bit of a dil?" (ABC, 1992).[3]

In this case, Gorton was a planned, in-studio guest on the program. Because he must have known what to expect out of the exchange, he was good natured, willingly (and admirably) played his part with good grace, and went along with the jokes. Some of the most memorable moments from *The Norman Gunston Show*, however, came from his "surprise" interviews with foreign celebrities, such as Paul and Linda McCartney, Muhammad Ali, and Sally Struthers, at press conferences and other media events. Because they were totally unaware of his character, many of these people were as much confounded by the person asking the questions as by how to answer the questions themselves. This was apparent in his interview with an initially puzzled and eventually irate Rudolph Nureyev, who told Gunston, "You should have stuck to Ballroom dancing and never [done] interviews," clapped his hands together, and ended the exchange by declaring the "whole thing is dismissed."

In a way, Gunston and his satirical approach reveals what could arguably be described as the "essence" of Australian humor. His irreverence, and polite disrespect for the powerful (or, to use Australian vernacular, "tall poppies") is core to the post-colonial antipodean myth of rebellion. This is illustrated well in this series of questions directed to a half-insulted and half-perplexed Warren Beatty at a 1975 press conference:

Gunston:	How long have you been here for?
Beatty:	I don't know, because my time is a little mixed-up, but I know I got here today.
Gunston:	Oh. And you haven't made it with any Australian ladies yet?
Beatty:	No. Have you?
Gunston:	Oh, no. I haven't got time for that. But I though you were a fast worker. What about the air hostesses, you know, on the way out? [*winks*]
Beatty:	The what?
Gunston:	The air hostesses, on the way out.
Beatty:	On the way in?
Gunston:	Yeah, yeah. From, you know, America, to Australia.
Beatty:	No. No.
Gunston:	I s'pose you haven't got time for it, like myself. You know, a star on the ascent and all that.
Beatty:	What do you do?
Gunston:	I have a national tonight show. I wanted you to come on it, you know, and do a bit of an interview . . .

---

[3] Although it is a mere coincidence, this exchange is eerily similar to Jon Stewart (in September 2006) offering Pervez Musharraf a cup of jasmine green tea and a Twinkie, and then asking him "Where's Osama Bin Laden?"

Beatty: Well, we'll do a bit of an interview here. You have a tonight show?
Gunston: Yeah, [I'm] sort of Australia's Johnny Carson. Sunday night, only on Sunday night.
Beatty: Only on Sunday night? Well, Carson is on, you know, five nights a week.
Gunston: Is he? Gee.
Beatty: How much time are you on every Sunday night?
Gunston: Ahh, 30 minutes. Anything you want to ask me?
Beatty: What time?
Gunston: Umm, 7:30.
Beatty: That's early.
Gunston: Yeah, yeah. Oh, yes, it's a family show.
Beatty: Children are still awake.
Gunston: Oh yeah. It's the bulk of my audience, I think. Mr Beatty, I know you've done 13 films over 15 years, haven't you?
Beatty: Ahh, yeah.
Gunston: Well, what do you do for a living? Like, how do you tide yourself over? [*Beatty shifts uncomfortably in his chair*] Do you write or anything like that? You don't have a tonight show, do you?
Beatty: Huh?
Gunston: You don't have a tonight show?
Beatty: No, no, no, no. I had thought of running a delicatessen for a while, on 3rd Avenue, but I have to ask this question, I don't mean to be rude.
Gunston: Yeah?
Beatty: Did you cut yourself shaving?
           (ABC, 1992)

Looking back at this interview, and what else remains of the show in publicly accessible archives, I am struck—particularly because the original three series aired long before I was even born—by what is a distinct echo from some of the Australian satirical news forms that would follow it. Particularly evident are the similarities to the work of *The Chaser*, who across their many television shows over the past decade, have regularly adopted a comparable ethos to Norman Gunston. They too have engaged heavily in the disruption of real-world media and political processes by, for instance, invading press conferences, intruding on the former Prime Minister John Howard's morning walks in increasingly bizarre ways, and making world head-lines in 2007 by passing heavy security in Sydney for the APEC conference with a "fake" motorcade (Harrington, 2012). During *The Chaser's War on Everything* (2006–2007, 2009), Andrew Hansen, for instance, would approach celebrities at press conferences under the guise of "Mr. Ten Questions," where he would ask a string of 10 humorous (and often insulting) ques-tions, but provide no time between each for a response. For example, he offended one member of the Backstreet Boys by inquiring, among other things, if the name of their group was "a sexual reference, because enduring your music is like being rogered[4] roughly from behind?" (ABC, 2006), and sparked some (largely manufactured) public outrage by asking "screen legend" Sophia Loren, "as the world's most refined actress, do you ever fart?" (ABC, 2007). This again reveals not only the Australian desire to mock the powerful and self-righteous but also the willingness to transgress social televisual boundaries. In fact, another key element of

---

[4] A euphemism for sexual intercourse.

31

The Chaser's War on Everything was its direct antagonism toward sensationalist or unethical news and current programs elsewhere on television (Harrington, 2010).

Although *The Norman Gunston Show* was not a fake *news* program as such (it intended instead to parody night time talk shows), it dealt with real people and serious events in mischievous ways (a fact perfectly illustrated by "the dismissal" discussed above) and played an important role in entrenching a "lack of respect for TV's conventions and formulas" (Turner, 1989, p. 37) as a defining trait of Australian television. McDonald's enthusiastic transgression of generic conventions and social expectations effectively marked out a space for future innovations. *The Norman Gunston Show* took the preexisting trend of "transgression" and, significantly, layered on top of it a new element of "fakeness" that effectively helped set down the roots for a variety of more specific news parodies that have followed in subsequent decades.

FRESH LEAVES: *NEWSTOPIA*

Newstopia[5] is perhaps best explained to an outsider as a comedy program presented in the form of a news show that aired on Australia's Special Broadcasting Service (SBS) over three series of 10 episodes each in 2007 and 2008. If Australian television is known for its "cheeky form of subverting generic expectations" (McKee, 2001, p. 20), then *Newstopia* was indeed an exemplar of Australian television, even if it did not earn a particularly large audience share or much lasting respect. Its host, Shaun Micallef, played the role of lone news anchor in a typical news studio (his desk formed the shape of Australia), commenting on the news, throwing to pre-prepared stories, or conducting interviews with in-studio guests.

Newstopia could be classified nearly as a contemporary televisual form of Dadaism due to the very unusual way it blended biting satire with "straight" comedy, almost anti-television jokes, and a strong degree of self-referentialism. It was semiotically rich, positively overloaded with sometimes nearly imperceptible visual jokes (many of them recurring "in-jokes" with its audience), and moved rapidly from one comedic posture to the next (in some cases from "worthy" satire to the outright bizarre in a matter of seconds). This has much to do with Micallef's absurdist and surrealist sense of humor, which is well illustrated in this example, where he ends a quite standard and serious announcement of the UN Envoy's arrival in Burma with an entirely unexpected, risqué joke:

> Micallef: [Ibrahim Gambari's] visit follows the expulsion of the UN's most senior official in Rangoon, Charles Petrie: a move regarded by some as a devastating blow to the UN Mission there. Gambari arrives with a serious message from UN Secretary General Ban Ki-Moon, "let the UN get on with what it does best: forcing underage girls into prostitution." (Series 1, Episode 5)

Although he mostly played the "straight man," Micallef's role was generally to surprise the viewer with injections of the strange and unexpected. For example, he quite seriously introduced one episode which included the line: "also tonight: why migrants are the main cause of racism" (Series 3, Episode 1). In the following case, he sets up to a "live" cross, with the expectation that the audience might be presented with some detailed analysis of a real election event. In the

---

[5]The show's title was normally capitalized as *NEWStopia*, but has been left here in standard form.

end, however, the cross is blindingly fast (again, breaking from the conventions of the news which would demand an extended discussion of minutiae), and used only as the punch line of a joke:

Micallef:	Well, Russia has had its elections, and next door the good people of Romania have also gone to the polls today. "Verity Elk" is in the tally room in Transylvania, and Verity, how's The Count going?
Verity Elk:	He's romped it in, Shaun.
Micallef:	Thanks Verity. (*Newstopia*, Series 2, Episode 3)

In this instance, as in many others, *Newstopia* offers a fictionalized, comedic twist on a real event. Another was the release of a frightening Al Qaeda training video which, in *Newstopia*'s version, detailed everything from the polite tea and coffee beforehand, to the PowerPoint presentations, the friendly team-building exercises, and a fun group photo at the end. The only difference here being that all of the attendees masked their faces and carried AK-47s or rocket propelled grenade launchers (Series 1, Episode 3).

As can again be seen in the following example, *Newstopia* had a deeply interwoven mix of the "real" and the "fake," using clever puns and its own spin on the news format:

Micallef: Well, the old saying "good things come in glass" might well apply to the coffin on display [. . .] at the Santa Maria Delle Grazie church [. . .] It's made entirely of glass except, presumably, the hinges inside. And inside is a very good thing indeed: the corpse of Padre Pio. So good he was made a Saint. Padre Pio was exhumed on the 40th anniversary of his death: a gesture he most certainly would've appreciated if he was alive. A Vatican forensics team dated his remains, and apparently had a wonderful evening. In life, The Padre had stigmata, which made it very difficult for him to play Twister. (*Newstopia*, Series 2, Episode 10)

While this absurdity punctuated the show, its defining premise—and the thing that set it far apart from most other parody news shows that have come before it in Australia—was its multilayered and extremely high degree of "fakeness."

All of the "guests" and the reporters filing the video stories were played solely by the same group of five actors: Ben Anderson, Nicholas Bell, Julie Eckersley, Kat Stewart, and Peter Houghton. At the end of each episode, these same actors would play members of the general public in a satirical take on a *vox pop* segment. In fact, the same actor might play several different roles on the show within the course of a single 25-minute episode.

Shaun Micallef himself also played a number of characters on the show. In many cases he would cross to a news story that he had voiced over in character; a common one was "Pilger Heston" (presumably a combination of John Pilger and Charlton Heston), who peppered news reports on any topic with loud, angry howls about "those damned apes!"—or with his imperson-ation of a real person (e.g., Christopher Walken). Perhaps the height of this strangeness came in his sporadic, extended, on-location interviews with special guests. In these interviews, Micallef would play both the interviewer, and would dress up and play the role of the interviewee as well.

Finally, among the commercials that would run during the show's ad breaks would be satir-ical ones created by the *Newstopia* team for real companies—in particular, for hardware chain Bunnings, which would advertise items for sale such as "other people's ointment"—fake compa-nies (such as the eco-friendly range of cleaning products from a company called "revive dead dolphins"), or previews for nonexistent shows on SBS such as "Inspektor Herring" (a clear reference to *Inspector Rex*) or "Tyrants and their Pets," which sent up the network's apparent obsession with documentaries about World War II.[6]

While *Newstopia* style was certainly unique, it did nevertheless share several similarities with a host of "fake" news shows that preceded it. Its entire cast of fake characters clearly harkens back to the comedic premise of Norman Gunston some 30 years before. The impersonation of political or media figures was a style likewise seen on *The Gillies Report* in the 1980s—most famous was Max Gillies' wicked impersonation of Prime Minister Bob Hawke—and the ongoing satire of John Clarke and Bryan Dawe. In their weekly segment on the highbrow ABC current affairs show *7:30*, Clarke pretends (without any actual impersonation, as such) to be a political figure in the news, answering Dawe's questions with the requisite amount of spin and feats of twisted logic.

Again in keeping with the "transgressive" tradition stretching back to *In Melbourne Tonight* in the late 1950s, *Newstopia* played constantly with the television format itself and the audience's expectations, often setting itself up as the target of ridicule. Here Micallef jumps rapidly between correctly and incorrectly playing the role of "straight" news anchor, that is, both following and breaking the genre for comedic effect, while discussing the 2008 US presidential election race with "political expert Marion Davies" (played by Nicholas Bell):

Micallef: While Barack Obama and Hillary Clinton battle it out to represent the Democrats in the November election, John McCain has been confirmed as the Republican nominee. At the moment, at 71, he's the second oldest first-time candidate to run for the office of US president: a situation which doesn't get any better later this year when the former Vietnam combat vet turns 72. If he becomes president, he'll be the oldest first-time US president in history. Now, Marion Davies, how far can McCain take this aging thing? It seems to be working pretty well for him so far.

Davies: Sky's the limit Shaun. If McCain is successful in his bid, and serves out his full four year term, then, according to our calculations, he could be up to 76 years old.

Micallef: Fuck.

Davies: We did some estimates, you know. We calculated that his likely age, should he continue to serve until the year 2048, would be 108 years old. Now that makes him not only the oldest US president, but also the third oldest person in the world.

Micallef: That's 2048 A.D.?

Davies: Yep.

Micallef: What about Hillary Clinton?

Davies: Well, she'll become, you know, the first female US President regardless of her age, but Barack Obama, on the other hand, that's an interesting case. Now, you elect him to the White House, he makes history as not only the youngest US president, but also the least-white president, and also the most-black president in the history of the United States.

Micallef: Right, so, triple threat?

Davies: Well, it's gonna be interesting.

Micallef: Should be *very* interesting, thank you very much Marion. [*leans over and politely kisses Davies on the cheek*] (Series 2, Episode 3)

---

[6]The first in this series, for example, teased an episode on "Hitler's Poodle."

As we can see, Micallef generally adopts the normative and well-established role of the rational anchor in contrast to Marion's inane commentary on trivial and ludicrous "facts," but he then disrupts that position with his completely unnecessary, "unprofessional" (and entirely unexpected) use of profanity to express his astonishment at his guest's analysis, and too with his highly unusual goodbye gesture to his guest. He transgresses the boundaries of "normality" in the television news sphere, surprising the audience into reflecting on what those boundaries are, and the reasons for their existence in the first place. It is another moment of parody "that employs exaggeration, often to the point of ludicrousness, to invite its audience to examine, evaluate, and re-situate the genre and its practices" (Baym, 2005, p. 269).

More importantly, however, *Newstopia* regularly leveraged its absurdist, satirical position to again transgress cultural limits and social mores. Amidst the fun and frivolity of the comedy was a frequently deployed dark sense of humor juxtaposed against real events to give the stories a high level of satirical critique. Here a story about an eating competition in the United States is placed into global perspective through a live phone cross to "Jordan Esterhaus" (Nicholas Bell), allegedly in Ethiopia:

Micallef:	A 24-year-old hospital orderly from California has set a new record for eating hot dogs. Billy O'Brien chowed down 61 hot dogs, including buns, in just 13 minutes, beating the old record by two. *Newstopia* correspondent Jordan Esterhaus is in the Somali region of southern Ethiopia. Jordan, what's the reaction been like over there?
Esterhaus:	Disappointment, obviously, Shaun. This is the 12th year this event has been staged, and, in that time, no Ethiopian has been in the top ten in the hot dog eating championships.
Micallef:	Why such an appalling record, Jordan?
Esterhaus:	Well, I think they struggle with the concept. They can't quite get their head around the notion of one person eating 61 hot dogs, instead of 61 people eating 61 hot dogs. It doesn't make any sense to them.
Micallef:	Well, they're not going to get anywhere in the international eating competitions with that mindset, are they?
Esterhaus:	Indeed.
Micallef:	Perhaps officials from the International Federation of Competitive Eating need to go over there and conduct some clinics [to] pass on their knowledge?
Esterhaus:	Yes, or just the hot dogs.
Micallef:	To practice on, you mean. Good idea.
Esterhaus:	But at least in the meantime the Americans have provided these people with plenty of instructional news footage, of how to stuff vast quantities of food down one's gullet in record time.
Micallef:	Yes, well let's hope the Ethiopians learn something from it, about how we do things in the west. (Series 2, Episode 8)

The same goes again in the following segment, which sends up the news media's almost orgiastic obsession with wealth, joking that a movement from the world's most wealthy person to the third most wealthy is seen as some kind of devastating blow by the people from *Forbes* magazine. Here, "Tony Pearon" from *Forbes* magazine is played by Ben Anderson:

Micallef:	The *Forbes* top 500 rich list is out, and it's not good news for Microsoft founder Bill Gates. Tony Pearon from *Forbes*. Tony . . .
Pearon:	That's right Shaun, old Gatesey's been knocked out from the number one possie by fellow US billionaire caucasoid Warren Buffett, who, despite giving away the bulk of his money

a year ago to Bill Gates and his wife, still has more money. It doesn't make any sense at all, mathematically, it just shows how freakin' appalling things are right now for the Gatemeister at the moment. In fact, he didn't even get second place this year: that went to some phone cat from Mexico. And it's uncertain at this stage, Shaun, just how Gates intends to rebuild his shattered financial empire.

Micallef: What about the bottom 500 list, Tony? What's happening there?

Pearon: Well, Afghani nonagenarian Afeeza Douad is most impoverished again, for the third year running, with personal assets of a bottle top, and a three centimeter bit of string. [*Holds up a copy of the magazine and looks at the camera*] *Forbes* magazine: go for it! (Series 2, episode 3)

In both of these examples, the "fakeness" of the show allows the stories to be discussed in frank terms, highlighting the universally flippant way that the news media covers events that can only come about through Western privileges of extraordinary wealth and nearly limitless supplies of food. By taking news stories such as these, which would normally receive no critical discussion, nor precipitate even the smallest measure of self-reflection by the journalists covering them as "news," the show is imbued with an overall tenor of responsibility, social justice, and rationality that is sadly absent in the mainstream media.

CONCLUSION

The intention of this brief analysis has been to sketch out some of main traits of "fake" news in Australia and historicize the genre within a wider tradition of "transgressive TV." As the discussion of *The Norman Gunston Show* and *Newstopia* suggests, news parody as a tool for political and cultural satire does indeed have a very strong tradition in this country. If news parody is a global television language, then is there such a thing as an Australian accent on this language? At the risk of being reductionist, I would argue that one can identify a single narrative about news parody's history in Australia: that it more frequently and more substantially transgresses the fine line between the "real" and the "fake" and is more likely to leave the audience wondering which is which. Whereas the quotation marks around the word "fake" are important in most contexts, as they denote the lose and complicated sense of the word, in this country it is probably more correct to just refer to these programs as *fake news*. Whereas *The Daily Show with Jon Stewart* has become the center of much positive discussion around the concept of "fake" news (see, e.g., Feldman, 2007; Jones, 2005), a more apt comparison between North America and Australia in this case might be with the work of fake newspaper (and now website and TV program) *The Onion*: where the relationships to events in the "real" world are more tangential than direct. If anything, this just further highlights the need for media, communication, and entertainment scholars to more fully appreciate regional specificities when discussing a broad term such as "fake" news.

Finally, it is useful to consider what the point of all this "fun" might be. If "fake" news really is a part of the Australian television landscape, then what "good" might the genre serve? While it would be tempting to dismiss the examples highlighted in this article as *less real* and therefore inherently *less worthy* than some of the more prominent international reference points which have helped bring the notion of "fake" news into the public consciousness, I would contend that to do so would be to underestimate the importance of "fakeness," not just as a comedic device or rhetorical camouflage, but also as a social tool and an avenue for a greater understanding of genre.

Paul Achter (2008) notes that comedy can oftentimes provide a comfortable way for people to initially discuss upsetting or confronting issues. While there was a period in 2001 shortly after the 9/11 terrorist attacks in New York and Washington, D.C., when laughter was seen as taboo (that it was literally "too soon" or disrespectful), comedy shows and, in particular, *The Onion* were in fact at the forefront of helping citizens begin to understand, discuss, and re-think the terror attacks in a wider political and social context. So, even in the case of highly fictionalized parodies where there is no real "surface-level" information, the audience is still afforded the chance to reflect on the deeper cultural questions raised in (and by) the *form* of the satire.

Similarly, news programs do not always have to generate new information but can be significant for their ability to interpret and frame news created by other sources (Harrington, 2010). There is an immense amount of value in a show such as *Newstopia* as a form of what Gray calls "critical intertextuality": antagonistic satire with the power to "re-evaluate, ridicule, and teach other genres" (Gray, 2006, p. 4). Gray draws on the work of David Buckingham, who argues that much greater emphasis should be placed "on how the text situates the viewer *in relation to* 'information,'" or "how it defines and constructs the experience of 'becoming informed,'" rather than simply judging news programs on their ability to deliver news to the viewer (Buckingham, 2000, p. 18, emphasis added). "Fake" news, in its finest forms, strips back the pretense that television news is "transparent or 'unmediated'" and makes the viewer realize "the ideologically or politically aligned character of the perspective from which the television 'eye' surveys the world" (Turner, 2000, pp. 89–90).

So, even in those cases where everything is "fake," the absurdity and contraventions can in fact make us think very carefully about the real world. Thus returning to *Newstopia* for one final time, we can see the type of juxtaposition which invites viewers to reflect critically on the often misplaced news values of the mainstream media:

Micallef:	Life in Baghdad might have presented its challenges under the regime of Saddam Hussein, but how has the continued presence of western forces changed things? Blair Francz reports. And does so for us now.
Francz [Peter Houghton]:	It's been a hellish few years in Baghdad, but the past three months have been particularly difficult for the locals. They've had to cope with the distressing images of Brittany [sic] Spears' performance at the MTV Awards, and disturbing rumors of a rift between Prince Mary and Princess Fredrick [sic] of Denmark. At least there's been some relief on that front: the latest intelligence suggesting the marriage is harmonious, the couple still very much in love. But tragedy is never far away here. Speak to any family in Iraq, and they'll all express the same fears: will Heather Mills and Paul McCartney reach an amicable settlement? Is Owen Wilson going to be OK? Will Shane Watson's wretched run of injury come to an end? Half of the children here have never heard of Nicole Ritchie [sic]. If aid, or *Ralph* magazine, doesn't arrive soon, some of them never will. Blair Francz, in Baghdad, for *Newstopia*. (Series 1, episode 5)

The "Blair Francz" character places the audience in an awkward position here, as his remarks force us to consider what count as "problems" in the first world, and to think about how they absolutely pale in comparison to the infinitely deeper and more serious problems confronting those stuck in a Middle Eastern war zone. If only for a moment, we might just re-think our own priorities, as well as those of the news media.

McKee has described the 1990s program *Frontline* as a "meta-text" because it was "an important text in popular culture's continual self-interrogation" that "allowed popular culture to discuss the production of popular culture" (McKee, 2001, p. 294). I would contend that the potential value of Australian "fake" news more generally should be seen in the same light. It is a fun, irreverent, self-reflexive, sometimes frivolous form of popular culture that mirrors a highly irreverent national consciousness and which often reflects very deeply upon who we are as a people.

REFERENCES

Achter, P. (2008). Comedy in unfunny times: News parody and carnival after 9/11. *Critical Studies in Media Communication, 25*(3), 274–303.

Australian Broadcasting Corporation. (1992). The Gunston tapes. Sydney, Australia.

Australian Broadcasting Corporation. (2006). The Chaser's war on everything: 1.1 [DVD recording]. Sydney, Australia.

Australian Broadcasting Corporation. (2007). The Chaser's war on everything: 2.1 [DVD Video Recording]. Sydney, Australia.

Baym, G. (2005). *The Daily Show*: Discursive integration and the reinvention of political journalism. *Political Communication, 22*(3), 259–276.

Buckingham, D. (2000). *The making of citizens: Young people, news and politics.* London, England: Routledge.

Cox, P. (2006). *Great moments in Australian television.* Sydney, Australia: Powerhouse Publishing.

Feldman, L. (2007). The news about comedy: Young audiences, *The Daily Show*, and evolving notions of journalism. *Journalism, 8*(4), 406–427.

Gray, J. (2006). *Watching with The Simpsons: Television, parody, and intertextuality.* London, England: Routledge.

Harrington, S. (2005). The 'democracy of conversation': *The Panel* and the public sphere. *Media International Australia Incorporating Culture and Policy, 116*, 75–87.

Harrington, S. (2010). Chasing reporters: Intertextuality, entertainment and public knowledge. *Media International Australia, 134*, 121–130.

Harrington, S. (2012). The uses of satire: Unorthodox news, cultural chaos and the interrogation of power. *Journalism: Theory, Practice and Criticism, 13*(1), 38–52.

Jones, J. P. (2005). *Entertaining politics: New political television and civic culture.* Lanham, MD: Rowman & Littlefield.

McKee, A. (2001). *Australian television: A genealogy of great moments.* Melbourne, Australia: Oxford University Press.

Sternberg, J. (1995). Signs of *The Times*: Television current affairs as "meaning and pleasure." *Metro Magazine, 101*, 43–54.

Stockbridge, S. (2000). The strategies of audience capture: The case of Network Ten. In G. Turner & S. Cunningham (Eds.), *The Australian TV book* (pp. 190–200). Sydney, Australia: Allen & Unwin.

Strauss, N. (2006, November 30). Man behind the moustache. *Rolling Stone*, 59–63.

Turner, G. (1989). Transgressive TV: From *In Melbourne Tonight* to *Perfect Match*. In J. Tulloch & G. Turner (Eds.), *Australian television: Programs, pleasures and politics* (pp. 25–38). Sydney, Australia: Allen & Unwin.

Turner, G. (1996). Post-journalism: News and current affairs programming from the late '80s to the present. *Media International Australia, 82*, 78–91.

Turner, G. (2000). Television news and current affairs: "Welcome to Frontline." In G. Turner & S. Cunningham (Eds.), *The Australian TV book* (pp. 89–102). Sydney, Australia: Allen & Unwin.

No Strings Attached? *Les Guignols de l'info* and French Television

Waddick Doyle

This article discusses the French puppet news program *Les Guignols de l'info*, one of the oldest and most significant satirical television news shows in the world. It combines historical, semiotic, and political economy approaches in assessing the show's contribution to the scholarly debate on news parody. *Les Guignols* is explained in terms of the transformation of the French network television system and the creation of Canal+. It represented a new mix of genres and assisted network Canal+ to counterprogram successfully and build a brand identity. This, in turn, shaped the political economic framework, legitimatizing commercial television as being in both the national and the public interest. The article considers questions of the relationship among genre, truth, and branding from a political economic perspective.

Les Guignols de l'info, perhaps the world's oldest continuous television news satire, has captured considerable audience share and is widely regarded as having considerable political impact. In this article I wish to examine *Les Guignols'* influence on French television by examining the history of the show and its contribution to the development of the news satire genre, how this was used in counterprogramming, and the consequent shaping of the identity of the brand of its host network. This, I argue, helped in the transition of the media system from a state-owned one to a mixed private/public system and also changed the conception of truth inherent in television news with an effect of desacralizing politics and the state.

France has had a number of programs that could fit into the categories of fake and satirical news. These include the puppet show the *Bébête* show, which was on TF1 the highest rating network in France (TF1 was the first public network until privatized in 1987). A program similar to the American *The Daily Show*, *Le Vrai Journal* (the true news) featuring Karl Zero was broadcast between 1996 and 2006 on Canal+. Nothing, however, can compare to the perennial success of *Les Guignols de l'info* (hereafter referred to as *Les Guignols*), a parody puppet version of France's leading news program read by a puppet of the historic anchor Patrick Poivre D'Arvor. The original news anchor is known by his initials PPDA, but the puppet newsreader is known as PPD. Inspired by the British comic puppet news show *Spitting Image* (1984–1996), *Les Guignols* has become a national institution in France. The day after the presidential elections in both 1995 and 2002, it reached extremely high audiences—over 15% of the national audience on each occasion (Hecker, 2004). It achieved equally high audience figures in 2000 when a rumor circulated that it was closing down (*Stratégies,* 2000). The show began in 1988, and now is in its 23rd year. In 2010, after 22 years and in a very competitive market, it still had an 8.5% market share and 26% of the 15–34-year-old market (*Le Post,* 2010).

Les Guignols has far outlasted the British show of which it was once an imitation. *Les Guignols,* as opposed to many other satire news shows, was not a stand-alone program but an eight-minute segment inside a longer program called *Nulle Part Ailleurs* ("Nowhere Else"), which appeared in prime time on Canal+. It was therefore part of the brand identity that constructed Canal+, France's first private channel, as different from its competitors because it had programming that could be found nowhere else. The show's title thus reinforced the originality of the channel's programming that was innovative and broke many genre rules. Canal+ could be explained to an American public as a mixture of Comedy Central and HBO. Most programming on Canal+ was pay TV available only to subscribers, just as HBO is in the United States. On the other hand, *Nulle part ailleurs* was free to air and could be seen by all French television viewers. It was the public face of the network during the peak viewing time of 7:00–9:00 p.m., the key portion of the French programming schedule. *Nulle part ailleurs* was discontinued in 2001, and the show which replaced it, *Journal du Cinema,* was discontinued in 2004. However *Les Guignols* survived and continued. It was never a free-standing program but always part of a container program: a genre more common in France, Italy, and South America than in the English speaking world which for several hours mixes talk, variety and other genres.

Since 2004, *Les Guignols* has been part of another container program called *Le Grand Journal* ("The Big News") which is broadcast for two hours every weeknight. *Les Guignols* continues to be presented by the puppet PPD, even though PPDA, the human being, retired and is no longer the anchor of the TFI news. PPD has taken on a life of his own and continues as a popular presenter even after the disappearance of the human version. *Les Guignols* and its anchor have become as much as an institution in French national television as the *téléjournal* of TF1, France's most viewed news program.

Les Guignols has also become a format that is imitated in other countries by direct format transfer (Moran, 2009): in Spain, Canal+ *Spain* produces *les Noticias del Guiñol*; in Portugal, there is *Contra-Informação*; in Cameroon, *Les Guignols de l'Afrique*; and in India, as discussed by Kumar in this collection, *Gustakhi Maaf*. In these cases, the program's format is used as part of a legal agreement to export a form where the intellectual property of *Les Guignols* is recognized. In other countries, there are also shows that follow the format closely but do not have a licensing agreement such as *Douma-Krati* in Lebanon, *Gli sgommati* in Italy, *Kulky* in Russia, *Hurra Deutschland* in Germany, and *Gustakhi Maaf* in India (see Kumar's contribution to this special issue).

The show lasts only eight minutes and consists of figures that are either political, show business, or sporting personalities in the form of caricature puppets. PPD introduces the guests and interviews them. Currently, he begins the show with the line "welcome to the ancestor of the internet," but formerly he began with "you who believe everything they tell you on television: good evening." Thus the show clearly has defined itself as the television news for skeptics, a form of counter information, a different model of truth. Furthermore, it is counterprogrammed against the very show it parodies at 8:00 p.m. In French slang, the evening news is referred to as *La Grande Messe* ("High Mass"), referring to the religiously regular way French audiences have watched the news since the 1960s. Hence *Les Guignols'* irreverent version is in direct competition and has itself become a type of counter-ritual for non-believers in network news. The show is so popular that the whole week's series is rebroadcast in a single free-standing program on Sunday at lunchtime known as *Le Dimanche des Guignols* ("Guignols Sunday"), with PPD always ending with the line "now you can turn off the TV and do something normal."

HISTORY

Les Guignols was first screened in 1988 but initially did not satirize the news of the day and was called *Les Arènes de l'Info*. It replaced a program called *JTN*, also a news parody but without puppets. Canal+ network decided to combine *JTN* with a copy of the English show *Spitting Image*. Many different talents including traditional puppet makers were employed, but perhaps the most striking contributor was Yves le Coq, a mimic and voice impersonator. In its early days, the program was recorded three weeks in advance, so its content was often out of date. After 1989, however, *Les Guignols* included live content and was thus not just a satirical reflection on current affairs but also an actual copy of a news format. At this point the name was changed to *Les Guignols de l'info*.

The decision to create the show was a risky one because it was counterprogrammed directly against *La Bébête Show*, the other satirical puppet show based on *Spitting Image*, which was broadcast on TF1 before the evening news. *Les Guignols de l'info* consisted of a mock news program with puppets whereas *La Bébête Show* was a program mocking politicians with puppet versions of them. The innovative element of *Les Guignols* was that it parodied both the news and anchors suggesting collusion between politicians and the media. The choice of mimicking France's best-known newsreaders and TF1 news was a successful one. After being counter-programmed against *La Bébête Show*, *Les Guignols* was moved to the 8:00 p.m. timeslot and was counterprogrammed against the news itself. Canal+ also began to counterprogram[1] against TF1 in general.

Les Guignols became spectacularly popular with the beginning of the first Gulf War. In 1991, France was part of the coalition that participated in the war, and the French media, particularly TF1, took a position in favor of the allied intervention. *Les Guignols,* on the other hand, had a fairly aggressive anti-American stance, and invented a puppet called *Monsieur Stallone* (based on American actor Sylvester Stallone, star of the *Rambo* movie franchise) who represented US global violence. He first appeared as a US Army officer and then as a corporate executive for the fictitious *World Company* representing the collusion of American military and economic interests, a theme that clearly struck a cord with the French public. Russell (2011) sees the first Gulf War as a key moment in the transformation of journalism, and it is clear that this was a key moment in France as well. A large part of the French general public found the reporting of the war on France's main stations unbelievable, with its surgical strikes and video game images. *Les Guignols* mocked the news coverage mercilessly, presenting the war as an advertisement for a videogame financed and designed by the American military.

The disaffection with the coverage can be attributed to many factors, including the historic anti-Americanism of both left and right, France's large Muslim and Arabic speaking population,

---

[1]Counterprogramming is the strategic use of programming scheduling to maximize target audience and sometimes to decrease the size of the competing network's audience.

and the long and tragic history of the Algerian conflict. All of these factors made the French public skeptical about the invasion of Kuwait and sensitive to the satire of the news provided by the mainstream stations. More importantly, it established *Les Guignols* as a program with a reputation for telling a version of events that many identified as more honest than that promoted by the traditional news media. This was accentuated when *Les Guignols* took an aggressive stance against TF1, and its management. *Les Guignols* caricatured Patrick Le Lay, the director of TFI and a key figure in the promotion of commercial television with a puppet version, an agent of the fictional *World Company* run by the Sylvester Stallone puppet. By insisting on the inauthenticity of the other private network based entirely on advertising, *Les Guignols* and Canal+ reinforced its image as authentic truth teller, despite itself being a private network (which the French public was quite suspicious of due to its economic imperatives).

Les Guignols rose quickly to capture 10–14% of the national viewing audience, some three million viewers (Hecker, 2004). By 1992, *Les Guignols* was drawing audiences away from France's most watched *téléjournal* on TF1. In the mid-1980s, private television was a new phenomenon in France where the system, as in other European countries, had consisted of three national publicly owned television networks. The new private television stations became the place where news parody genre was developed. This served the purpose of attracting audience but also helped create an image of irreverence for authority and a sense of freedom that helped justify the existence of the new networks. Thus, *Les Guignols* helped define Canal+ within the general economy of television in France. *Les Guignols* is Canal+'s critical "lead-in." Ksobiech and Tiedge (1986) define "lead-in" as the key counterprogramming moment where a network attempts to attract an audience for the evening's viewing. Typically it is the evening news, which draws the audience on a regular basis.

All of this was achieved at a relatively low cost. Kerloc'h (2009) explains how *Les Guignols* is produced with a budget of 15 million Euros a year, a large staff of writers (normally three at a time), puppeteers (more than 33), impersonators, costume makers, and technical staff. Cartoonists draw figures that are then turned into latex puppets, baked, and then painted. The show has a stock of more than 320 puppets covering most of France's important political, cultural, and social figures. Each stringless puppet is manipulated by two people, one who controls the arms and one the face. Often the show produces fictional skits, which include the construction of decors, as well as the interviews by the puppet anchor PPD. As Kerloc'h (2009) notes, the program's creator, Alain Duverne, says that the puppet format provides far more freedom than computer-generated images because they are supple and can react to the news very quickly, producing a bulletin at the same time as television news. In 2011, the show did however begin to use computer-generated images of less known figures.

CARICATURE AND FRENCH CULTURE

Les Guignols has now entered firmly into French popular culture and language. Certain expressions have been adopted, for example, *"espice de connasse,"* a vulgar play on words originally used by the Guignols to mock the Taliban's attitude to women, but was subsequently adopted as derogatory slang for women. Other phrases such as *"a Ciao,"* the greeting given by the puppet PPD, have become popular expressions. Children often imitate figures from *Les Guignols*, including Health Minister Roselyne Bachelot's caricature of feigned surprise saying, "Ah Boooon," indicating her ignorance and surprise about everything.

Although *Les Guignols* is part of the worldwide tendency toward news satire (as detailed in this special issue), it also corresponds to key elements of French culture in several regards. First, it is a complete imitation of the news on TFI, the former leading public station in France, which was privatized in 1987. Second, the name *guignol* refers to the age-old French cultural puppet show from Lyon, a French *Punch and Judy* that is still very much alive today. In any Parisian park or in any village in summer there will be the traveling spectacle of *Guignol*, the furtive puppet causing chaos and being chased by the police shouting, "you cannot catch me," while children shout to the police where he is. On *Les Guignols*, until recently Osama Bin Laden played the role of the uncatchable *guignol*. The title of the program thus fits with a French tradition of marionettes and puppets associated with what Bahktin (1941) called a carnivalesque inversion of authority and mocking of established power. France is often described as a monarchical republic and has an old tradition of mocking its absolute authority. McCormick and Pratasik (1998) explain the history of the puppet as an instrument of subversion in French history during the French revolution. The puppet shows were improvised and often referred to current events. Clark (1982) recounts how Napoleon's nephew, Louis-Napoléon Bonaparte, was elected President of France in 1848 after the revolution and in 1851 declared himself Emperor in a coup d'état. His secret police tried to silence the opposition but Lyon's *Guignol* made relentless fun of him. The police tried to make all puppeteers submit a written text before any performance. Thus, subversion linked to *Guignol* and puppets has a long tradition.

What is more, *Les Guignols* combines puppetry with caricature, another strong tradition in French culture. Sandy Petrey (2005) analyzes Phillippon's caricatures of King Louis Philippe during the 1830s. When charged with sedition, Phillippon said that his drawing was not one of the king but of a pear as there were no royal insignia. The pear became a symbol of resistance to Louis-Philippe's rule and Stendhal remarked that France's walls were covered with pears. The censors banned pears and then they even banned rabbits without ears that looked like pears. In a headline worthy of today's *Guignols*, the newspaper of the day announced: "Censors ban dumb animals. It is practically suicide."

One of France's oldest and most popular newspapers is *Le Canard Enchaîné* (Martin, 2001), a satirical newspaper based on wordplay, cartoons, and investigative reporting. It is famous for mock interviews, scandals, courageous journalism, and scathing sarcasm. In 2011, it ran a fictional column authored by "Carla B.," mocking the presidential couple (referring to Carla Bruni, wife of President Nicolas Sarkozy). In many ways *Les Guignols* is a postmodern televisual version of the *Canard Enchaîné*.

POLITICS AND POLITICIANS

Since 1989, *Les Guignols* has caricatured every major event and personality of international and French public life. George Bush was cast as an ineffectual idiot dominated by his parents, and Monsieur Stallone was the director of the World Company. The Pope was shown as ineffectual and aided by none other than Cardinal Stallone. Arab dictators all had puppets: Kaddafi, Mubarak, Ben Ali, and Bouteflika were all shown as complicit with the French political ruling elite. *Les Guignols* has also played an important role in presidential elections. In 1995, it was accused of making former French president Jacques Chirac appear likeable and attractive despite representing him as a heavy beer drinker and liar, whereas the socialist candidate Lionel Jospin was depicted as well-meaning but boring and ineffectual (Collovald & Neveu, 1996; Hecker,

2004). In 2002, 15% of voters said the show influenced their choice (Hecker, 2004, p. 164). That election resulted in a runoff between Chirac and Le Pen, the leader of the extreme right Front National, who was only ever depicted on *Les Guignols* as a pitbull barking ferociously. Controversy arose around the *Guignols* because French law states that if election results are announced before the closing of polls, the election is invalid. *Les Guignols* announced the election result 15 minutes before closing, claiming that they wished to force a re-election to rid France of the embarrassment of the ultra-right Le Pen being a candidate in the second round. Their tactic had no effect. The electoral commission ruled that the results announced by puppets could not be taken seriously, showing that the conception of genre influences the way policy and legal bodies interpret the role of journalism

Les Guignols had acquired such significance in French society that the public took its anti-fascist stance as justification for disrupting the elections. The logic of *Les Guignols* was like that of Canal+, one of disruption, including disrupting clichés and ideas of truth, as well as programming schedules. The creators of the show can be seen as following a situationist logic, disrupting the habits of daily life against a political power that has come to work through spectacle.

This comes as no surprise, in that Bruno Gaccio, the chief scriptwriter of *Les Guignols*, was himself from a revolutionary background. In the 2007 presidential election, Gaccio courted controversy when it was reported that he wanted to openly campaign against President Sarkozy, who is depicted in the show as an ambitious, self-seeking treacherous *nouveau riche*, subservient to American interests. Being openly partisan may appear surprising to the non–French reader, but the right to satire and free speech is strong in France, where many media are also openly partisan. As Barbrook (1995) points out, France has a different notion of media freedom from English speaking countries; France's notion is based on individual freedom of expression and also on the idea of allowing the plurality of ideologies in the press. Thus the French state subsidizes both Catholic and Communist newspapers on the grounds of supporting a plural democratic state. Readers and viewers choose media outlets in full awareness of their partisan role (see Murschetz, 1998). The legitimacy of these media come simply from their role in the democratic process. Despite its partisan attitude, *Les Guignols'* legitimacy also came from its audience ratings.

PROGRAMMING AND GENRE

As this special issue demonstrates, news parody is a worldwide phenomenon that operates on the cusp of fictional and truth genres. Parody often reveals the actual form of genre by pushing it to its limits. Canal+'s image became associated with the novelty of remix culture based on genre mutations. *Le Grand Journal* itself could be identified by the different genre mutations included within it, such as *Les Guignols*, another parody show entitled *Le Petit Journal*, *le Zapping* (a remix based on the previous day's television), a talk show with prestigious guests, a parody weather show, and aggressive interviews with politicians. *Les Guignols* is scheduled exactly half way through the program. The second half, which features more guests and music, is called *Le Grand Journal La Suite*. It concludes with the comic segment *Service Après-Vente*.

In 1993, *Les Guignols* won two national television awards (Sept d'Or) for the best variety show as well as the best entertainment show (Jost & Spies, 2004). Interestingly, the television awards classified it generically as "entertainment" when clearly its role was increasingly political and news oriented, with an anti-war, anti-American, anti-TF1 identity. For example, in a special edition on December 9, 2009, the show involved an interview with Monsieur Stallone, the puppet in charge of selling war, chewing gum, and Chevrolet cars. He explains how the World Company invented "surgical strikes" and other terms and refers to the viewers as *cons* (idiots), correcting himself, then calling them *con-sommateurs* (consumers). Hence the show mocks the way television viewers are increasingly seen as consumers and not as citizens while at the same time it could be argued it was exactly part of that process.

Les Guignols remixed genre by combining real news stories that are mimicked as they break on the other networks. Every day three or four subjects are chosen from the news and the text is finalized by 5:00 p.m. when the puppets are chosen. The puppeteers then rehearse until the show goes live at 8:00 p.m. or sometimes two or three minutes before. The show not only competes for audience with network news, but it also conforms to the time constraints and actual pressures of a newsroom. The show has the authority of both telling the news while denouncing the official version of it. The production is clearly satire and although it often includes elements of fiction inspired by blockbuster movies, it is always about the news of the day and is thus able to convey a sense of immediacy.

NEO-TELEVISION

Umberto Eco (1985) called the genre-bending phenomenon of mixing news and fiction, *neo-television*. He explains that in the news the newsreader is expected to tell the truth. To prove it, he or she looks straight at the audience; in fiction, however, the viewer looks at characters in profile and the characters never look directly at the viewer. The then-new genres of talk shows and chat (in Italy, from where Eco is writing) broke up this dichotomy by conforming neither to the rules of fiction nor information. Eco linked this transformation to the proliferation of private television in Italy after 1980. Neo-television was encouraged by the rise of private networks. Italy in the 1980s was Europe's first deregulated, or more precisely "aregulated," television system, and the new private networks attracted attention to themselves by breaking down the distinction between news and entertainment (Doyle, 1989). The Italian Constitutional Court only allowed private channels if they were local, and the court ruled that only national public television could provide *informazione*, the genre usually used to talk about news. Advertisers wanted access to national markets, and therefore new programs appeared which bent the law and were not exactly "news." This enabled the creation of pseudo-national networks. I argue that neo-television led to the transformation of genre categories and that the law had to adapt to these new categories. The transformation of the public's definition of, or expectations for, program types in turn is closely related to how they see truth and information. *Les Guignols*'s mixing of news and puppetry, and caricature with poignant war stories on France's first private network did exactly the same thing. Genre remix and satire television redefine the news, the truth, and perhaps then, the nation.

In France, the transformation of genres has played a significant role in the rise of private television. French academic discussion of *Les Guignols* has centered either on its electoral influence (Groupe de St. Cloud, 1995; Hecker, 2004) or on questions of genre. Jost and Spies (2004) regard *Les Guignols* as an example of "reflexive television." Jost's (2007) analysis of television genres suggests a triangle between the authentic, the fictional, and the playful. *Les Guignols* finds itself between the three. Spies, meanwhile, focuses on the authenticity claims that underlie both news and satire. By translating statements from one genre to another, the program makes the public aware of how much one's acceptance of the truth value of a given statement depends on the rules of the genre in which the statement is uttered. Hence belief in the news comes not just from its words, but also from the style of the news desk, the anchor, and so on. In its news parody, *Les Guignols* reveals the fictional elements present in the news, and thus helps undermine the authenticity of news by showing its artifice.

Many academic studies of fake or parody news have tended to deal with questions of political influence and the way that information is treated. In the United States, this occurs in the framework of questions of political communication (Baym, 2005, 2009) or the transformation of journalism (Russell, 2011). Baym (2009) argues that "traditional" news was presented as the authoritative word, limiting other avenues of inquiry, and imposing narrative closure. News needs to maintain a position that is objective and expository. *The Daily Show*, he claims, emphasizes contradictions and inconsistencies in official discourses. Gaines (2007) demonstrates how this is done through the semiotic technique of continuity, exposing different forms of contradiction.

Baym (2005) argues that parody news uses "techniques drawn from the genres of news comedy and television talk show to revive a journalism of critical inquiry and advance a model of deliberative democracy" and that it opens the "potential possibilities of innovative forms for journalism in the 21st century" (p. 257). These shows reach disaffected audiences. Gray, Jones, and Thompson (2009) argue that satire challenges news publics to examine, question, and play with politics rather than simply to consume it, revealing the spectacular nature of news and restoring critical awareness.

Russell (2011) points out that many scholars have argued for the social and political value of this type of news. Hence she argues, along with Boler and Turpin (2007), that a type of ironic citizenship has arisen with an ethos and aesthetics of remix as a genuine subversive challenge. She links the rise of parody news to new forms of citizenship, political engagement, and journalism. This is in line with Eco, who argued that neo-television gives the private sector legitimacy over the public. News parody arrived in France at a key moment in the transformation of the political economy of broadcasting from a state system to a mixed system with public and commercial sectors. In the United States, Albarran, Chan-Olmsted, and Wirth (2005) argue that many transformations in the nature of US television programs were encouraged by cable networks, leading to a renewed importance of channel brand identity. American news parody is linked to the rise of cable television targeting young people and to the identity of the Comedy Central network (see Jones, 2005) as *Les Guignols* is linked to Canal+ in France. *Les Guignols* provided a new genre of satire news to French television that challenged dominant ways of perceiving truth, nation, and power.

NATION, NEWS, AND LEGITIMACY

Historically, television news helped legitimize national television as it contributed to the formation of national consciousness. Tunstall (2008) has argued that what remains resolutely national in our globalized media world is news. Historically, the nightly news program was linked to national television networks as the key moment leading into the evening's entertainment. This was true in television systems across the world, creating or reinforcing imagined communities of national citizenry in the same way that Benedict Anderson (1987) argued that the novel and the newspaper were central in creating a sense of national community. Somehow as French people sat in front of the television at 8:00 p.m., they knew that the majority of the other 60 million people were doing the same thing. They were watching the same news together simultaneously. In addition, this news was principally about what happened in the previous 24 hours and reinforced a sense of simultaneity, the sense that national community was real, alive, and active. Anderson refers to newspaper reading as a silent ceremony where one is aware that other people are reading the same newspaper (p. 35). Emphasizing the point further, in France, the news was called the television newspaper, *le télejournal*. The television news thus helped to create or reinforce the idea of the nation state, not only as unquestionable reality but as the basic community with which the audience identified.

In addition France associates the nation very clearly with the state and this notion has dominated the history of French broadcasting (Kuhn, 1995). Nation and citizenship are not conceived as ethnic entities but as ones linked to the constitutional order of the state. Until 1981, television news reflected this in its clear subservience to the interests of the state and often to the government (Barbrook, 1995). Canal+, when it was created in 1984, was the first network in France not to have a news program and not to be a national government-owned network. It thus involved a change in the practice of the news and thinking about what the national was (Doyle, 2004).

Consentino, Doyle, and Todorova (2009) have argued that the parody program *Striscia La Notizia* played an important role in legitimizing Berlusconi's networks in Italy (see Consentino's contribution to this special issue as well), while *Goposdari Na Efira* helped legitimize private broadcasting in Bulgaria. In France, I suggest, *Les Guignols'* generic transformation would similarly change the status of authority over truth and allow private television to be seen as a legitimate broadcaster worthy of public support. It also made the public broadcaster *France 2* and the former public broadcaster TF1 lose some of their credibility as sources of news.

Public broadcasting in all European countries depends on a tax on households called the *redevance* in France or a license fee in Great Britain. The existence of public broadcasting depends on the public perception that it is in the national and public interest, providing news and contributing to national cohesion and culture. In the 20 years since the creation of *Les Guignols*, the notions of both nation and public have much changed. This is in part a product of both changing technologies and changing economic circumstances. French television has moved away from national networks and opened to cable, satellite and internet, and the state has become less and less able to govern national broadcast systems. In this situation national television news has lost some of its authority, its capacity to authorize truth challenged by international news networks and online news services as well as satirical news programs on new networks.

Audience segmentation has lead to the decline of television as a central civic space for national deliberation (see Katz, 1996). In the European, and particularly French context, the emergence of satirical news coincides with the decline of public television as a primary civic space and the rise of private networks dependent on *brand* identity. Power in turn shifts away from the national broadcaster and towards an economic model of private competitive television, which airs competing notions of truth. Jones (2010) and others have pointed out that the edge of news parody is its power to show the inconsistencies offered by those who claim the authority to speak the truth about events crucial to the nation-state. In so doing, *Les Guignols* not only gave the private Canal+ network brand identity, media attention, and political importance, but it also helped *authorize* private television broadcasting in general.

TEXT AND GENRE

Chambers (1984), following Walter Benjamin, argues that all stories require a form of social authorization. Until the rise of the novel, stories were authorized by the state or the church. The novel, he argues, was able to avoid such forms of authorization by seducing an audience prepared to pay for it. Its authorization came from the market. Chambers argues that the novel was a text that shaped its context through commodification and encouraging a new type of reader. I argue that *Les Guignols* and news satire in general have had a similar function in the last 20 years. They have changed the way television news is authorized by shifting the authority to a critical general public and away from the state. This also has an influence on the framing and shaping of the audience's understanding of truth.

Jones (2007) points out these processes are linked to new subjectivities and the rise of what he calls monitorial citizens. Citizens are no longer conceived of as individuals of a nation who seek information to help make rational choices but rather as groups—audiences to be defined, "known," and pleased. To that I would add that these groups increasingly form postnational allegiances. Satire news and *Les Guignols* participate in the rise of a new vision of truth and meaning as well as a new political economy of television and perhaps a changing form of subjectivity and understanding of truth.

Jost (2007) defines three essential genres of television: authentic, playful, and fictional. Each has a different relation to the viewer and a different way of conceiving truth. National television had news, documentary, and information programs, which were positioned as authentic, as well as fiction and game shows, which were not. Satirical television combines elements of all three genres. *Les Guignols* included elements from fiction marked by reference to famous movies (as well as the basic fact that the protagonists were all puppets), elements of the authentic (e.g., a news desk, and the structure of television news), and elements of play (e.g., a studio audience and a host cracking jokes). This generic mix complicates the perception of authority and assumptions of truth.

News satire exposes what used to be considered truth as either fiction or game, and in turn establishes itself as telling truth of another order. Showing the falsity and hypocrisy of those in power, in essence it exposes the fictional nature of the news and in so doing makes a claim to its own capacity to tell a hidden truth. Thus it not only authorizes itself as an authentic text, but it helps to authorize the brand identity of the network, and invites the audience into a new way of thinking of itself. In the context of the United States, Jones (2010) argues that networks and their brand identities are correlated with affective political stances and have become elements of cultural identification with, for example, Fox News speaking to and for the political right while the satirists Jon Stewart and Bill Maher seem to provide "an alternative set of relationships" for the political left (p. 3). One sees something similar in France, where Canal+ has taken a left stance and TF1 to the right. The decline of state owned networks meant that new commercial networks had to create a distinct exciting and perhaps seductive brand that has been able to woo viewers away from previously regular habits. *Les Guignols* has played a central role in this.

CONCLUSION

Historically, French television has been strongly cultural and educational, with a tradition of being obsequious to political power. The legislative conception of Canal+ was itself bold and different with an image of creative innovation. The station fit into a cultural logic where French films and television would be supported by the state against imports. *Les Guignols* fits the bill for the station's image. It contributed to its legitimacy and its success.

By the mid 1990s, Canal+ was on the crest of a wave and was so successful that it had become bigger than its parent company, Havas. It was the market leader in subscriber television in Europe with 4.5 million subscribers in France and 14 million in Europe (Palmer, 1999, p. 143). It had set up subsidiaries in Spain and Poland, established arrangements with other cable networks across Europe, and was broadcasting to Africa with Canal+ Horizons.

Les Guignols had long mocked globalizing America with its portrayal of "The World Company" but now Canal+ was to become a leading element of Vivendi, which, when it took over Universal, became the second largest communications conglomerate in the world. Suddenly it seemed that French national interest could be represented by a French corporation, and not the state. Vivendi's glory was to be short lived. By May 2002, Vivendi-Universal had followed the internet bubble and its share price fell 70%. However *Les Guignols* continued to function as part of a creative and dynamic corporation and provided the network the legitimacy of an Anti-American leftist satirical program as well. Canal+ was seen in the national interest and indeed helped redefine what constitutes the national. *Les Guignols* thus cannot be understood simply in terms of mocking the news or conveying information. Rather it must be seen in terms of how it created a brand that itself shaped the identity of its network and accelerated the turn away from a political economy of television based on state-controlled broadcasters speaking to and for the public, and toward a global communication economy based on network brands competing for audiences.

REFERENCES

Albarran, A., Chan–Olmsted, S. M., & Wirth, M. (2006). *Media management and economics handbook*. New York, NY: Lawrence Erlbaum and Associates.

Anderson, B. (1987). *Imagined communities*. London, England: Verso.

Bahktin, M. (1941). *Rabelais and his world*. Bloomington, IN: Indiana University Press.

Barbrook, R. (1995). *Media freedom: The contradictions of communication in the age of modernity*. London, England: Pluto Press.

Baym, G. (2005). *The Daily Show*: Discursive integration and the reinvention of political journalism. *Political Communication*, 22(3), 259–276.

Baym, G. (2009). Real news/fake news: Beyond the news/entertainment divide. In S. Allan (Ed.), *The Routledge companion to news and journalism studies* (pp. 374–383). London, England: Routledge.

Boler, M., & Turpin, S. (2007, June). *Ironic citizenship or coping with complicity in a spectacular society*. New Network Culture Theory Conference. Amsterdam, The Netherlands. Retrieved from www.meganboler.net/publications/

Chambers, R. (1984). *Story and situation: Narrative seduction and the power of fiction*. Minneapolis, MN: University of Minnesota Press.

Clark, T. J. (1982). *The absolute bourgeois: Artists and politics in France*, 1848–1851. Princeton, NJ: Princeton University Press.

Collovald, A., & Neveu, E. (1996, September). Les Guignols ou la Cricature en abyme. *Persée*, 48, 87–112.

Consentino, G., Doyle, W., & Todorova, D. (2009). Tearing up television news across borders: Format transfer of news parody shows between Italy and Bulgaria. In A. Moran (Ed.), *TV formats worldwide* (pp. 203–221). Chicago, IL: University of Chicago Press.

Doyle, W. (1989). From deregulation to monopoly: A cultural analysis of Italian television. (Unpublished doctoral dissertation). Griffith University, Brisbane, Australia.

Doyle, W. (2004) French television and Canal+. In J. Sinclair (Ed.), *Contemporary world television* (pp. 74–77). Berkeley, CA: University of California Press.

Eco, U. (1985). *Sette Anni di Desiderio*. Milan, Italy: Bompiani.

Gaines, E. (2007). The narrative semiotics of *The Daily Show*. *Semiotica, 166*, 81–96.

Groupe de Saint Cloud. (1995). *L'image candidate à l'élection presidentielle de 1995: Analyse des discours dans les medias*. Paris, France: L'Harmattan.

Gray, J., Jones, J., & Thompson, E. (2009). *Satire TV: Politics and comedy in the post-network era*. New York, NY: New York University Press.

Hecker, M. (2004). *La presse française et la première guerre du golfe*. Paris, France: L'Harmattan.

Jones, J. P. (2005). *Entertaining politics*. Latham, MD: Rowman and Littlefield.

Jones, J. P. (2007). Citizenship, politics, and television panel. Unboxing Television Conference, Boston, MA: Massachusetts Institute of Technology. Retrieved from http://unboxingtv.org/provocations/unboxingtv_jjones.pdf

Jones, J. P. (2010). *Entertaining politics: Satiric television and political engagement*, 2nd edition. Latham, MD: Rowman and Littlefield.

Jost, F. (2007). *Introduction à l'analyse de la television*. Paris, France: Ellipses.

Jost, F., & Spies, V. (2004). *La télévision dans le miroir: théorie, histoire et analyse des émissions Reflexives*. Paris, France: L'Harmattan.

Katz, E. (1996). And deliver us from segmentation. *Annals of the American Academy of Political and Social Science, 546*(1), 22–33.

Kerloc'h, A. (2009, March 16). La souplesse du latex au service de l'humour. *20 Minutes*.

Ksobiech, K., & Tiedge, J. (1986). The "lead-in" strategy for prime time TV: Does it increase audience? *Journal of Communication,36*(2), 51–63.

Le Post. (2010, September 14). Record pour le Grand journal et les Guignols de l'info. Retrieved from http://www.lepost.fr/article/2010/09/14/2220387_record-pour-le-grand-journal-et-les-guignols-de-l-info.html

Kuhn, R. (1995). *The media in France*. London, England: Routledge.

Martin, L. (2001). *Le Canard enchaîné*. Paris, France: Flammarion.

McCormick, J., & Pratasik, B. (1998). *Popular puppet theatre in Europe, 1800–1914*. Cambridge, England: Cambridge University Press.

Moran, A. (2009). *TV formats worldwide*. Chicago, IL: University of Chicago Press.

Murschetz, P. (1998). State support for the daily press in Europe: A critical appraisal. *European Journal of Communication, 13*(3), 291–313.

Palmer, M. (1999). Multimedia multinationals: Canal Plus and Reuters. In M. Lecomte & M. Scriven (Eds.), *Television broadcasting in contemporary France and Britain* (pp. 140–168). Oxford, England: Berghahn Books.

Petrey, S. (2005). *In the court of the Pear King: French culture and the rise of realism*. Ithaca, NY: Cornell University Press.

Russell, A. (2011). *Networked: A contemporary history of news in transition*. London, England: Polity.

Strategies. (2000). *Record pour le grand journal et les Guignols de l'info*. Retrieved from http://www.strategies.fr/actualites/medias/r57436W/audience-record-pour-les-guignols-de-l-info.html

Tunstall, J. (2008). *The media were American: U.S. mass media in decline*. New York, NY: Oxford University Press.

The Comical Inquisition: *Striscia la Notizia* and the Politics of Fake News on Italian Television

Gabriele Cosentino

This article presents a discussion and analysis of the most prominent fake news show on Italian television, *Striscia la Notizia*, to demonstrate how it can effectively mount critiques against the political class, expose institutional inefficiencies, and mobilize audiences for matters of public interests. In order to analyze *Striscia*'s original brand of journalism, the article starts with a thorough account of the historical conditions that have fostered its rise to prominence. The second part of the article is based on a textual analysis of a number of segments from various episodes, which I selected in order to provide an account of the techniques, themes, and language adopted by the show. By providing both theoretical and empirical knowledge, I therefore wish to interrogate the ways in which fake news programs such as *Striscia* can create effective sites for citizens to engage with matters of public interest, while in the process challenging political institutions and the traditional role of mediation of official news outlets.

PUPPETEERING AS ALTERNATIVE JOURNALISM

Italian journalism is full of colorful myths about itself. For example, the "giornalista dimezzato" (Pansa, 1977)—the journalist split in half—has traditionally been a popular expression for the external constraints imposed on the professional independence of the Italian press. It suggests that the average Italian journalist is only 50% independent, with the rest of his or her abilities controlled by politics or finance. Another famous myth is that of the "1500 readers" (Forcella, 2004), the elite circle of business executives, politicians, members of the clergy, and academics that supposedly constitute the only readership of an Italian journalist. In the 1980s, formulas with strange code names such as "zebra" or "telephone number" were followed to hire or appoint journalists, as part of the larger phenomenon of "lottizzazione"[1] in public television RAI—the practice of assigning editorial or administrative positions along religious and party lines (Padovani, 2005).

A more recent and striking example of this mythology of the Italian press is the notion that one of the most trusted investigative journalists in Italy is a chubby red puppet that goes by

---

[1]The term comes from the Italian verb "lottizzare," which means to create "lotti" (lots) within a geographical area or a property. Inside Italian public broadcaster RAI, it came to identify the practice of assigning editorial or administrative positions along party lines. The "zebra" formula for example meant that journalists representing lay or catholic parties had to alternatively fill positions, creating the effects of "zebra stripes" in the structure of the staff.

the name of Gabibbo (Brambilla, 2004). Speaking with a thick accent from the city of Genua, Gabibbo is the creation of the program *Striscia la Notizia*, a pioneer in the increasingly popular fake news genre (Baym, 2005). Undoubtedly, the mixing of politics and popular culture in Italy has produced extravagant manifestations, from the election of a porn star to parliament in 1987 to the more recent scandals involving current Prime Minister Silvio Berlusconi. Within the characteristically Italian "theatre of politics" (Stille, 2006), it therefore may not be surprising that citizens trust a puppet as a legitimate source of information on current affairs and see it as a good representative of their discontent with political scandals or institutional wrongdoings.

So how did the Gabibbo manage to become a trusted voice in the Italian media, and what does its popularity entail for the relationship among television entertainment, journalism, and political communication in Italy? With this question in mind, this article discusses the most prominent fake news show on Italian television, *Striscia la Notizia*, in an effort to demonstrate how it can effectively mount critiques against the political class, expose institutional inefficiencies, and mobilize audiences for matters of public interests, all within a unique blend of entertainment and information.

As an early example of the fake news genre, *Striscia la Notizia* developed in the late 1980s within the specific conditions of the Italian broadcasting system and its relation with politics, characterized by a public service broadcaster, RAI, traditionally subservient to government parties, and by a highly concentrated private sector. The anomalous nature of the Italian broadcasting system is further seen in the ownership of a majority share of the main private television network, Mediaset, by current Prime Minister Silvio Berlusconi, who can by virtue of his position also wield significant influence on the public broadcaster. The unique current conditions of Italian television broadcasting are the product of the deregulation of national private television that followed the liberalization of the broadcasting system in the mid 1970s and early 1980s (Hallin & Mancini, 2004). The deregulation allowed the broadcasting system to be reconfigured, in less than a decade, into a duopoly, with public television RAI competing for audience and advertising investment with private conglomerate Fininvest. Since the late 1980s, *Striscia la Notizia* (henceforth referred to simply as "*Striscia*") has performed critical work required for transforming the attitude of Italian audiences toward state institutions in general, and public television in particular, in turn legitimating and empowering private commercial broadcasting. The traditionally pedagogic role of RAI's networks, undermined by the cultural transformations of the 1970s and 1980s, was challenged by the parodic, irreverent, but also somehow emancipatory language of entertainment programs.

Antonio Ricci, *Striscia*'s creator and main producer, argued that his program contributed to a redefinition of public service broadcasting, which he saw as no longer being about the representation of state institutions and political parties but rather of the demands and aspirations of the viewing publics (Maffioletti, 2008). Indeed, many of *Striscia*'s reports are based on a critique of the incompetence of institutions, including state television. Inquiries into political corruption, drawing on a populist animosity against government officials, are frequent, too. By often championing the claims of consumers' advocacy groups, the fake news show further seems to support a libertarian ethos based on free market capitalism and democracy.

By examining in detail the political-economic conditions that contributed to the emergence of this type of alternative news, this chapter suggests that *Striscia*'s success needs to be read in light of the growing relevance in liberal democracies worldwide of television programs blurring the boundaries between entertainment and information, and in turn as a consequence of the crisis of authority suffered by traditional news sources (Riegert, 2007; van Zoonen, 2005). The limited academic attention that fake news programs such as *Striscia* have received in Italy (Cosentino, Doyle, & Todorova, 2009; Giudici, 1998; Mascio, 2002) belies the surprisingly important role the show plays in the sphere of Italian broadcast journalism, and the trust it enjoys in the eyes of public opinion.[2] In particular, *Striscia* is Italy's most striking example of how the "discursive integration" (Baym, 2005) of formerly separate genres such as satire, variety show, and news has created durable and effective sites for the circulation of political information, public participation, and inquiry into actions of institutional power.

In recent years, media studies and political communication scholars worldwide have shown growing interest in such alternative journalistic outlets. While the term "fake news" has been offered to encapsulate the essence of this new genre, that label has often been criticized for being inadequate, as it belittles the credibility that shows such as *Striscia* in Italy or *The Daily Show* and *The Colbert Report* in the United States have gained in their respective domains of broadcast journalism and political communication (Baym, 2005; Jones, 2005). Nonetheless, fake news remains a useful category insofar as it articulates a tension between the uniqueness of such alternative news outlets on the one hand, and the common "assumptions about . . . authentic or legitimate set of news practices" (Baym, 2005, p. 261) on the other.

The title of this article, "The Comical Inquisition," refers to the approach that *Striscia* adopts when questioning the actions of politicians and institutions, which is both entertaining and aggressive. Such unprecedented hybridization between slapstick-style comedy and the vocal championing of citizens' rights in the face of institutional scandals is *Striscia*'s unique take on journalism. In open contrast with the tradition of journalism of public service broadcaster RAI, *Striscia* absorbed the entertaining language of its parent Fininvest network and put it in service of an odd but effective news organization. The article's title also echoes the historical role of the Catholic Inquisition as a symbol of a prosecuting attitude in the name of a higher moral authority. With this allusion I suggest that *Striscia*, by championing the cause of citizen-consumers, situates its public in a position of power vis-à-vis often disarrayed and corrupt institutions, particularly those associated with the Italian state. As argued by the show creator (Ricci, 1998), *Striscia* claims to act as the best representative of the political will of its audience, redefining the notion of public service according to the cultural and economic logic of private television.

In order to analyze *Striscia*'s original brand of journalism within the current landscape of mediated politics in Italy, the article starts with a review of the historical conditions that have fostered *Striscia*'s rise to prominence. The second part of the article offers a textual analysis of a number of segments from various episodes, which provide an account of the techniques, themes, and language that the show adopts to advance its critical function vis-à-vis the political class, and to emphasize its singularity with respect to traditional information outlets. By providing both theoretical and empirical perspectives, I therefore wish to interrogate the ways in which fake news programs such as *Striscia* can create effective sites for citizens to engage with matters of public interest, while in the process challenging political institutions and the traditional role of mediation of official news outlets.

---

[2]According to a 2010 Demos-Coop survey on information sources and public opinion in Italy, *Striscia* enjoys the highest percentage of trust of any newscast or public affairs show on Italian television. See http://www.demos.it/a00511. php. For a discussion on the survey result, see Diamanti (2010).

STRISCIA'S PLEDGE: TO BE FUNNIER THAN RAI'S JOURNALISTS

Striscia airs live on weekdays and recorded on Saturdays at around 8:30 p.m. on the national channel Canale 5, part of Berlusconi's television network. Behind the entertaining veneer of a hybrid between satirical news and a variety show, *Striscia*'s unique formula blends elements of investigative journalism, television parody, and comedy. The standard setup of the show features two "anchormen" introducing various correspondents, with frequent entertaining intermissions, such as comedic skits by the anchors and dance numbers by the "veline"[3]—two girls originally introduced to bring the anchors the news stories, who have become icons of contemporary Italian popular culture and its (often demeaning) representation of women. With the exception of the Gabibbo puppet, original pieces of news gathering are often introduced by correspondents, while the most humorous segments or gags are performed by a variety of other characters.

One of the most consistently successful programs on Italian television, averaging around six million viewers per day, *Striscia* started in 1988 on the youth-oriented channel Italia 1 owned by Berlusconi's corporation Fininvest, later to become Mediaset (Tanzarella, 1988). The following year, *Striscia* was moved to the more popular Canale 5 channel, counter-programmed against the traditional time slot of the 8:00 p.m. newscast on RAI Uno, the most important program of the main national public network. The show's creator, Antonio Ricci, claimed he wanted to create a variety show that was "nazional-popolare" ("national-popular"), in his interpretation of Gramsci's concept (Ricci, 1998, p. 65), which would also include journalistic elements.

Ricci is well-known for having borrowed ideas and practices from the Italian left—from Situationism to the neo-Marxist critique of culture—to put them at the service of the commercial networks, which he envisioned as sources of liberation from the cultural and ideological constraints of state television (Panarari, 2010). As Ricci proclaimed at the time of *Striscia*'s launching, the goal of the show was to "attempt the impossible: to be funnier than Bruno Vespa," one of the most prominent journalists at RAI (cited in *Striscia La Notizia*, 1988). Despite the humorous tone, the statement hinted at a larger strategy behind the show's creation, namely the competition between Fininvest and RAI. During the mid 1980s, Fininvest's status as national network was still openly questioned. Most of its success was based on its ability to directly challenge RAI's previously undisputed authority and to transform Italian television from a public monopoly to a duopolistic system. Since the early 1980s, the competition between the two has centered on the acquisition of prized content and talent, strategic counter-programming, and parody. The first network to engage in this strategy was Berlusconi's Canale 5, which was able to establish nationwide cultural legitimacy through its capacity to attract large audiences both by programming popular entertainment and by systematically experimenting with genres (Doyle, 1989). Parody programs poking fun at their competitors also played a vital role in the overall strategy, as Ricci's *Drive-In* successfully challenged and innovated upon RAI's tradition of the "varietà."

By the late 1980s, the competition for audience share between private and public broadcasters had reached a point of balance—the so called "Pax Televisiva" ("television peace"; Stille,

---

[3]The word "veline" is a playful reference to the practice by the Ministry of Popular Culture during the Fascist era of issuing directives, named "veline" on the news that were allowed to be released (from the thin type of paper used, "carta velina" in Italian). After *Striscia* popularized it, the term has become synonymous with attractive showgirls on television, and the velina has become an icon of contemporary Italian popular culture, often associated with a sexist and demeaning representation of women.

2006). Fininvest, though, was still fighting for the legal rights to have a fully legitimate national television network, which was officially granted only in 1990 by a highly contested regulatory framework.[4] A key element in the cultural and political legitimization of the network was the ability to broadcast news programs. However, at the time of *Striscia*'s introduction, Fininvest and the other private networks were prohibited from broadcasting live news. Until the 1990 broadcasting law, previous regulation had ruled that live news was the exclusive privilege of public television. Due to this legal impediment, and since Fininvest's networks were perceived as mostly entertainment based, Fininvest developed the strategy of introducing news combined with comedy. At the same time, awareness was spreading within Italian public opinion about the political agendas behind the RAI networks, and consequently the credibility of their newscasts was seriously undermined (Padovani, 2005). Focused on exposing the political subservience of public television, *Striscia* participated in Fininvest's strategy to escalate the competition by attacking the public network on its strongest, yet most sensitive spot: the legitimacy of its newscasts.

With this goal in mind, *Striscia* parodied the form of public service broadcasting news and exposed its complacency with official politics. According to Ricci, "the program was born with the goal of revealing the lack of credibility of television, attacking the newscasts, which are the programs that claim to have the highest authority" (*La Repubblica*, 2007). Referencing the traditional model of public service television, Ricci (1998) continued: "The television of the past was a highly ideological television. [. . .] You'd be watching the newscasts, thinking to simply receive news, instead they're selling you a political idea, and a car too" (p. 8). In turn, mixing journalism parody, the exposing of sloppy reporting, and an original form of news gathering based on viewers' spontaneous contributions, *Striscia* would create a new journalistic formula.

Since the start, *Striscia*'s model of confrontational journalism had been constantly mixed with absurd parody and entertaining skits. Amongst the various characters and puppets in the show's cast, the most famous is the Gabibbo, which has become one of the main symbols of the show. Ricci (1998) recalls that the Gabibbo was born as an ironic take on the "loudmouths" who were becoming popular on Italian television in the early 1990s, such as talk shows hosts and pundits with a "quarreling, threatening attitude" (p. 58). From a mere parody of television pundits, the Gabibbo has unexpectedly evolved into the avenger of the common people. On several occasions, city councils, volunteers, or factories groups have called on the Gabibbo to support their causes, and *Striscia* now offers a telephone hotline, "SOS Gabibbo," which viewers can use to reveal consumer fraud, inefficiencies in public administration, or similar issues. To further support his argument that the show is an alternative form of public service broadcasting, Ricci claims that "thousands of citizens prefer to file a complaint to the Gabibbo than to state institutions" (Ricci, 1998, p. 60).

NEWS PARODY AS POLITICAL LANGUAGE

Beginning with the season of collective action during the 1970s (Ginsborg, 1990) that led to the liberalization of television, and increasingly during the "lottizzazione" of the 1980s, Italian public opinion started to grow increasingly skeptical of the reliability of RAI journalists and

---

[4]Law 223, issued on August 6, 1990, is commonly referred to as "Legge Mammì." See http://www.difesadellinformazione.com/leggi_e_provvedimenti/15/legge-n-223-del-1990--legge-mammi-/.

their ability to perform a watchdog function vis-à-vis institutional powers. This trend reached a peak during the 1992–1993 Tangentopoli political scandal, which nearly swept away the political establishment that had ruled for the first 40 years of the Italian republic. Public television suffered a severe crisis of authority as it became evident that RAI's news editors had ties with the corrupt political class (Padovani, 2005). The critique of official news that *Striscia* had started in 1988 appeared prescient of the crisis of legitimacy suffered by public service journalism and, more generally, by the Italian political and cultural elites.

It has been noted that fake news programs seem to take on greater importance at times when confidence in the national news is challenged by scandals or other traumatic events (Baym, 2005; Cosentino et al., 2009). In the United States, *The Daily Show* emerged as an important site of public inquiry in the post 9/11 period, when mainstream media largely sided with the Bush administration and failed to question the government over the issue of weapons of mass destruction as a justification for the military intervention in Iraq in 2003. Similarly, *Striscia*'s popularity grew in the early 1990s when the crisis of the political class was accompanied by the collapse of the ideological domination of Catholicism and Marxism.

In the delegitimization process that political and state institutions underwent in the early 1990s, it is not surprising that parody and satire were employed to criticize the authority of party politics and of official news programs. In my reading, the emergence of this type of critical discourse is intimately related to the transformations in the political economy of television. While public news performed the essential work of establishing "imagined communities" of national citizenry (Anderson, 1983) as envisioned by the political class ruling in the postwar period, by breaking conventions and unmasking the fabrication of official news, private television challenged the authority of national public television. At the same time, *Striscia* was crucial in assisting commercial television in establishing a new type of national popular culture more closely tied to consumerism and to transnational flows of television practices and, later, to a new political order embodied by Berlusconi's party Forza Italia, which originated within the milieu of the Fininvest television network (Porro & Russo, 2001).

Against the Italian tradition of partisan journalism characterized by an open allegiance to a political party or movement (Hallin & Mancini, 2004), the creators of *Striscia* understood that in the milieu of commercial television, only audience ratings could guarantee editorial freedom. As Ricci (1998) admits, "*Striscia* is kept alive during the most difficult times by its popularity among audiences and advertisers. [. . .] We need to constantly look for the public, door to door" (p. 65). The respected Italian television critic and academic Aldo Grasso (1997) provocatively extends the argument:

> *Striscia* [. . .] is the only believable newscast. Its authority derives from two unique factors in the history of journalism. *Striscia* has the largest, most competent, most cooperative network of informants that any news outlet ever had. And most of all, for free. People cooperate with *Striscia* for fun, out of rage or for the need of expressing themselves. [. . .] *Striscia*, an antagonistic show, is the most effective money machine ever invented by Italian television. As long as it delivers revenues, it can do anything it wants. (p. 37)

Operating outside the traditional ideological constraints of political journalism, and effectively hybridizing entertainment and information to attract large audiences, *Striscia* has thus produced a two-fold political innovation. On the one hand, it has reformulated the notion of public service by decoupling it from state institutions and basing it instead on the demands and tastes of the general audience (Cosentino et al., 2009). On the other hand, it has elevated parody as a form of political language, enabling an unprecedented critical attitude towards the language of broadcast journalism, and more generally of the institution of public television.

The informative and satirical work of *Striscia* thus carries political content, but it rarely takes an overt political position. The show remains beyond traditional party politics, rather insisting on the empowerment of its public as both consumers and citizens. More importantly, the show has generally steered clear of covering controversies involving Mediaset founder and majority shareholder Berlusconi. Such an ambivalent position—aggression toward traditional parties and institutions; complacency with its employer—has been the preferred target for the critics of the show. Particularly since Berlusconi entered politics in 1994, and later in 2001 as he consolidated its power with a strong victory in the general elections, *Striscia* has been particularly cautious in covering the frequent judicial issues and the scandals surrounding Berlusconi. While Ricci has often claimed that the show is only accountable to his public, it is nonetheless obvious that Berlusconi, as the de facto executive of the Mediaset network, has received far more favorable treatment than have other politicians, a position for which *Striscia* has been often criticized (e.g., Panarari, 2010).

According to Ricci, counter-information and advocacy are byproducts of a broader, more ambitious goal of *Striscia,* that is, to redefine television's pedagogic role. By critiquing television journalism, particularly on public television, *Striscia* "attacks the whole broadcasting system (which has in journalism the main source of credibility, authority and self-legitimation)" (Giudici, 1998, p. 424). Ricci and the other authors of *Striscia* understood that the most sensitive target of political criticism was not so much the political class per se but rather the representation of politics offered by the television system. Therefore, alternative journalism for *Striscia* is only important insofar as it helps question the authority of television. To Ricci, "counter-information is only [. . .] one of the means to unmask the fictions of the television language" (Giudici, 1998, p. 424). I will discuss this aspect of the show in greater detail in the following section, which considers examples of one of *Striscia*'s most popular segments—the airing of discarded "outtakes" or "found footage" from various television programs, which the show uses to expose the aspects of fabrication, falsity, and contradictions inherent to the representation of politics on television.

Ricci, formerly a high school principal, openly admits to having a didactic approach to television production, with the goal of teaching viewers to be skeptical about the objectivity of television and its claims of truth. Thus *Striscia* has exposed numerous cases of omissions and fabrications by national television journalism. Often, its targets have not only been national but also important international networks. In one early example, at the time of the Gulf War in 1991, *Striscia* revealed that a CNN correspondent from Tel Aviv was wearing a gas mask without any real need, deceitfully suggesting that the Iraqi army was using chemical weapons against Israel. With respect to this, Ricci argues that "all journalists are like followers of Nietzsche, who believed that there are no truths, only interpretations. You'd think that you're freely watching the world from your window, but somebody has selected the angle and the frame for you. [. . .] If the spectacle is not there, it is fabricated" (cited in *La Repubblica*, 2001).

By countering the traditional educational model of public service broadcasting and by openly disassembling the mechanisms of journalistic practices, *Striscia* claims to address the viewers as savvy users of media. *Striscia*'s viewers are indeed routinely involved in the deconstruction of official texts, as well as in the production of critical texts. *Striscia* is thus among the pioneers of the use of what is now commonly referred to as "user-generated content," such as amateur videos, notifications by viewers, and content from local or independent channels. Ricci admits that more than 90% of the content of *Striscia* is suggested or provided by users, and that the show's hotline and website receive an average of "600 messages per day, 60% of which concern cases of fakes or television mistakes, indicating the presence of a savvy television audience" (Giudici, 1998, p. 424). The important role given to users' contribution in discovering and submitting stories covered by *Striscia* may explain the show's currently high level of trust among the Italian public. The unique relation that *Striscia* has with its viewers indicates widespread discontent among the public of the forms of mediation provided by traditional information outlets, as well as a growing interest in programs that can create the conditions for a more engaging and participatory approach to the discussions of matters of public interest.

TELEVISION OUTTAKES AS ALTERNATIVE POLITICAL COMMUNICATION

Mimicking the fragmented narrative of mainstream news, the standard format of *Striscia* is a collection of disconnected segments. Some are single news reports while others are episodes of recurring segments. Frequently these are reports based on the exposure of errors and omissions by official newscasts, examples of inefficiency of public institutions, fraud during television programs, parodies of famous politicians or journalists, denunciations of scandals, and the stigmatization of embarrassing public performances by celebrities or politicians.

The clips are often accompanied by cartoonish sound effects and humorous visual elements that enhance the comedic tone of the reports, even when serious issues are covered. The correspondents often dress in an unpretentious and informal style, and speak in a simple language when addressing regular people exposing government abuses, corporate frauds, or deceptive marketing techniques. While the show targets politicians from both ends of the political spectrum in a similarly ironic and critical way, it appears to be more aggressive with minor or younger politicians, and more deferential with more powerful ones. As noted, the references to Berlusconi are usually innocuous jokes about his flamboyant style, and rarely address more sensitive political issues.

A common and popular feature of *Striscia* is its airing of "fuorionda,"[5] an Italian term from the television jargon indicating "found footage" from live or recorded transmissions that did not air. "Fuorionda" often contains outtakes or segments from interviews, reports, or live shows that reveal embarrassing or controversial incidents involving public figures, celebrities, or politicians. "Fuorionda" are based on discarded "leftovers" of the television flow, thus performing the type of critical "disassembly" of the medium that Ricci claims is one of *Striscia*'s main objectives.[6] Of the many different segments featured by Striscia, I chose to focus on this particular type because it offers the most straightforward and unfiltered exposure of the representation of politicians on television, as well as of the role of mainstream news and public affairs programs. By exposing and making fun of controversial footage that either was edited out or went unreported, the show attacks the reliability of official news outlets, creating viewer awareness of the hidden motives

---

[5]This literally means "off the air."

[6]While *Striscia*'s producers have, to date, never openly revealed how they obtain the outtakes, in his book *Striscia la Tivù*, Ricci (2008) hints that he used special equipment to intercept the low-frequency transmission of Emilio Fede newscasts, TG4, one of his favorite targets.

behind politicians' public statements or decisions and about the editorial and political logics driving broadcast journalism.

Here, I analyze three examples, all of which expose compromising actions by politicians. The first and most famous example is from 1994, while the other two are more recent, from 2008 and 2010, respectively. In all three, politicians were caught exchanging confidential information or contradicting their public statements with their behind-the-scene actions, thus causing their "backstage" behaviors to collide with official statements or positions. To emphasize the controversial content of the "fuorionda," *Striscia*'s hosts introduce the various segments with background information about the significance of the footage in the context of a wider political situation, and ironically comment on the contradictions and sensitive aspects that are inherent to the segment.

The first outtake, which aired on November 25, 1994, is widely regarded as the most effective example of the ability of this type of television technique to publicize a controversial political exchange. The episode aired during Berlusconi's first term as prime minister, at a time of widespread uncertainty about the strength of the coalition he had assembled to run for the 1994 presidential election, with tension mounting between his main allies, the former fascist party Alleanza Nazionale and the federalist party Northern League (Stille, 2006). The clip showed Berlusconi's party Forza Italia's spokesperson, Antonio Tajani, sitting in a television studio with Rocco Buttiglione, leader of the now-defunct Catholic Partito Popolare Italiano (Italian People's Party, or PPI). The clip opened with a conversation between the two politicians while they waited for an interview with journalist Emilio Fede of Fininvest's newscast *TG4*. Commenting on the results from the recent local elections, Buttiglione analyzed the data with satisfaction, surprised to realize that his party performed better than expected. He immediately suggested to Tajani that Forza Italia and the PPI should join forces, in an attempt to reconfigure the Polo della Libertà coalition, which at the time was considered too unstable and controversial to last.

Striscia host:	Let's follow the developments of their behind the scene dealing,[7] something that would make Machiavelli pale in comparison.
Tajani:	There is a new political class that does not know how to do politics, our members of parliament don't know how to do politics.
Buttiglione:	That's why we need to create a party together. You know that I always had good words for you. We can do experiments for the next regional elections. You should join us in the north of Italy, and ditch the Northern League.
Tajani:	We must let the situation become ripe.
Buttiglione:	So that Fini[8] will be weakened, because now he's too strong and too dirty. He needs to become cleaner, and weaker.[9]

What made the outtake particularly effective as an element of criticism is that in the interview that followed the exchange shown by the outtake, Buttiglione openly contradicted what *Striscia* viewers had seen him previously discussing with Tajani, announcing that his party was ready

---

[7]The Italian word is "inciucio," a term used to refer to an informal and often controversial agreement among political parties or factions.

[8]This refers to Gianfranco Fini, leader of Alleanza Nazionale, post-Fascist right wing part and member of the Polo delle Libertà coalition in 1994.

[9]See RTI (1994).

to enter into a coalition with Forza Italia's main opponent at the time. *Striscia*'s airing of the outtake had the twofold effect of ridiculing the politicians involved in private "dealing," while at the same time delegitimizing the newscast that broadcasted the actual interview, which appeared to be based on an outright lie.

Interestingly, a few weeks after this outtake aired, among much controversy both in the media and within the political system, the Northern League withdrew its support from Berlusconi's party, causing the collapse of the Polo delle Libertà coalition, and the end of Berlusconi's first term as prime minister (Roncone, 2009). While there is no evidence suggesting that the airing of the episode is linked to the Northern League's withdrawal of political support from Berlusconi's coalition, it is still undeniable that the outtake caused a political stir at the time, particularly because of the novelty of such a form of disclosure (Dipollina, 1994).

Another more recent example of an outtake aired by *Striscia* that revealed controversial dynamics of televised political communication occurred on a 2008 episode of the political talk show *Omnibus,* which airs on the private television network *La 7*. The topic of the exchange recorded by the outtake was the appointment of the president of the Parliamentary Commission in charge of overseeing RAI, a sensitive political body with important cultural and political responsibilities. The three politicians featured on the show were Massimo Donadi of the small center-left Italia dei Valori (IDV) Party, Italo Bocchino of the center-right Popolo della Libertà (People of Freedom, or PDL) party, and Nicola Latorre of the Partito Democratico (Democratic Party), the main Italian center-left party. The clip opens with Donadi criticizing the center-right coalition for its appointments to the Parliamentary Commission. While Donadi is talking, the clip shows Latorre taking a copy of a newspaper sitting on the desk in front of Bocchino, on which he starts scribbling some notes. When finished, he watchfully nods to Bocchino, inviting him to read his notes.

Striscia's host:	Now look at what happens. Upon reading the message, Bocchino asks the show's host for the right to speak, possibly to repeat what Latorre just suggested to him. In order not to be caught by the cameras, Bocchino turns the newspaper upside down. To be even safer, like a secret agent Latorre takes the newspaper back from Bocchino, tears apart the page, and hides the "pizzino."[10]
Bocchino:	I just would like to remind you that for the appointment to the Constitutional Court, we proposed Pecorella, and you said: "Change the name or else we won't vote for him." We did accordingly—showing a sense of responsibility—and suggested the candidacy of Frigo.
Striscia's host:	This sounds as a precise attack against the center-left, and in particular against the IDV. Is it possible that Latorre would suggest to Bocchino what to say against the IDV? There's something shady going on here. And if this is the case, it means that between Veltroni and Di Pietro we have reached the moment of "strappo."[11]

---

[10]"Pizzino" is journalistic jargon indicating brief messages, often written in encrypted text, used by the Sicilian Mafia for high-level communications.

[11]See RTI (2008). Veltroni was at the time the leader of the PD, and Di Pietro is still currently the leader of IDV party. The word "strappo" is a pun on the double meaning of the verb "strappare," which literally means "to tear apart," for example, a piece of paper, but also in political terms it means to "break away" from a coalition or a common platform.

Striscia's host suggested that the tip given by Latorre to Bocchino served as a deliberate attack from the PD against the IDV, which, although both center-left, are often at odds on several topics. The outtake is noteworthy because it revealed how the behind-the-scene relations among political allies and political competitors are often more complex than what politicians tend to manifest. In this case, it is striking to see a member of the main center-left party providing an effective argument to his opponent, in order to hit the smaller center-left party, possibly because of more general political disagreements within the same coalition.

The third outtake aired on April 14, 2010, and showed the newly elected governor of the Lazio region, Renata Polverini, having a private chat after a public meeting with Vincenzo Zaccheo, mayor of the city of Latina, near Rome. In a thick Roman accent, Polverini greets Zaccheo in a warm and ironic way:

Polverini:	Hi Vincenzo, you brought just four votes to me!
Zaccheo:	I love you, I believed in you. . . . You know I went swimming to the island of Ventotene, and I got 57 votes for you.
Polverini:	I know, I know.
Zaccheo:	Please don't forget about my daughters.
Polverini:	Are you kidding? Tomorrow I'll start my new daily planner, I'll start going around . . .
Zaccheo:	And most of all, don't give any public contract to Fazzone . . . he lost 15-thousand votes.
Polverini:	Don't worry.
Striscia's host:	Did you get it? Polverini has just been elected governor, and she is already "fixing" the place. And, since she's at it, she takes a good recommendation for the children of her friends. . . . And by the way, let's keep the unwelcome people out of the way. Who is this Fazzone? He is a politician from Fondi, near Latina, and a powerful senator for the PDL. He was formerly part of Forza Italia, and allegedly he organized a protest of the Forza Italia members of the city council against Zaccheo, who was formerly a member of the AN party. It really looks like a showdown among historical factions of the Popolo delle Libertà.[12]

This clip is particularly noteworthy as it provides proof of controversial dealmaking, specifically Zaccheo asking Polverini to "remember his daughters" after he pointed out that he delivered votes for her. Further, the clip stigmatizes the dynamics of political appointments and agreements on public works, as per Zaccheo's request that Polverini not assign public contracts to Fazzone. Interestingly, in the aftermath of the clip's airing, 22 members of the Latina city council resigned to protest the mayor's behavior in his exchange with Polverini (*Il Messaggero*, 2010).

The three clips presented offer a valuable albeit controversial picture of backstage political maneuverings that clash strikingly with the often-polished image of politicians and the rhetoric of political communication on television. *Striscia*'s outtakes thus act as a powerful critical tool in the process of unveiling the mechanisms shaping the political sphere, showing its viewers how often politicians contradict their official statements with hidden scheming and bargaining. *Striscia* thus appears to be playing a twofold function. On the one hand, it reveals the limits of the representation of politics on television, exposing the operations of fabrication and falsification

---

[12] See RTI (2010).

that are inherent to the language of television, particularly of official newscasts or public affairs programs. On the other hand, however, it legitimizes the very medium, especially in its more entertaining or satirical genres, by emphasizing how the self-critical ability of television serves as a guarantee of empowerment of citizens vis-à-vis the political class, ultimately strengthening the authority of the medium in general, and of entertainment programs such as the fake news shows in particular.

CONCLUSION: IS FAKE NEWS REAL NEWS?

What has occurred in Italy with *Striscia* since the 1990s has recently become increasingly visible in other countries. The emergence of fake news as a legitimate and trusted site of political communication appears to be linked to a larger set of transformations affecting traditional alignments between television and politics in liberal democracies worldwide. In Italy, the deregulatory effects of broadcasting liberalization historically accelerated the hybridization of genres. The role currently played by *Striscia* within the sphere of broadcast journalism likewise has been deeply connected with the transformation of the Italian broadcasting system and its relation to party politics.

Analyzing the conditions that have contributed to the popularity of *The Daily Show* in the United States, Baym (2005) points out that technological, economic, and cultural factors are causing a "wider breakdown [. . .] of traditional boundaries and social structures." As a result, there is an increasingly visible "lack of distinction between the public and private spheres, public affairs and popular culture, and information and entertainment." Referencing the work of Michael Delli Carpini and Bruce Williams, Baym further argues that the "dissolution of such borders is in part a recognition of the arbitrary nature of those distinctions and a challenge to the structures of political and social power upon which those borders ultimately depend" (p. 262).

By addressing viewers as savvy readers of media texts, skeptical of institutional information sources and able to detect or expose falsifications or errors, "fake news" programs such as *Striscia* or *The Daily Show*—despite emerging in different historical and political contexts—perform a similarly significant redrawing of the limits of public discourse. The rise to prominence of fake news as a viable source of political communication thus demonstrates that the "discourses of news, politics, entertainment, and marketing have grown deeply inseparable, and [. . .] are being melded into previously unimagined combinations" (Baym, 2005, p. 262). With the blurring of the distinction among genres, the power structures that relied on previous separation among roles, hierarchies, and discursive practices are also called into question, opening up new possibilities of participation in public affairs for new types of information outlets and, with networked digital media, increasingly for citizens.

However, despite Ricci's claim about his supposed editorial freedom, shows such as *Striscia* are subject to the political and economic constraints of commercial television, which depends on advertising revenue. This aspect needs to be interrogated in light of the implications of two decades of neo-liberal politics, which in Europe as elsewhere have favored deregulatory policies in the media sector to the detriment of the role of traditional public institutions. Thus Ricci (1998) has argued that "television should not operate as window on the world, but as a point of view on the market" (p. 8). Here he sums up the economic and political ideology to which programs such as *Striscia* subscribe. *Striscia* has effectively unmasked the "fictions" of traditional public service journalism and television. In the process, however, it has reinforced an equally powerful fiction: the consumerist culture promoted by commercial television. While Ricci has often distanced the overall editorial orientation of the show from Berlusconi's politics, *Striscia*'s heavy emphasis on the critique of state institutions, on entertainment as a viable outlet of public discourses, and on the ubiquitous presence of scantily clad women seem to fit well with the type of ideological and cultural imaginary that in Italy has emerged over the past two decades around Berlusconi. One of *Striscia*'s most vocal critics, Italian journalist Gad Lerner, has in a recent public discussion referred to Ricci as the "Dante of Berlusconism," or the poet laureate and main author of Berlusconi's political language (*Corriere della Sera*, 2009).

Arguably, no single form of representation of public affairs—neither the official news on public television RAI nor the fake news programs on Berlusconi's private television networks—can legitimately claim to be more objective or trustworthy than the other. What distinguishes them is the type of language used to reflect and support different political agendas and cultural projects. While traditionally close attention has been paid to the role that newscasts have in promoting different political agendas, still relatively little scrutiny is given to the equally important role played by fake news shows within the public sphere. Therefore, just as *Striscia* has gained credibility by teaching its public not to take the "puppet journalists" of "real news" too seriously, by the same token the puppet journalists of fake news, such as the Gabibbo, should be instead taken more seriously, and watched closely by politicians, journalists, and academics alike.

REFERENCES

Anderson, B. (1983). *Imagined communities: Reflections on the origin and spread of nationalism*. London, England: Verso.

Baym, G. (2005). *The Daily Show*: Discursive integration and the reinvention of political journalism. *Political Communication*, 22(3), 259–276.

Brambilla, C. (2004, November 13). Premio-choc a Striscia la Notizia. *La Repubblica*. Retrieved from http://ricerca.repubblica.it/repubblica/archivio/repubblica/2002/11/13/premio-choc-striscia-la-notizia.html

Corriere della Sera. (2009, September 26). Lerner: Ricci ha creato la lingua berlusconiana. Retrieved from http://archiviostorico.corriere.it/2009/settembre/26/Lerner_Ricci_creato_lingua_berlusconiana_co_9_090926072.shtml

Cosentino, G., Doyle, W., & Todorova, D. (2009). Tearing up television news across borders: Format transfer in news parody shows between Italy and Bulgaria. In A. Moran (Ed.), *TV formats worldwide* (pp. 203–219). Bristol, England: Intellect.

Diamanti, I. (2010, October 25). Tv, la 'vita indiretta' degli italiani a picco la fiducia in Tg1 e Tg5. *La Repubblica*. Retrieved from http://www.repubblica.it/politica/2010/10/25/news/diamanti_tg-8403346/

Dipollina, A. (1994, November 27). Ho mostrato cos'è la politica. *La Repubblica*. Retrieved from http://ricerca.repubblica.it/repubblica/archivio/repubblica/1994/11/27/ho-mostrato-cos-la-politica.html

Doyle, W. (1989). From deregulation to monopoly: A cultural analysis of the formation of Italy's private television monopoly. (Unpublished doctoral dissertation). Griffith University, Brisbane, Australia.

Forcella, E. (2004). *Millecinquecento lettori*. Rome, Italy: Donzelli.

Ginsborg, P. (1990). *A history of contemporary Italy*. London, England: Penguin.

Giudici, S. (1998). *Striscia la Notizia*: Molto vista e poco studiata. *Problemi dell'informazione*, 23(3), 417–426.

Grasso, A. (1997, December 2). "Striscia": i furti e la forza del fatturato. *Il Corriere della Sera*. Retrieved from http://archiviostorico.corriere.it/1997/dicembre/02/Striscia_furti_forza_del_fatturato_co_0_9712029442.shtml

Hallin, D., & Mancini P. (2004). *Comparing media systems: Three models of media and politics*. Cambridge, England: Cambridge University Press.

Il Messaggero (2010, April 15). Comune di Latina nella bufera, decade il sindaco Zaccheo dopo Striscia la Notizia. *Il Messaggero*. Retrieved from http://www.ilmessaggero.it/articolo.php?id=98217

Jones, J. P. (2005). *Entertaining politics: New political television and civic culture*. Lanham, MD: Rowman and Littlefield.

La Repubblica. (2001, February 23). I falsi dell'informazione protagonisti a Striscia. Retrieved from http://ricerca. repubblica.it/repubblica/archivio/repubblica/2001/02/23/falsi-dellinformazione-protagonisti-striscia.html

La Repubblica. (2007, October 6). Il Tg1 festeggia i 20 anni di Striscia. Retrieved from http://ricerca.repubblica.it/ repubblica/archivio/repubblica/2007/10/06/il-tg1-festeggia-20-anni-di-striscia.html

Maffioletti, C. (2008, September 20). Ricci, lezioni di satira: "Grillo? Rischia di fare l'imbonitore." *Il Corriere della Sera*. Retrieved from http://www.corriere.it/spettacoli/08_settembre_20/ricci_lezioni_di_satira_a81669b0-86c1-11dd-bd39-00144f02aabc.shtml

Mascio, A. (2002). *Striscia La Notizia*: Sotto Il Segno del Tapiro. In U. Volli (Ed.), *Culti tv: Il tubo catodico e i suoi adepti*. Milan, Italy: Sperling & Kupfer.

Nadeau, B. (2010, November 15). Italy's woman problem. *Newsweek*. Retrieved from http://www.thedailybeast.com/ newsweek/2010/11/15/bunga-bunga-nation-berlusconi-s-italy-hurts-women.html

Padovani, C. (2005). *A fatal attraction: Public television and politics in Italy*. Lanham, MD: Rowman and Littlefield.

Panarari, M. (2010). *L'egemonia sottoculturale. Da Gramsci al gossip*. Turin, Italy: Einaudi.

Pansa, G. (1977). *Comprati e venduti*. Milan, Italy: Bompiani.

Porro, N., & Russo, P. (2001). Berlusconi and other matters: The era of "football-politics." *Journal of Modern Italian Studies*, 5(3), 348–370.

RTI. (1994, November 25). *Striscia la Notizia*. Milan, Italy: Mediaset. Retrieved from http://www.striscialanotizia. mediaset.it/video/videoll.shtml?2007/11/poli20.wmv

RTI. (2008, November 11). *Striscia la Notizia*. Milan, Italy: Mediaset. Retrieved from http://www.striscialanotizia. mediaset.it/video/videoll.shtml?2008/11/C_35_video_8160_GroupVideo_filevideo.wmv

RTI. (2010, April 14). *Striscia la Notizia*. Milan, Italy: Mediaset. Retrieved from http://www.striscialanotizia.mediaset. it/video/videoflv.shtml?2010_04_poli14.flv

Ricci, A. (1998). *Striscia la tivú*. Turin, Italy: Einaudi.

Riegert, K. (Ed.). (2007). *Politicotainment: Television's take on the real*. New York, NY: Peter Lang.

Roncone, F. (2009, December 2). Microfoni accesi, tutte le parole "sfuggite" da Buttiglione a Visco. *Il Corriere della Sera*. Retrieved from http://archiviostorico.corriere.it/1994/novembre/27/adesso_insieme_troppo_forte_sporca_co_ 8_9411271824.shtml

Stille, A. (2006). *The sack of Rome: Media + money + celebrity =power = Silvio Berlusconi*. New York, NY: Penguin.

Striscia La Notizia. (1988). Giornale radio. Retrieved from http://www.striscialanotizia.mediaset.it/bin/18.$plit/ P_35_56_indexstory_listapdf_itemName_0_binary.pdf

Tanzarella, M. (1988, November, 6). Un tg in sette minuti: Le notizie da ridere di Antonio Ricci & Co. *La Repubblica*. Retrieved from http://ricerca.repubblica.it/repubblica/archivio/repubblica/1988/11/06/un-tg-in-sette-minuti-le-notizie.html

van Zoonen, L. (2005). *Entertaining the citizen: When politics and popular culture converge*. Lanham, MD: Rowman and Littlefield.

Localizing *The Daily Show*: The *heute show* in Germany

Katharina Kleinen-von Königslöw

Guido Keel

The recent success of the *heute show*, a German adaptation of *The Daily Show with Jon Stewart,* on the one hand exemplifies how in this globalized age a foreign format can successfully be adapted to a country's own political, cultural, and journalistic context, even in a genre as notoriously culture-bound as political satire. On the other hand this success story also illustrates how perceptions of political satire appear to have shifted in Germany, allowing for a greater degree of playfulness and thus attracting a new, younger audience to the genre and, in the long run, to a critical perspective on politics and media.

In a recent global poll Germans have been voted "the least funny nationality" (Casciato, 2011). Either blissfully unaware of this deficiency or in defiant protest, German viewers flock by the millions to the wide range of comedic programming offered on German television, in particular to made-for-Germany comedy formats. Whether viewers from abroad would find this fare funny and enjoyable is an open question, since even in this globalized age humor, and in particular political humor, remain culture-specific concepts.

Thus even though the history of German television programming is basically a history of the continuous import, adaptation, and sometimes export of television formats from and to different countries in the world, and in particular from the United States and Great Britain, importing a political satire program poses great challenges. In this article we take a closer look at how the *heute show*, based on *The Daily Show with Jon Stewart*, has been adapted to the German political, media, and journalistic culture and how the local context and the foreign role model both inhibit and enable the political and social potential of this news parody format.

Academic (and public) interest in "Satire TV" has been blossoming in the United States in recent years (Baumgartner & Morris, 2008; Baym, 2010, 2005; Gray, Jones, & Thompson, 2009; Jones, 2010; Tenenboim-Weinblatt, 2009). In Germany, comparable television formats have been discussed in innumerable master and diploma theses, but academic scholars have been hesitant to concern themselves with material on the fringes of the field of political communication. A few studies focus on the German tradition of political cabaret, but less prestigious forms of political satire have received virtually no attention (e.g., Rosenstein, 1994). This article will attempt to break with this tradition and instead connect its analysis of the German localization of *The Daily Show* to the Anglo-Saxon academic debate on the political and social potential of satire television in all its variants. It shall thus illustrate how the *heute show* represents a shift in the German understanding of political satire, which in recent years has moved closer to the British/US tradition of political satire, making more room for playfulness and laughter in the discussion of political failings. This in turn opens the genre for a new, younger audience for which it may prove to be the urgently required introduction to the realm of political public debate and contestation.

GERMAN PERSPECTIVE ON POLITICAL SATIRE

A commonly cited characterization by George A. Test (1991) ascribes four necessary elements to modern satire: aggression, play, laughter, and judgment (p. 14). Though some authors have suggested rewordings or additional traits, for example, "required prior knowledge" on part of the audience (Caufield, 2008, p. 9) in order to distinguish political satire from other forms of political humor, there appears to be a certain consensus on these key traits in the Anglo-Saxon academic discussion of satire. The German perspective, however, differs significantly—a difference that is even more striking as both scholarly traditions trace their understandings of satire back to the shared cultural heritage of the satirists of Ancient Greece. Still according to the main German satire theorist Jürgen Brummack (1971), satire is composed of attack, norm, and indirectness (p. 282).[1] While attack and aggression, judgment and norm clearly relate to the same characteristics respectively, play as a stylistic device is replaced in the German definition by the far less "playful" indirectness, and laughter as a reaction to satire is missing completely. In the further discussion of indirectness as a stylistic device, laughter does play a role (Behrmann, 2002), but it is not considered to be an essential part of the definition of satire.

This omission may in part be due to a greater reluctance of German scholars to be associated with seemingly nonserious phenomena; nevertheless, it should not be taken as an indication that German satire is in fact humorless and does not entice laughter. Rather, it reflects the strong feeling of earnestness, seriousness, a sense of mission, and even cultural distinction which plays an important part in the German tradition of political satire, but may appear quite alien to the genre for foreign observers. This tradition was mainly formed by political cabaret shows, which developed in the early 20th century. Originally these shows also included somewhat risqué numbers and musical show elements, but soon their main focus became biting social and political critique. While there exist comical-entertaining or artistic/aesthetical forms of German cabaret as well (Budzinski & Hippen, 1996), the main implication of the German word "Kabarett" is hence "political satire": Small groups or single performers use a series of parodies, sketches, satire, political songs, and rants criticizing the current state of politics and society (usually from the left) to entertain, educate and mobilize their (usually rather select) audiences. Political cabaret requires a comparatively high level of political knowledge and can be quite paternalistic in tone,

---

[1] In German: "Angriff, Norm, Indirektheit." Authors' translation.

often transporting a sense of seriousness: "This is important!" "This is not fun!" "This is a serious problem that we are making fun of!"

With the introduction of television, this tradition of very "serious" political satire produced a strong tension between expectations of the performers, broadcasters, audiences, and politicians, which can be traced throughout the history of German television satire.

A BRIEF HISTORY OF GERMAN TELEVISION SATIRE

Germans themselves may not be considered particularly humorous, but they have always cherished media comedy. When television was re-introduced to Germany in the 1950s as a public service institution, its charter included a mission to inform, educate, and entertain. Thus, fortunately for fun-starved German viewers, entertainment and comedy programs were available from the start, long before the launch of commercial TV in the late 1980s. The position of political satire, however, has been much more contested.

1950s to 1980s: Political Satire as a Contested Rarity During the Duopoly of Public Television

For the first 30 years of its existence, German television consisted chiefly of two national public channels. While these provided plenty of entertainment programming, they were financed by licensing fees and could easily be put under pressure by politicians either through unofficial channels or through their supervising boards of governors, whose members were representatives of social and political groups, associations and parties, as well as the churches.[2] With the support of the German judicial system characterized by strong protections against libel and in general a conservative and paternalistic outlook, there was rather tight political control on what Germans were allowed to laugh *about*. Any form of political satire quickly came under scrutiny of the political establishment, which displayed a strong will to control and sanitize humor in a new medium deemed extremely powerful (for a captivating summary see Behrmann, 2002; Rosenstein, 1994). In some cases this led to on-air censorship of particularly controversial acts, as well as television bans of certain cabaret artists. But more importantly it also led to the early demise of the two main attempts to establish made-for-television political satire programs. In 1963 the series *Hallo Nachbarn* ("Hello Neighbors") was introduced on the first channel, ARD.[3] Based on the BBC production *That Was The Week That Was*, it contained fake news, fake documentaries, and critical chansons. Mirroring the fate of its British role model, the show was discontinued in 1965 due to protests from both major parties. The second channel ZDF (an abbreviation of "Second German Television") launched in 1973 *Notizen aus der Provinz* ("Notes from the Periphery") consisting of satirical monologues as well as re-dubbed and re-edited news footage of politicians. Despite

---

[2]As regulation allowed only 20 minutes for commercials per channel and day, the channels were relatively independent from advertisers' pressure.

[3]The first German television channel is called Das Erste or ARD, an abbreviation of Arbeitsgemeinschaft der öffentlich-rechtlichen Rundfunkanstalten der Bundesrepublik Deutschland ("Working Group of Public Broadcasting Stations in Germany"), which is an organization consisting of (currently) nine regional public broadcasters.

its overwhelming popularity—it reached audience shares of 45%—two of its episodes (on abortion and terrorism) never aired due to intervention "from above" and it was yanked in 1979 for siding too strongly with the political left (Budzinski & Hippen, 1996, p. 250). It was the last satirical format to air on ZDF for almost three decades.

ARD, however, had the structural advantage that its content was produced by regional affiliates, resulting in a rather diverse mixture of more conservative and more experimental programming. In particular, regional stations situated in traditionally left-wing federal states were more open to political satire, for instance the monthly satirical cabaret show *Scheibenwischer* ("Windshield Wiper") by the Berlin station of ARD. Modeled on the British *Not the 9 O'Clock News,* ARD also introduced *Rudis Tagesshow* in 1981. Produced for national distribution by the regional station Radio Bremen, the most-beloved entertainment host of the time Rudi Carrell presented fake news items and comedy sketches as a news anchor in a setting similar to the station's (and the nation's) most important newscast, *Tagesschau*. The show was extremely successful but only rarely touched on political issues. Still it caused a noteworthy diplomatic scandal in 1987 with Iran in reaction to a sketch depicting veiled women throwing underwear at a figure implied to be Ayatollah Khomeini.

1980s–2000s: Political Satire Replaced by the Comedy Boom as Commercial Television Is Established

By the time commercial television was introduced in the mid-1980s, political satire had been relegated to the regional public service channels which made use of their position somewhat secluded from national scrutiny to provide room for political cabaret acts and to develop a number of rather edgy and unique satirical shows (which met a quick demise whenever they were promoted to national distribution on the main channel of ARD due to a mixture of increased scrutiny and political pressure as well as a failure to attract a larger audience). While commercial channels did make an effort (and in part succeeded) to scratch at the monopoly of public channels on political information by producing regular newscasts as well as political talk-shows and magazines, they steered clear of politically charged formats for comedic programs. Looking predominantly to the United States for inspiration, they introduced the concept of "stand-up comedians" to the German audience and a number of comedy shows such as *RTL Samstag Nacht* (1993–1998, inspired by *Saturday Night Live*), *Freitag Nacht News* (1999–2006, also RTL), the *Wochenshow* (1996–2002, Sat.1—relaunched in June 2011), and *Switch* (ProSieben, 1997–2000, on air again as *Switch – Reloaded* since 2007).

All of these contained, among other things, parodies of newscasts and used clips of politicians in their sketches. However, it was always the fame and publicity that made politicians an easy target for parody and satire, not the political content of their statements. An exception has been the first successful German late night show host Harald Schmidt, who started out on the commercial channel Sat.1 in 1995 with a nearly identical adaptation of the *Late Show with David Letterman*. In time the show developed a distinctly German profile, playing to the almost pathological need for cultural distinction of the German bourgeoisie; for instance, one episode was presented entirely in French and another crafted as a reenactment of Shakespeare's *Hamlet* using Playmobil figurines. But part of its appeal to German media critics and the intelligentsia lay in the acerbic political wit of Schmidt's stand-up routine at the beginning of each show. Nevertheless over the years and many changes in format and even broadcasting channel, the show lost much of its political drive and impact. The host of the other longtime successful late night show in Germany, Stefan Raab, never had any political ambitions with his format *TV Total* on ProSieben (since 1999).

Late 2000s: The Re-Politicization of Television Comedy?

In 2007, public channel ZDF decided to end its almost 30-year hiatus from political satire and introduced *Neues aus der Anstalt* ("News from the (Mental) Institution") where two regular and several guest comedians take turns dissecting political issues. In 2009 it added the *heute show* and in 2011, another politically satirical talk show to its roster. Whether this program re-orientation is part of a larger trend toward a re-politicization of television comedy still remains to be seen. So far the *heute show* has been attributed with revitalizing the genre of political satire, while media critics claim that the longtime late night show host Harald Schmidt has been revived by the competition (e.g., Brauck, 2009). The relaunch of the weekly parody format *Wochenshow* on Sat.1 in June 2011 may also have been inspired by the success of the *heute show*. Nevertheless, political satire currently remains limited to the three ZDF shows and the regional public broadcasters, commercial stations continue to make Germans laugh about everything but politics.

A LIGHTER TAKE ON POLITICAL SATIRE? INTRODUCING THE *HEUTE SHOW* TO GERMANY

ZDF, the second largest national German public channel, started its new foray into news parody rather tentatively in 2009 with two pilot episodes of the *heute show* on May 26 and June 23, followed by a first season of monthly episodes from September 8 to December 30 the same year. With growing confidence, the show started its second season with a weekly slot on Friday night around 11:00 p.m., the exact time depending on preceding programs. To keep fans interested during the summer break, weekly mini news updates (called *heute show spezial* [2009] and *heute show xxs* [2011]) have been presented by one of the show's fake correspondents and broadcast on the web and in 2011 also nationally on ZDFinfo, ZDF's cable news channel.

But why would a large public broadcaster primarily associated with Volksmusik shows and high-budget adaptations of Rosamunde Pilcher novels take the risk to invest in a news parody format likely to offend quite a number of its core viewers? The main reason is that the two national public channels (and their large portfolios of regional and special interest channels) are facing mounting public pressure questioning the stations' reliance on licensing fees, in particular as their audience shares are continuously declining. In 2010 both channels finally fell behind the main commercial competitor RTL (Zubayr & Gerhard, 2011). At the same time, they are having trouble attracting a younger audience. The average viewer of ZDF is 61 years old compared to the 46 years for RTL viewers (AGF/GfK, 2011). Programming the *heute show* has thus been a strategic decision to appeal to younger viewers through intelligent, sophisticated political satire, and at the same time to underline the "public value" of the channel.

This public value of political satire, however, has only recently been recognized by broadcasters as well as politicians. They have noticed the increasing relevance of satirical news shows such as *The Daily Show* and *The Colbert Report* in the United States—both of which are available online in Germany. A weekly summary of highlights from *The Daily Show* is also shown on German cable TV. Broadcasters and politicians have taken particular note of how, in the United States, those shows have managed to reach the growing demographic of politically disinterested citizens. This is relevant for Germany, which has seen a decline in party membership and voter turnout over the last decades.[4] Thus while politicians and public broadcasters still retain some reservations concerning the potentially disruptive or alienating effects of political satire, these are beginning to be overruled by the need to reach the segments of society which have been alienated by the traditional coverage of politics in the news, and which at the same time are quite familiar with the satirical news programs in the United States.

As a result of this, ZDF's director has been very supportive of the show. When, after a promising start, audience response fell below expectations during the first season, the show was still allowed time to develop its own voice and audience niche. Whenever the show caused political controversy or ran into legal troubles, the channel's management issued a formal reprimand, but it never questioned the value or the existence of the show itself. Moreover the show was allowed to model itself as closely as possible on the main newscast of ZDF which is called *heute* ("today")—the title *heute show* is thus both a play on *The Daily Show* and the main regular newscast. Furthermore it could integrate other important aspects of the channel brand such as the *Mainzelmännchen*, cartoon figures ZDF has been using since 1963 and whose appearances in the *heute show* are often not exactly G-rated. This represents a clear break from former channel guidelines according to which political satire had to be clearly labeled to protect the audience from misunderstandings. At the same time their very imaginative use is an excellent illustration of the new level of playfulness of political satire demonstrated by the *heute show*: Until recently these cartoon figures would have been considered too childish to illustrate political points, but now they can kill Bin Laden as part of a doorbell prank.

The show is so closely associated with the channel that in its current format, it could not be broadcast on any other station. This may hinder its effort to connect to a younger audience, given ZDF's image as the retired people's channel. However, this association with a national channel greatly increases the show's credibility as "serious" political satire. Despite a clear convergence in program content and styles, German viewers still associate the public channels more strongly with well-researched, fact-orientated journalism (Zubayr & Geese, 2011). In addition, the majority of politicians and people on the street will be far more likely to talk to a journalist with a ZDF microphone than one from a commercial station.

LOCALIZING THE *HEUTE SHOW* IN GERMAN MEDIA CULTURE

Formally, the *heute show* is a very close adaptation of the US original *The Daily Show with Jon Stewart*, from the studio furnishings to the composition of each episode (with the important

---

[4]While party membership increased after World War II until the 1970s, it has been on a steady decline since then, decreasing from 2 million members of political parties in Western Germany (of a population of 61 million) in the mid-1970s to 1.4 million in 2009 (population 82 million) (Bundeszentrale für politische Bildung, 2009; Gabriel/Völkl, 2005). The same is true for voter participation: Numbers went up between 1949 and 1972 from 78.5% to 91.1% in national elections, before declining again to 70.8% in 2009 (http://www.bundeswahlleiter.de).

exception that until recently there were no interviews with "real" politicians or experts). A show usually lasts 30 minutes without commercial breaks, since these are not allowed on public broadcasting in Germany after 8:00 p.m. The program starts with an introductory jingle modeled from regular newscasts, and then the camera moves into the studio to focus on the anchor Oliver Welke at his desk (see Figure 1).

After a brief introduction, Welke typically proceeds to discuss approximately five topics chosen for the episode. Each topic is illustrated with a symbol photo or graphic, usually with a funny word play, or a montage of photos and graphic elements, in the background. The topic is then presented in a mixture of actual reporting of the facts and ironic and humorous comments. Often, snippets of regular TV news programs are used, sometimes consisting only of single words. The fast montage of these snippets turns statements of politicians or other public figures into pointless repetitions of talking points or absurd contradictions. The anchorman not only presents the news but also reacts to the humor or the absurdity of it with comments or simply his mimics. The whole presentation of news, including mimics and expressions of astonishment and disbelief, is done in the same style as Jon Stewart's presentation of the news (e.g., Baym, 2005; Jones, 2010).

The anchor himself may not be as central to the *heute show* as Jon Stewart is to *The Daily Show*, but Oliver Welke is the face of the show, and he also serves as its spokesperson. As he is already well known to the German TV audience as presenter of various other TV shows, mainly sports and comedy shows, and still works as a presenter/commentator of key soccer games for a commercial German broadcaster, he provides an easy entry point into the world of political satire. In violation of the still-prevailing image of political cabaret artists, he does not appear to be particularly intellectual, politically aggressive, or self-righteous. He is the guy who used to talk to you about soccer and other fun things and now offers his views on political issues in a

FIGURE 1 The anchor presents selected news of the week accompanied by illustrations and word plays, adding a humorous touch to the story. In this case, along with the news of the killing of Osama Bin Laden, President Obama is shown as "Schützenkönig" ("King of Marksmen"). Screenshot was taken from ZDF and used with permission from Prime Productions (color figure available online).

similarly unpretentious manner. This is aided by the fact that in contrast to Jon Stewart and to the rest of the *heute show* staff, Welke has not developed a noticeable role or persona; he appears (and is perceived by the audience) as "himself."

As on *The Daily Show*, many of the topics are also covered by reports from fake correspondents or fake experts in the studio. These are played by well-known comedians using a pseudonym. While the use of fake correspondents/experts in general has been modeled on *The Daily Show* (and other US formats), their personas have been adapted completely to German media and journalistic culture. The senior, disgruntled, and jaded foreign correspondent is probably the figure most accessible to non-German viewers; the others all represent well-known aspects and stereotypes of the German culture. There is the fastidious, but pointless statistics expert (as a general critique of the inherently German fixation on numbers and statistics), the typical East German (easily identifiable by his poor taste in clothing, his Saxon accent, and his air of whiny resignation and disaffection), the admiring supporter of Chancellor Merkel, and the Turkish reporter (representing the largest group of immigrants in Germany).

In general, the *heute show* is embedded in German media culture, drawing inspiration for its jokes from a broad range of cultural phenomena. Some of its humor requires an intimate knowledge of German (media) history, for example, by playing with headlines and magazine covers that have gained an iconic status, such as the first cover of the German satire magazine *Titanic* after the German reunification. For the generation 30 and older, it holds sometimes a nostalgic appeal. Due to the 30 years of public television duopoly, most Germans share memories of important television events that had audience shares of 60% or higher. Thus when the *heute show* uses popular entertainment shows from the German past as props, such as *Der große Preis* (1974–2003) or *Wetten dass..?* (the number-one Saturday night family show on German television since 1981), it taps into this sense of common cultural history. However, this also makes it a distinctly *West* German format. Many of its cultural references can only be understood with a West German (media) background, and the caricature of an East-German as a pseudo-correspondent also appeals more to West Germans.

THE *HEUTE SHOW* AND GERMAN JOURNALISTIC CULTURE

Hallin and Manicini (2004) characterized German journalistic culture as more partisan than that of the United States, but recent developments in the American media appear to suggest otherwise. So far nothing remotely comparable to US talk radio or *Fox News* has developed in Germany. National newspapers exhibit some political leanings ranging from the left (*tageszeitung*) to the right (*Die Welt*), but none openly promotes specific parties or candidates, not even the right-leaning tabloid *Bild*. In particular on television and radio, most programs and their journalists subscribe to a doctrine of fairness and civility that is due, in part, to the regulations governing public stations (and with less strictness, also the commercial channels). Given the absence of any controversial media pundits, the *heute show* is thus left with decidedly less provoking material to dissect or a distinct target for its media critique.

In absence of a divided, partisan media landscape, the show criticizes in general the inadequate, sensationalized, and personalized reporting in German media by exaggerating exactly these aspects, either through a montage of clips from regular news shows or by parodies of regular news elements. It also attacks the downside of this doctrine of fairness and civility—a blandness and artificial, disengaging neutrality. Exemplary for this critique is the regular segment featuring commentator Gernot Hassknecht, played by the actor Hans-Joachim Heist. He delivers editorial comment on current topics, a format German viewers are familiar with, since for important issues, chief-editors or directors of regional TV subsidiaries regularly deliver comment as part of the regular newscast on the national public stations. These comments are formally separated from the presentation of the daily news through the elaborate measures taken to ensure that viewers do not mistake them for "real" news. They are introduced formally by the news anchor: "And now a commentary from regional station chief XX." The comments are then presented in front of a different backdrop and with the insert "comment by XX," while a (not particularly aggressive or opinionated) comment is read in a rather neutral, distant voice. In his parody, Hassknecht starts his comment with a balanced report on the facts of an issue, but then talks himself into a flaming rage (much like *The Daily Show*'s Lewis Black in "Back in Black"), until he is cut off by a still frame of the channel's logo, with comforting music indicating a short interruption in the program.

There are stronger forms of political commentary in the German media, but they are more likely to be found in niche outlets such as the political satire print magazines *Eulenspiegel* and *Titanic* (both with a circulation of about 100,000). In particular *Titanic* has created quite a few political scandals and a number of iconic covers and headlines that found their way into mainstream media reporting and popular culture. The *heute show* thus gained significant political credibility by adding the former chief-editor of *Titanic* to its staff. Martin Sonneborn regularly takes on "interview missions" where he ventures with his trademark earnestness into terrain mostly ignored by regular journalists. He interviews neo-Nazi extremists and members of the Marxist Forum (the openly Marxist wing of a small left wing political party), he portrays a Santa Claus workshop as a terrorist training camp, and he intrudes in the houses of simple citizens claiming the need to film their homes for the new service "Google Home View."

Sonneborn represents a more controversial, polarizing approach to journalism, which can be seen as a reaction to the well-mannered, well-balanced media culture in Germany. He also caused the only legal case surrounding the *heute show* when he interviewed a pharma lobbyist in 2010 about the price of drugs in Germany, pretending to be from ZDF's regular newscast *heute*. In the interview, the lobbyist made statements about the quality of drugs from Chinese pharmaceutical companies, but then said he did not want to be shown on TV. Nevertheless, the segment was used by the *heute show*. As a result, the lobbyist lost his job, and Sonneborn and the *heute show* were reprimanded by the head of ZDF. However, in an interview, Welke pointed out that his show had shown the mechanisms of lobbying in a new light, stressing that this kind of background information should be shown on regular TV news but isn't (Leurs, 2011). He thus sees his show as a form of criticism of the regular news programs on TV, a standpoint he shares with his American role model Jon Stewart.

THE *HEUTE SHOW* AND GERMAN POLITICAL CULTURE

In a parliamentary democracy with currently five elected political parties (and 16 federal states clamoring for their share of the public debate), developing a news parody program that covers all relevant political actors and issues, while at the same time providing its viewers with a restricted range of recognizable, easy-to-understand objects of ridicule, has been a challenge for the *heute show*. To avoid further distractions, the show has a clear focus on national German politics, touching rarely on international topics, and then usually from a German point of view, looking at the German coverage of the event, or talking about the involvement of German politicians in the story.

Much more than its American role model, it criticizes and mimics politicians and parties across the political spectrum. The political opinions voiced appear to place it more on the left side of the political spectrum, but it displays no signs of loyalty towards the Social Democrats or even the Greens. In contrast to Jon Stewart, no specific political agenda has been discernible so far. However, the Free Democratic Party (FDP, the small partner of the CDU in government, which clearly favors free markets and privatization) has become a bit of a pet topic: It has been an easy target having lost its political representatives and voter support in breathtaking speed over the last year. At the same time the *heute show* provided some substantial criticism of the special (business) interest group legislation introduced by the party, such as a reduction in the value-added tax rate for the hotel industry.

While there has been much speculation and outrage about a possible "Americanization" of German politics and political communication, most scholars would refute that an actual "Americanization" has occurred. German political campaigning and campaign coverage appear to have adopted some American strategies, but only with significant modifications (e.g., Reinemann & Wilke, 2007; Schulz, 2005). As Pfetsch (2001) points out, German political communication culture remains much less media-centered compared to the United States. Party block voting is still the norm in German parliaments; hence, politicians have far less need to mobilize public opinion concerning specific issues outside of election times. Intense mediated policy controversies are therefore rare, leaving the *heute show*, again, with less enticing fodder.

Similarly despite a perceived increase in "politainment" (i.e., the blurring of lines between politics and entertainment), this phenomenon has not yet reached American levels. While in the United States the participation of politicians in entertainment talk shows such as Oprah or late night talk shows has become an accepted part of political campaigning, in Germany, politicians, media, and the public continue to have strong reservations. At the time of their appearance in popular entertainment programs, the popularity of politicians may increase temporarily, but in the long run, their image has suffered. The most recent victim of this is former Vice Chancellor Guido Westerwelle, whose appearance on the German *Big Brother* in 2000 made him vulnerable to charges of triviality and likely contributed to his expeditious fall from grace a year after being appointed vice chancellor in 2010. Politics in Germany, so it seems, is still a "serious" business. This in turn helps explain the reluctance of German politicians to be associated with a satirical program. In addition to their fear of losing control over their image in nonstaged interviews, the positive effect of such appearances is not yet clear.

It is for this reason that the producers of the *heute show* have not been able to integrate an interview with politicians in the show's regular set-up. So far there has only been one politician who dared to accept an invitation of the *heute show*. In the episode on May 13, 2011, Claudia Roth, head of the German Green Party and prominent member of the German parliament, was the first and so far only politician on the show. Her courage as a forerunner should not be overrated: Of all German parties, the politics of the Green party come probably closest to the opinions of the *heute show* and its viewers. In addition, the Greens had scored a major victory in a state election a few days before, becoming the strongest party in the large and prosperous state of Baden-Württemberg. She could thus expect kind treatment, and Oliver Welke most likely even exceeded her expectations. For most of the interview, he only talked about the fact that she was the sole politician who would dare to appear on his show. He treated her with exaggerated hospitality, giving her a huge bouquet of roses, and offering her a clock radio for each politician she would be able to motivate to appear on his show. Unfortunately, this uber-hospitality prevented Welke from raising any interesting issues with his guest.

THE *HEUTE SHOW*'S IMPACT ON GERMAN POLITICS, MEDIA, AND VIEWERS

The anchor Oliver Welke rather downplays the political aspirations of his show: "The common denominator of the show is more the spoofing of the powerful to the point where it hurts" (cited in Brauck, 2009).[5] And so far not much of an impact on national or regional politics has been discernible. The show has only reacted to political events and issues without setting an agenda of its own. Still both the political and the media system in Germany attribute it with an enormous amount of potential—often with direct references to its American role model. As a result, German politicians have become very much aware of the show. For instance, Finance Minister Philip Rösler's parliamentary speech on nuclear energy was countered by a member of parliament with this statement: "Mr. Rösler, you will find your speech line-by-line on the *heute show*" (Deutscher Bundestag, 2011, p. 12977). While in earlier episodes some of the lesser known and thus less sophisticated politicians appear to be somewhat flattered when asked a question by one of the most important German channels on their way to the Bundestag or at party conventions, recently the rising awareness of the show among politicians and society in general is clearly visible in a growing reluctance to participate in ad-hoc interviews, sometimes a distinct "Don't talk to them, they do satire!" can be heard in the background.

In the media the response to the first episodes was rather skeptical if not negative. Welke was considered to be a "case of blatant miscasting," and the show itself "a classical boss's brainchild that just doesn't work" (Mohr, 2009). This melted away quickly to a rather benevolent and enthusiastic reception. After only two years on the air, the *heute show* is now the standard that newly introduced formats have to measure up to. Some of the support, however, seems to be linked to a sense that the German public sphere needs a political satire show, needs its own Jon Stewart. Thus even though the *heute show* may not be as good as hoped for, it is at the moment seen as the best there is to be had in Germany.

The awards the *heute show* has received indicate how the show is not only perceived as a comedy but also as a journalistic format. It won the *Deutscher Comedypreis* ("German Comedy Award") twice, and in 2010 won the *Deutscher Fernsehpreis* ("German Television Award") and the *Grimme Preis*, the most prestigious award in the category of entertainment. But its team also was awarded the *Journalist of the Year* Award in 2010, because the *heute show*, according to the jury, is living proof that journalism and entertainment works on TV, without getting stuck in cheap jokes and puns (Disselhoff, 2010).

Outside the media critique columns, its impact has been rather small. There are some examples of successful sketches going viral or being taken up in other "serious" programs. For example,

---

[5]In German: "Der gemeinsame Nenner ist eher die Veralberung der Macht - bis an die Schmerzgrenze." Authors' translation.

the show's attempt to explain the validity of the different German value-added tax rates following the significant tax reduction for the hotel industry was picked up for an episode of the political talk show *Hart aber fair* on public channel ARD.

When the *heute show* started in 2009, it had promising ratings, with around 2 million viewers and a market share of around 15%. In the following months, the ratings dropped to about 1–1.5 million viewers per episode and market shares with single-digit percentages. Recently, the show has been able to break the 2 million mark again, even though the Friday night slot is a heavily contested time slot for TV comedy, and the overall trend indicates a steady growth of the audience (Markhauser, 2011).

Like *The Daily Show*, the *heute show* works with a live audience which adds atmosphere, laughter, and applause to the show. This is the most immediate involvement of the audience. However, the *heute show* goes beyond this. While on the official website of ZDF only the last episode of the show can be accessed (with up to 400,000 downloads per episode), older episodes and highlights of them can easily be found on YouTube, where ZDF officially uploads some episodes on its YouTube comedy channel *ZDFlachbar* ("ZDFlaughable") and fans upload clips of the show. These uploads are often commented on by YouTube users, sometimes resulting in several hundred, in rare cases even more than a thousand comments on an episode or a segment of it.

In general, comments on social media sites such as YouTube and Facebook show that many viewers appreciate the quality of the *heute show*. At the same time, the show is often compared to *The Daily Show*, and in such comparisons, the *heute show* is usually seen as the inferior copy of the original. Interestingly, while some see the show's weakness in the fact that it is too close to the American original, others complain that it is not living up to the standards set by *The Daily Show*, a comparison that is also often made in media articles on the *heute show*. For example, one critic of the show writes that while *The Daily Show* employs three non-white correspondents, the *heute show* only features white men and two (white) women (Wagner, 2010).

Overall, the favorite part of the *heute show* seems to be the segments featuring reporter Sonneborn and his bitingly sarcastic reports on serious issues, thereby not only making a mockery of the portrayed figures but also of the journalists whom Sonneborn is parodying. Many comments agree that with this kind of coverage, and with the kind of humor that is being used in the show in general, the TV station is attracting a younger audience than with its traditional news shows, a development greatly welcomed by both the younger audience and the TV producers.

As the American original is known and immediately accessible not only to a selected few elites but to a larger segment of the population, the *heute show* therefore is not judged on its own merits but rather in comparison to its US role model. This has important consequences for its evaluation by the viewers. On the one hand there may be consistent disappointment, as the *heute show* cannot live up to *The Daily Show*. It is a weekly not daily program, its staff is minimal compared to Jon Stewart's, it is not yet as established in the political system, it has less of a political impact, no political guests, and no political agenda. At the moment Oliver Welke and his team would never be able to mobilize a substantial number of "fans" for a rally to restore sanity or any other concern. On the other hand, knowledge of *The Daily Show* greatly increases the credibility and political weight of the show. People aware of the political impact of *The Daily Show* cannot dismiss the *heute show* as "just" a television show, for they know how much political clout this type of format can achieve.

CONCLUSION: POTENTIAL AND EFFECTS OF NEWS PARODY IN GERMANY

Political satire has a long tradition in Germany, mostly in the form of political cabaret, originally taking place in small theaters and clubs, and then transferred to television. However, it is a dated format that has not adapted well to the opportunities the medium of television has to offer or to a younger generation's habits of media use. Given this, the adaptation of *The Daily Show* may have come at an opportune moment. Whether it is due to the continuous import of American shows and formats, or to the easy accessibility of American culture on the internet, German viewers seem by now to have become quite "Americanized" in their tastes and thus more open to the treatment of "serious" matters in a more humorous way. The German understanding of political satire appears to be in the process of converging with the US and British approach to political satire: As a more playful and less grave satirical treatment of politics becomes possible, laughter moves to the center of German political satire, drawing in a wider pool of television viewers and recruiting new audiences to public political contestation.

The celebration of play and laughter in the *heute show* may, however, partially explain why the show's impact on politics has been minimal so far. For the moment one can only note an awareness of the show and its political potential among politicians, media critics, and parts of the population. Whether this awareness will transform into real political clout will strongly depend on the decision of Oliver Welke and his team to develop a clearer political profile and champion specific issues. Concerning the sense of earnestness and mission, it is actually Jon Stewart who comes currently closer to the traditional German understanding of political satire. If the *heute show* can hence develop the right formula—retaining its current level of playfulness and laughter, while finding a persistent, authentic line of attack and judgment, without falling back into the patterns of the old German political cabaret by sounding preachy and self-righteous—it can become a considerable force in the German public sphere.

REFERENCES

AGF/GfK. (2011). TV-Panel D+EU. Retrieved from http://www.agf.de/daten/

Baumgartner, J. C., & Morris, J. S. (Eds.). (2008). *Laughing matters: Humor and American politics in the media age.* New York, NY: Routledge.

Baym, G. (2010). *From Conkrite to Colbert: The evoluation of broadcast news.* Boulder, CO: Paradigm.

Baym, G. (2005). *The Daily Show*: Discursive integration and the reinvention of political journalism. *Political Communication, 22*(3), 259–276.

Behrmann, S. (2002). *Politische Satire im deutschen und französischen Rundfunk.* Würzburg, Germany: Königshausen & Neumann.

Brauck, M. (2009, December 19). Seh' ich aus wie ein Vollidiot? *Der Spiegel.* Retrieved from http://www.spiegel.de

Brummack, J. (1971). Zu Begriff und Theorie der Satire. *Deutsche Vierteljahresschrift für Literaturwissenschaft und Geistesgeschichte, 45,* 275–377.

Budzinski, K., & Hippen, R. (1996). *Metzler-Kabarett-Lexikon.* In Verbindung mit dem Deutschen Kabarett Archiv. Stuttgart, Germany: Metzler.

Bundeszentrale für politische Bildung. (2009). Mitgliederentwicklung der Parteien. Retrieved from http://www.bpb.de/themen/1YML48,0,Mitgliederentwicklung.html.

Casciato, P. (2011, July 6). Americans rated most hilarious in global poll. *Reuters.* Retrieved from http://www.reuters.com

Caufield, R. P. (2008). The influence of "Infoenterpropagainment": Exploring the power of political satire as a distinct form of political humor. In J. C. Baumgartner & J. S. Morris (Eds.), *Laughing matters: Humor and American politics in the media age* (pp. 3–20). New York, NY: Routledge.

Deutscher Bundestag. (2011, June 9). Plenarprotokoll 17/114. Stenografischer Bericht der 114. Sitzung. Berlin, Germany.

Disselhoff, F. (2010, December 22). Das sind die Journalisten des Jahres 2010. *Meedia*. Retrieved from http://meedia.de

Gabriel, O. W., & Völkl, K. (2005). Politische und soziale Partizipation. In O.W. Gabriel & E. Holtmann (Eds.), *Politisches System der Bundesrepublik Deutschland* (3rd ed., pp. 523–574). München, Germany: Oldenbourg Wissenschaftsverlag.

Gray, J., Jones, J., & Thompson, E. (2009). *Satire TV: Politics and comedy in the post-network era*. New York, NY: New York University Press.

Hallin, D. C., & Mancini, P. (2004). *Comparing media systems: Three models of media and politics*. Cambridge, England: Cambridge University Press.

Jones, J. P. (2010). *Entertaining politics: Satiric television and political engagement*. Lanham, MD: Rowman & Littlefield.

Leurs, R. (2011, March 4). *Komischer Typ. Financial Times Deutschland*. Retrieved from http://www.ftd.de

Markhauser, A. (2011). *Quotencheck: "heute show."* Retrieved from http://www.quotenmeter.de/cms/?p1=n&p2=50218&p3=

Mohr, R. (2009, May 27). *Wo bleibt der Wahnsinn?* Der Spiegel. Retrieved from http://www.spiegel.de

Pfetsch, B. (2001). Political communication culture in the United States and Germany. *The Harvard International Journal of Press/Politics*, *6*(1), 46–67. DOI: 10.1177/1081180x01006001004

Reinemann, C., & Wilke, J. (2007). It's the debates, stupid! How the introduction of televised debates changed the portrayal of Chancellor candidates in the German press, 1949 2005. *The Harvard International Journal of Press/Politics*, *12*(4), 92–111. DOI: 10.1177/1081180x07307185

Rosenstein, D. (1994). Kritik und Vergnügen. Zur Geschichte kabarettistischer Sendeformen. In H. D. Erlinger & H. F. Foltin (Eds.), *Unterhaltung, Werbung und Zielgruppenprogramme. Geschichte des Fernsehens in der Bundesrepublik Deutschland. Band 4* (pp. 159–185). München, Germany: Wilhelm Fink.

Schulz, W. (2005). Voters in a changing media environment: A data-based retrospective on consequences of media change in Germany. *European Journal of Communication*, *20*(1), 55–88. DOI: 10.1177/0267323105047670

Tenenboim-Weinblatt, K. (2009). Jester, fake journalist, or the new Walter Lippman?: Recognition processes of Jon Stewart by the U.S. journalistic community. *International Journal of Communication*, *3*, 416–439.

Test, G.A. (1991). Satire: Spirit and art. Tampa, FL: University of Florida.

Wagner, D. (2010, January 29). Wenn der Wegschaltfinger dreimal juckt. Retrieved from http://www.freitag.de/kultur/1004-medientagebuch-heute-show

Zubayr, C., & Geese, S. (2011). Die Fernsehsender im Qualitätsurteil des Publikums. *Media Perspektiven* (5), 230–241.

Zubayr, C., & Gerhard, H. (2011). Tendenzen im Zuschauerverhalten. Fernsehgewohnheiten und Fernsehreichweiten im Jahr 2010. *Media Perspektiven* (3), 126–138.

Transgressing Boundaries as the Hybrid Global: Parody and Postcoloniality on Indian Television

Sangeet Kumar

This article analyzes the role of political satire on Indian television through a comparative study of two satire shows (one each in Hindi and English). It investigates the process by which these shows, both based on successful Western formats, "Indianize" themselves and find audiences at a new cultural site. It argues that the shows adapt themselves to the Indian cultural milieu in distinct ways by aligning themselves along a postcolonial social rift that is differentiated by language. By appealing to these culturally distinct audiences and tapping into the unique sensibilities that each of them represents the shows construct hybrid identities from global formats in innovative ways. Through this exploration, this article ponders over the inherent paradoxes within global cultural flows and echoes calls for a dialectical approach to studying it.

That global formats must invariably tap into local cultural nuances to find audiences at new locations (Moran, 1998; Robertson, 1994; Straubhar, 2006) poses a much-needed correction to arguments about the unfettered flow of dominant cultural products (Schiller, 1992; Tomlinson, 1991). Analyzing the minutiae of the processes through which the global acknowledges and accommodates the local, however, allows us to extend existing theoretical explanations about the phenomenon of cultural globalization. This article explores that negotiation through a close comparative analysis of two news parody shows on Indian television. These shows are an exception within the television news landscape in India because comedy as a genre exists primarily in the nonnews entertainment channels. Airing in Hindi and English, respectively, within a relatively uncensored press system, the shows *Gustakhi Maaf* and *The Week That Wasn't* both engage with current political events in a light vein poking fun at politicians and satirizing political events across the country. Despite being based on successful Western satire programs, the shows have Indianized themselves through distinct modes of comedy that are targeted to different linguistic audience groups. Through analyzing their prevalent themes, their styles of humor, the characters they portray, and their formats, this article argues that the two shows replicate each side of a social split specific to India. This fissure is a colonial legacy, a remnant of an attempted social stratification to facilitate colonial rule in India, but one whose endurance in postcolonial times continues to fascinate and intrigue scholars (Rajagopal, 2001; Sunder Rajan, 1992).

As adaptations of Western formats, both shows illustrate a negotiation between structure and culture (Straubhar, 2006) but emerge from that negotiation inhabiting two ends on the spectrum of culturally distinct humorous styles. While globally successful formats have succeeded in India ever since Western media networks sought to capitalize on India's liberalizing media policy (Kumar, 2005, 2006; Punathambekar, 2010), in each instance (e.g., the *Millionaire* and the *Idol* franchises) their success has depended on their ability to allow space for local specificities to assert themselves making them "glocal" or the hybrid global (Canclini, 2006; Kraidy, 2002; Pieterse, 2006; Robertson, 1994). In the initial days of television liberalization, Western shows found small audiences among the urban elite but achieved mass popularity only after unshackling themselves from their rigid formats to Indianize.

This study investigates the case of political comedy, whose translation is tricky due to culturally coded category of humor. In India this translation is further complicated by a rich and ancient indigenous tradition of comedy and satire as a means of speaking truth to power. Its lineage can be traced to the ancient Indian theory of drama within which the tropes of *rasa* or moods includes the *hasya rasa* or the trope of comedy (Arogyasami, 1994; Schwartz, 2004; Vatsyayan, 2001). From its ancient origins to its ripening as a fully developed mode of political resistance during colonial rule (Freedman, 2009; Hasan, 2003), political satire has thrived in India prior to the airing of the two shows analyzed here. The notable contribution of these shows is popularizing the genre on television while also adapting already successful formats to India. While the Western tradition of satire has been well documented by scholars (Connery & Combe, 1995; Hutcheon, 1985), this article illustrates how the merger of these seemingly different strands of humor within the shows allows them to inhabit an interstitial space located between Western and Indian aesthetics of humor.

An analysis of Indian political satire must also locate its emergence within ongoing changes in the country's political landscape. Despite being a multiparty democracy that theoretically allows for equal representation and accountability through a system of checks and balances, India has entered a phase of extreme disillusionment with its political institutions and their ability to represent and empower the weakest in society. Instances of egregious abuses of power by politicians for personal gain have galvanized civil society leaders to take to Gandhian forms of national protest, forcing the state to negotiate with them for stringent anti-corruption laws.[1] If political satire is a particularly apt mode of resistance during periods of "social and political rupture" or those of "manufactured realities" (Gray, Jones, & Thompson, 2009, p. 15), then the current political impasse in India provides ample cause for its thriving. It allows for a "momentary form of aggression" (p. 12) against institutions of power that otherwise remain largely unaccountable and unreachable for the common people. This political impasse provides ammunition for programs of satire to tap into and build upon the disillusionment.

---

[1] An ongoing stalemate between the Indian government and veteran social activist Anna Hazare on his demand for a strong anti-corruption bill had just ended at the time of the writing of this article. Hazare's fast-unto-death mobilized India's youth leading to unprecedented simultaneous protests in multiple cities and eventually forcing the government to accept his demands.

SATIRE AND PARODY IN INDIAN HISTORY

Within India's tradition of theater, the earliest discussions about humor are present in Bharata's *Natyashastra*, the ancient treatise on the theory of drama (Vatsyayan, 1996). A body of texts authored by the sage Bharata, the Natyashastra is dated between 200 BC and 200 AD and covers a range of topics around theater. Bharata classifies humor as one of the eight *rasas* (mood-effects) that can be created through drama. For Bharata the comic sentiment arises from the erotic that is "the happiness or pleasure" that is "connected with desired objects" (quoted in Arogyasami, 1994, p. 155). The Natyashastra lists several devices through which laughter can be created, with juxtaposition and mimicry being two of them. Having given rise to a rich body of debate and deliberation on various aspects of theater, Bharata's original text remains one of the key inspirations for contemporary Indian drama. The presence of humor as a theatrical trope in ancient India provided a foundation for it to flourish in subsequent years and legitimized its presence in public and distinctly political spaces. The witty verbal duels between the Mughal emperor Akbar (1542–1605) and his court advisor Birbal are a prominently recurring theme within India's historical tales (Naim, 1995) and provide a clear instance of the use of humor to speak truth to power.

This history of political humor in India seeks to underscore the indigenous tradition of satire within which the shows are embedded. In modern India, the existence of satire and parody as a means of political commentary has existed at least since the inception of an opposition press during the consolidation of the British Empire. The origin and initial development of the Indian press was directly associated with resistance against the British rule as several current newspapers were founded during the movement, and movement leaders often wrote for these newspapers to mobilize public opinion (Parameswaran, 2009). Hence contrary to being set up for advertising or financial profit, the founding of newspapers in India was directly connected to ongoing social and political movements (Sonwalkar, 2002). Given their anti-establishment stance, they had ample space for forms of political critique including humor and satire. In tracing the history of political humor in India, Freedman (2009) finds several instances in the news media when British rule was resisted through the use of satire, leading to the earliest charges of sedition and instances of press censorship. The ubiquitous political cartoon that continues on the front pages of most Indian newspapers today came to India with British rule and became a tool of "protest, agitation, and peaceful revolution" (Freedman, 2009, p. 131).

Not surprisingly the interactions between a preexisting and culturally distinct satirical style present in the local language presses and the one introduced through the English press was a productive alliance. In North Central India, the prevalence of a rich literary tradition in Urdu around the cities of Lucknow and Delhi helped inspire rich political satire in English as well. The debut of *Awadh Punch* (a weekly started in 1877) marked the launch of India's own political satire magazine along the lines of the British *Punch* magazine. Historian Mushirul Hasan (2003) claims that with the launch of the weekly "political satire, hitherto disguised, became a legitimate form of experience." Even though targeted primarily against the British Empire, the magazine was equally unsparing in its criticism of self-seeking Indian politicians and those Westernized Indians who either helped the British in governance or imagined themselves to be equal to them.

This historical lineage gives Indian political satire strong roots in the independence movement. In postcolonial India that tradition has continued with renewed vigor, making political cartoonists such as R. K. Laxman, Abu Abraham, Sudhir Dar, and Unny popular figures. The launch of the political satire journal *Shankar's Weekly* in 1948 (a year after India gained independence) points to the persistence of that tradition. That satire thrived during colonial rule reflects its tendency to flourish during increased censorship and totalitarianism, as direct and obvious political criticism is easier to regulate than the ambiguous and grey zone of satire and parody (Baym, 2005; Gray et al., 2009; Griffin, 1994). In India, the infamous period of the suspension of democratic process and the imposition of the "emergency" (1975–1977)[2] is remembered equally for the censorship imposed on newspapers and for caricatures of the politically powerful in newspaper cartoons (Freedman, 2009). This brief history of humor in general, and political humor in particular, helps us situate the two shows within a larger trajectory of intermixing politics and comedy in India.

SITUATING THE HYBRID GLOBAL IN INDIAN TELEVISION

Inspired by successful formats abroad and launched within short periods of each other on competing networks, the two shows analyzed here are prime instances of political humor on Indian television today. *The Week That Wasn't* (launched in 2006 and henceforth referred to as *TWTW*) airs weekly on Sunday nights. Hosted by the comedian Cyrus Broacha, it is a mix of news parody and skits that poke fun at news events by caricaturing and impersonating characters in the news. The show airs for 30 minutes each Sunday night on the network CNN-IBN, a 24-hour news network produced in collaboration with CNN. *Gustakhi Maaf* ("Excuse the Transgression"; launched in 2003) is a satirical puppet show in Hindi that airs for four minutes twice a day and then is compiled together to create a half hour show called the *Best of Gustakhi Maaf* on Sundays. It airs on *NDTV India*, a 24-hour news channel in Hindi. Current host Brij Bhushan Shukla, the only human character on the show, introduces each skit and provides his own interpretation of political events. NDTV (New Delhi Television) and IBN (India Broadcasting Network) are rival networks operating out of New Delhi,[3] both of which offer a bouquet of channels catering to news and entertainment. Both networks also run competing news channels in Hindi and English. Since *Gustakhi Maaf* runs on the Hindi channel of NDTV and *TWTW* runs on the English channel of IBN, they are indirectly in competition despite being in different languages.

TWTW is loosely based on the format of the American news parody program *The Daily Show*, while *Gustakhi Maaf* is a copy of the successful French puppet show *Les Guignols de l'info*[4] ("News Puppets") that has run for more than 25 years on French television. Similar to the styles of Jon Stewart on *The Daily Show* and Stephen Colbert on *The Colbert Report*, *TWTW* follows the format of humorous video montages of news footage, fake reporters pretending to do on-location reporting, and fake "experts" pontificating on news events of the day/week. Similar to Stewart's straight-faced interviews, the reporters and experts on *TWTW* too begin in all seriousness (after having their expert credentials declared by Cyrus) until he begins to feign

---

[2]The Emergency is the only period in India's postindependence history when normal democratic processes were suspended through a diktat by the central government. It led to a political backlash and the overthrow of the Congress party that had been continuously in power since independence.

[3]A former NDTV editor and anchor Rajdeep Sardesai launched CNN-IBN. Ever since its launch the two networks have been in a heated rivalry.

[4]This is discussed by Doyle in this collection.

surprise at the ridiculousness of their answers. The juxtaposition of a serious news format with inexplicable and perplexing behavior or answers is the key to laughter on the show.

Akin to Stewart's constant penchant for ridiculing his own show through self-deprecating humor, *TWTW* also regularly indulges in self-bashing aimed to point out that its creators do not take themselves too seriously. A particular case in point is its celebration of 200 episodes in October 2010. As a part of its celebration, the show conducted interviews with several celebrities as well as journalists from the IBN channel on which *TWTW* aired. Almost every interviewee either feigned ignorance about the show and its anchor or dismissed it while hurling expletives. In one particular scene, the network's top executives in an editorial meeting show complete ignorance about the program and its anchor Cyrus. In another, the chief film critic on IBN reviews *TWTW* and gives it a rating of 0 out of 5. In an expanding and fiercely competitive television landscape caught in a ratings war (Kohli-Khandekar, 2006; Sanghvi, 2011) and featuring outlandish claims about the relative success of networks and shows, this self-deprecating attitude, even coming from a parody show, stands out as odd.

As opposed to the unofficial and informal relationship between *TWTW* and the American *TDS*, *Gustakhi Maaf* is an officially sanctioned Indian version of the French *Les Guignols*. The launch of the Indian version was preceded by a training workshop in which technicians and producers from the French show visited Delhi for over a month and taught their Indian counterparts (including the current anchor of the show) the skills of creating and maintaining the puppets. The program began with a short four-minute clip each weekday, but due to its rising popularity the frequency was increased to twice a day and later to three times a day before settling on a regular schedule of telecasting twice a day (the second one repeats the first airing).

Les Guignols and *Gustakhi Maaf* have identical-looking puppets as the technique of gradually constructing and then maintaining the cast was transferred to the Indian staff during the workshop. It currently takes about 25 days for the staff at *Gustakhi Maaf* to build a puppet and add it to the show's repertoire. Given the time and labor involved, the process of adding a puppet to the show depends on following the public actions of politicians and celebrities to gauge their ability to stay continuously in the news.

An innovative way in which the team has added a uniquely Indian flavor to the show is by confronting the real life characters (mostly politicians) with their puppets or that of their rivals. These face-offs have been extremely popular since coaxing a celebrity or a politician into conversations with their puppets (who speak as their alter ego) invariably leads to hilarious situations. "In these situations we realized that politicians respond best when the puppets speak in the plural 'us' as though the person and the puppet were one and the same," explains Shukla (personal communication, September 4, 2011). Among the topics between puppet and politician are strategies for the future, "malicious" media allegations, and private conversations presented as though the real people are speaking to themselves. Not all politicians take this face-off sportingly and the team has also had rude encounters in the process. When confronted with her political rival's puppet at a political event, the politician Uma Bharati was visibly upset and refused to engage in any conversation. Later, however, when mollified she agreed to a long conversation with her puppet (but not with her rival's) (Shukla, personal communication, September 4, 2011). For the most part, publicity hungry politicians jump at these opportunities, especially during election time.

Besides these face-offs between puppets and real people, the show has also introduced a distinctly Indian ethos through the use of musical numbers from Hindi movies. The cultural dominance of the film industry in India ensures that popular songs from successful movies provide readily available metaphors for explaining political events that the show frequently deploys to amplify themes of love, betrayal, and loyalty to describe shifts in political coalitions and changes in personal fortunes in Indian politics. The writers on the show routinely write their own lyrics set to the tunes of popular numbers from movies.

As is evident, *Gustakhi Maaf*'s success must be attributed as much to its borrowed format as to the innovative ways in which it has managed to reflect uniquely Indian themes and motifs. These adaptations allow it to resonate with Indian audiences especially in the nonmetropolitan areas of the country. "News reporters from our network who travel to rural areas frequently narrate instances of immediate recognition when introducing themselves from the same channel that airs *Gustakhi Maaf*," explains Shukla (personal communication, July 8, 2011). The diverging ways in which both the comedy shows have Indianized themselves points to the unique case of the Indian audience as well as the fragmented Indian national identity itself. The historical processes instrumental in creating this fractured identity inform the analysis of the two shows.

THE POSTCOLONIAL FISSURE

An attempt to analyze popular cultural artifacts created in Hindi and English (the two most spoken languages in India) must engage with the role of language in general and English in particular in postcolonial India. Scholars have argued that the elitist role played by English in colonial India has only been further entrenched in postcolonial India (Sunder Rajan, 1992) where the English and non-English speaking populations form two oppositional sides of a "split public." Rajagopal (2001) coined the phrase to analyze the rise of right-wing Hindu nationalism in the 1990s. He concludes that the ideologues on the right accentuated an already existing fissure in Indian society to create a popular base. On one side of this divide is the elite, English-speaking, usually upper class, often urban, ostensibly liberal, and secular India. This English-speaking India often comprises a "well-networked national elite" that has "a sense of being bearers of the agenda of modernization" (p. 159). The other India comprises the vernacular speaking, religious minded, rural and traditional India, often at odds with the discourse of secular modernity espoused by "liberal" English speaking elites.

This divide is rooted in India's colonial history, when a mediating class was created through the limited and controlled diffusion of the English language. This elite class continues in postcolonial times, reproducing a fissure most readily apparent in the competing English and non-English media. While the urbane, English press claims to speak in the name of "reason" and "liberty" and other European enlightenment ideals, that discourse is challenged by a vernacular press consumed by the rural majority, who fail to participate in the idiom of Western modernity. The vernacular press' resentment toward English language media arises because the latter's "inability to access the values and beliefs of the vernacular realm was then a form of sanctioned ignorance, a sign of privilege rather than handicap, portending none of the usual consequences of ignorance" (Rajagopal, 2001, p. 163). These contestations over modernity that pit the liberal elite and the "anti-modern" masses against each other have been analyzed in other settings as well (Frank, 2004; Kraidy, 2008, 2009) but the Indian case is set apart by its colonial roots and linguistic divide.

The cultural landscape of India replicates this social divide with, on the one hand, the existence of a westward-looking cultural milieu whose primary language is English and, on the other, a locally rooted culture that exists in non-English languages. The two shows analyzed here resonate with opposing sides of this social split and display a notable difference in emphasis and content. Their comparative analysis brings out three crucial areas of difference—a split between urban versus rural focused stories, a divergence along linguistic lines, and a difference in emphasis on Indian versus Western themes. These points of departure are not accidental but allow us to identify the target audiences for the shows and the ways in which the codes of humor operate differently within those demographic groups.

India versus Bharat

Both shows feature stories about national news events, but the English-language *TWTW* shows a clear emphasis on urban themes, while the Hindi *Gustakhi Maaf* is geared towards events that concern a more rural audience. The difference between the globally known English name "India" as opposed to the Hindi name "Bharat" is an apt metaphor to describe the two Indias that the shows represent. This difference, while hardly surprising, leads to quite different aesthetics of humor.

Urban-themed events recently covered on *TWTW* include union strikes in the airline industry, the upscale party scene in cities, details of Hollywood and Western celebrities' lives, sex scandals involving the rich and famous, and references to social networking websites. These topics are likely to resonate instantly with a newly expanding westward-looking, upwardly mobile population created from two decades of economic liberalization in India. In fact, at the very beginning of the show, its host Cyrus Broacha introduces it as being telecast from "a garage in Malabar Hill," which is one of the most expensive residential locations in Mumbai and whose name would be unknown to most Indians in rural India. By invoking this location (while also mocking itself by falsely stating that it airs from a garage), *TWTW* seeks to connect with a city-centric audience able to differentiate between the class connotations of different city neighborhoods. Even as it frequently includes urban topics, one rarely finds references to events in small town India, regional politics and politicians, or issues and controversies related to religion or caste that are frequent sources of conflict in India. These omissions, when juxtaposed with the topics the show does emphasize, allow us to paint a picture of the demographic of *TWTW*.

Gustakhi Maaf, however, frequently picks on news stories that would be of interest to a more rural audience. Given its format of a puppet show often including musical skits, *Gustakhi Maaf* frequently toys with themes and ideas that draw upon religion, ancient mythology, agricultural issues, and politics of the regional states. A case in point is a recent show that featured a poor farmer's family and sought to take aim at Rahul Gandhi, the son of Sonia Gandhi who is the chairperson of the Congress party currently in power in India.[5] As the de-facto heir to the party, the skit portrayed him as an ancient prince waiting for his chance at power, even as he toured around the country ostensibly showing sympathy to poor farmers while devouring (in the spirit of sharing) the little amount of food they had during their meals. The skit features a scene where the puppet Rahul re-enacts an event from the ancient epic tale of *Mahabharata* in order to find a bride. The choice of this ancient tale of Rajas and princes, familiar to most Indians, also uniquely

---

[5]No relation to M. K. Gandhi, the leader of India's freedom struggle.

taps into a religious sensibility that is predominant within the rural areas. The skits of *Gustakhi Maaf* also frequently caricature regional politicians, presenting comic analyses of local election results. Their puppets enact tales of love, loyalty, betrayal, and despair with suggestive Hindi songs in the background referencing Bollywood plots. The frequent use of Hindi movie songs and Urdu couplets called *shayari* (a form of poetry recital common in North India) in their skits gives *Gustakhi Maaf* an aesthetic of humor that is culturally distinct from the "sophisticated," linguistic-based humor largely present in *TWTW*.

The difference in the target audience for the two shows is made possible by the phenomenal expansion of the television audience after the loosening of state control on Indian television beginning in the 1990s (Kumar, 2005, 2006; Thussu, 1999, 2007). Unlike the unified captive audience for the state controlled *Doordarshan*, the privatization and expansion of the television space has relied crucially on an invitation to the "other" India to join in as participative audiences (Punathambekar, 2010). Transforming the televisual space in India, this expansion has allowed for niche targeting of audiences along linguistic and cultural lines that both *TWTW* and *Gustakhi Maaf* seek to achieve.

The Language of Humor

Both shows play upon the linguistic and accent diversity within India to create humor. While *TWTW* uses the distinction between the Hindi and non-Hindi speaking populations, *Gustakhi Maaf* taps into the variations and dialects within Hindi itself. Given the rich multiplicity within the linguistic space in India, the issue of language creates ample opportunities for jokes aimed at politicians and celebrities. For *TWTW* the inability to speak English, or in the correct accent, is a frequently recurring cause for ridicule. A case in point is the show airing June 26, 2011, in which the Indian Finance Minister Pranab Mukjerjee's accent is exaggerated to create comic effect. Even though the person ridiculed on the show is not the minister himself but his spokesperson, it is clear that the show makes the latter stand in for Mukherjee as the skit repeatedly exaggerates his accent and makes fun of his inability to speak grammatically correct English. Moreover the skit, which is based on allegations of Mukherjee's office being spied upon through a wiretap, ends when the spokesperson mentions that bugging his office was a useless exercise as no one could understand what he was saying anyways. The joke is clearly targeted at the finance minister's thick accent that is at odds with the polished Anglicized accent considered "proper" within the English-speaking world of *TWTW*.

Several of the show's jokes are language based relying on puns or phrases that require an advanced familiarity with the language. For instance, Cyrus recently (May 8, 2011) poked fun at a politician by saying that "he put his foot in his mouth" and adding, "and it fit perfectly well." In yet another instance he clarifies accusations against the Prime Minister by saying that instead of calling him a "lame duck," he was actually a "sitting duck." An earlier episode about the President's visit to China played on the phrase "bull in a China shop." Many of these linguistic wordplays also utilize a uniquely Indian way of speaking English that may be lost on speakers of English in other nations. In an interview celebrating 150 episodes of the show, Cyrus interviews Kunal Vijaykar, an actor on the show, who frequently uses words/phrases such as "motherswear," "one nut loose," and "get your kidney checked." Each of these phrases, even though spoken in English, are translations of common Hindi phrases that have been incorporated into the lexicon of Indian English and are far more likely to resonate with an Indian speaker of English than English speakers from other countries.

Similarly, the use of language on *Gustakhi Maaf* relies on regional variations in Hindi accents to create humorous situations. These depictions rely on stereotypical conceptions about regional accents and privilege a North Indian way of speaking Hindi over other regions' accents. Distinctions from the norm are marked either by overtly Sanskritized "pure" Hindi that sounds comically highfalutin or by an Anglicized Hindi that is interspersed with English words. While the former is often used to mock a purist right-wing position, the latter is used to ridicule an elite incapable of speaking in Hindi without using English words. On the show, both religious gurus (e.g. well known yoga guru Baba Ramdev speaking in accentuated Hindi) and English speaking politicians (e.g., Rahul Gandhi using English words when speaking) are frequently the target. The attack on politicians unable to speak Hindi is a surreptitious condemnation of the elites in the English speaking India who either cannot speak Hindi or avoid speaking it in order to mark social distinction. It is a way to reassert the primacy of Hindi, the language of the program, within the political discourse of the country.

The complex politics of English in postcolonial India are not merely symbolic but also have material stakes as language and accent become means of upward social mobility (Sonntag, 2009). While certain regions in India (specifically in Southern and North Eastern India) have welcomed the hegemony of English as a counter to the dominance of Hindi, regional parties in the North have opposed that imposition as they see English as a vehicle through which the English-educated elite perpetuate their rule. It is also a potent issue in the electoral politics of India with some regional parties frequently threatening legislation against the use of English and others seeking a more widespread role for it to counter the dominance of the North over Southern India. The different ways in which the two shows deploy linguistic difference in India to humorous effect allow us to interrogate the political stakes masked behind the comedic gesture. While English remains an aspirational language for all, there is a clear disdain against those who differentiate themselves on the basis of the supposed cultural capital the language and a certain accent gives them.

Looking Inside versus Looking Outside

Related to the issue of language is the emphasis each program places on foreign versus domestic stories. Aimed towards an English speaking urban audience, *TWTW* is focused on foreign stories and events far more than *Gustakhi Maaf*. Its jokes and skits ridicule foreign (usually Western) celebrities and politicians almost as often as they pick on Indian targets. This tendency to focus on Western stories shows the extent to which the show's targeted demographic already consumes and is familiar with non-Indian news and cultural events.

Cyrus's headline announcements during the show on January 23, 2011, exemplify this. He mentions news about Steve Jobs' indefinite leave from Apple as well as visits by global celebrities Bill Gates, Warren Buffet, and Sarah Palin to India. One often finds *TWTW* using Western news and social context beyond celebrities to tell its jokes. In a show celebrating 150 episodes, Cyrus creates an imaginary setup where he hosts the Oscars and continuously pokes fun at the audience. He refers to his American audience and says that one sees lots of them in India adding, "We call them lost." As for Americans in the United States, "We call them jobless." Commenting on another news report that noted that a certain section of the US population blamed the recent Japanese tsunami on retribution for their attack on Pearl Harbor, Cyrus claims, "but these are the same people who kept the show *Two and a Half Men* running for eight seasons!" The reference to the Charlie Sheen show is noteworthy because were it not for the recent scandal involving him, the show would be quite unknown in India. In a single joke he ties together several cultural and news events that are US-specific and hence foreign to Indians unless they regularly consumed American popular culture through media or travel. These jokes rely on an existing knowledge base about the United States, presumably created due to the global proliferation of US culture through Hollywood and globalized television that *TWTW* is both inspired by and a beneficiary of.

The desire created by this access is frequently tapped into by *TWTW* and in sharp contrast to *Gustakhi Maaf*, it is Hollywood and not India's own film industry that is the source for plotlines and themes to be parodied. An instance of this is a skit inspired by news that James Bond would be shooting his next film in India. In the skit, Bond (played by Cyrus) goes around discovering what the show would consider to be the most remarkable things about India seen from a Western perspective. To begin, Bond visits a high-society party where upper-class women are talking in whispers about the fact that they illegally employ underage maids for household work. Having made note of this common malpractice in India, Bond moves to a bar where he is informed that he can only be served drinks if he is over the age of 25 (referring to recent legislation in the province of Maharashtra where the city of Mumbai is located). Bond then moves to the popular Juhu beach in Mumbai expecting to meet women there but instead only comes across a few drunken men dancing to Bollywood songs. This short skit is notable because it picks up on those aspects of Indian life that the makers of the show perceive would strike a Westerner as odd. The skit therefore refracts the Western gaze on Indian society. More importantly, the interstitial space that the show occupies allows it to reflect the gaze back onto the West as it simultaneously mocks both the oddities of India and the Western gaze that would find certain things to be odd.

As opposed to this, the Hindi show *Gustakhi Maaf* rarely uses or makes reference to events and celebrities from the West. In the rare case this occurs the reference is strictly in the realm of politics and rarely popular culture. The most frequent non-Indian context mentioned on the show is that of India's neighbor Pakistan, which given its rivalry with India in the realm of politics and cricket, continues to occupy a large share of the conversation in Indian media. The show regularly takes a dig at the country's internal instability and its close relationship with the US with frequent skits that show presidents of both countries meeting in private to plan their public strategy. The most recent of these skits occurred after the killing of Osama Bin Laden. The skit offers a prehistory of the killing as it shows former US President George Bush teaching the former Pakistani President Pervez Musharaf to feign public anger against the US presence in Pakistan in order to allay opposition against him. The skit then repeats the exact scenario with the current Prime Minister of Pakistan Yousuf Geelani first practicing in private with President Obama and then publicly getting an apology out of him after feigning displeasure. The message about the failure of the Pakistani state is clear and is part of efforts by the show to create Pakistan as India's inferior Other.

Aside from references to Pakistan, mentions of Western news and personalities are a rarity on *Gustakhi Maaf*. This difference in emphasis points to a more globally oriented consciousness on *TWTW* that is at odds with the more domestic emphasis on *Gustakhi Maaf*. The audience for *TWTW* is differentiated not only by language but also by an affluence that allows them to physically inhabit a cosmopolitan interstitial "scape" due to their ability to travel (Appadurai,

1990). This space is defined not merely by a mobile culture but also by subjects who are themselves not neatly identified by the classical markers of nation, language, and place. That the movement of cultural products finds sustenance from an increasingly itinerant audience whose global mobility complicates their ideas of home points to the cyclical nature of global processes.

CONCLUSION

Globalization is an inherently contradictory process, one that Frederic Jameson (1998) has called a "never ending series of Paradoxes" (p. 75). To hold a single position on it as always true is to push away others that would seem just as plausible and seemingly evident. Arguments that explain a particular phenomenon or object of study seem contradicted when tested against another. Looking at globalization through the provisionally separated lens of culture already throws up conflicting positions that are best seen as being in an "inseparable Opposition" and in a continuous dialectical interplay (Jameson, 1998; Kellner, 2002). Global cultural flows have been theorized both through the lens of them being a cleverly maneuvered imposition (Dorfman & Mattelart, 1975; Miller, 2005; Schiller, 1991; Tomlinson, 1991) and from that of a productive fusion of ideas (Garcia Canclini, 2006; Pieterse, 1994). These seemingly contradictory positions on the phenomenon provide a cautionary charge for scholars to relentlessly contextualize their object of study.

In exploring the distinct ways in which the two shows have Indianized themselves and in aligning that difference along a historically situated postcolonial social rift, this article points to the innovativeness engendered within global cultural exchanges (Havens, 2005). It responds to the invitation of scholars who see the global amalgamation of culture as a story of gain rather than one of loss. In so doing it takes seriously Pieterse's (1994) contention that the coming together of cultures in a syncretic mix, while frequently seen as erasing global difference, could also be seen as emphasizing similarities. The latter perspective begins with the position that cultural texts must meet the threshold of a bare minimum resonance with audiences in order to be translatable to new locations. A text entirely at odds with the cultural sensibilities prevalent at its new site may arouse initial interest but will invariably meet opposition and face steep odds unless it allows space for local specificities to seep in. The category of humor is a helpful heuristic tool in this investigation as it allows for the interplay of sameness and difference to emerge quite clearly. Causes for laughter around the world are both common as well as culturally contingent and the two shows analyzed here show this duality at play.

They display humor strategies that could have worked in a different cultural setting as well as those that are specific to the cultural framework of India. The most prominent instances of the former, found already embedded in the borrowed formats for both shows are juxtaposing incongruities and mimicry. As *TWTW* relies on professional reporters and "experts" to do and say the incomprehensible and *Gustakhi Maaf* allows respectable public figures to be caricatured through puppets, they both rely on the juxtaposition of seemingly incompatible elements to create laughter. Moreover the puppets in *Gustakhi Maaf* as well as the characters on *TWTW* are also copies of an original that they mimic with a "critical ironical distance" (Hutcheon, 1985) thus subverting the original through parody. The tropes of juxtaposition and mimicry commonly seen in Western aesthetics of comedy are also deeply embedded in the ancient Indian treatise on drama the Natyashastra (Arogyasami, 1994) and hence point to the commonalities within the category of humor. Focusing on it affirms Pieterse's (1994) contention that cultural globalization hinges as much on similarities as it does on difference. Exploring the two shows as a story of gain must emphasize how the genre of political comedy is enriched through its interaction with a new cultural site.

This account of gain however must be tempered simultaneously with the caution that we not eschew power imbalances within global cultural flows. Tomlinson (1991) reminds us that arguments about universalism within global culture discount the power of Western media institutions to distribute their cultural products worldwide. Speaking specifically of comedy, he conjectures that "the force of this argument is seen when we think that no Mongolian or Balinese comedian has been suggested, by Western critics, as striking the chord of common humanity" (p. 53). Cultural products presented as resonating globally often have particular origins, but their ability to mask their particularity is the artifice through which they operate. Unraveling this device is an equally valid endeavor for the study of cultural globalization. To hold contradictory positions simultaneously in tension as we analyze the process unfolding before us gives us a more situated understanding of the paradoxes within the process of cultural globalization. Celebratory accounts of gain must continuously be complicated by well-documented advantages that political-economic arrangements accrue for certain culture producing sites (Miller, 2005). This cautionary prodding warns us of the pitfalls of seeing cultural intermixing as an equal and benign interplay where the success of some over others points to an inherent superiority.

Theories of hybridity are perhaps most valuable in their critiques of essentializing moves that seek to present an immutable conflation of culture with place. These critiques (Gupta & Ferguson, 1992) are urgent in cases of nationalistic attempts to limit and police cultural expression with the intent to limit political freedom. By arguing that cultures have always already been in a flux and creolized, they allow alternative imaginaries to be legitimized and gain from global exchanges. Yet when this very argument of hybridity is deployed to further particular and commercial interests (Kraidy, 2005), nationalism and even essentialism of a particular kind (Eide, 2010; Spivak in Grosz, 1990) become a strategic vantage point from which to oppose those impositions. Allowing these tensions within theories of hybridity to animate our analysis of global cultural flows helps contextualize our findings and move our understanding of the phenomenon from the conjectural to the concrete.

REFERENCES

Appadurai, A. (1990). Disjuncture and difference in the global cultural economy. *Theory, Culture & Society*, 7(2), 295–310.

Arogyasami, M. (1994). Shakespeare's treatment of comic sentiment (Hasya Rasa): An Indian perspective. In F. Teague (Ed.), *Acting funny: Comic theory and practice in Shakespeare's plays* (pp. 153–163). Cranbury, NJ: Associated University Presses.

Baym, G. (2005). *The Daily Show*: Discursive integration and the reinvention of political journalism. *Political Communication*, 22(3), 259–276.

Canclini, N. G. (2006). Hybrid cultures, oblique powers. In M. G. Durham & D. Kellner (Eds.), *Media and culture studies: Keyworks* (pp. 422–444). Malden, MA: Blackwell Publishing.

Connery, B., & Combe, K. (Eds.). (1995). *Theorizing satire: Essays in literary criticism*. New York, NY: St. Martin's Press.

Dorfman, A., & Mattelart, A. (1975). *How to read Donald Duck: Imperialist ideology in the Disney comic*. New York, NY: New York International General.

Eide, E. (2010). Strategic essentialism and ethnification: Hand in glove? *Nordicom Review, 31*(2), 63–78.

Frank, T. (2004). *What's the matter with Kansas?: How conservatives won the heart of America*. New York, NY: Metropolitan Books.

Freedman, L. (2009). *The offensive art: Political satire and its censorship around the world from Beerbohm to Borat*. Westport, CT: Praeger Publishers.

Gray, J., Jones, J. P., & Thompson, E. (2009). The state of satire: The satire of state. In J. Gray, J. P. Jones, & E. Thompson (Eds.), *Satire TV: Politics and comedy in the post-network era* (pp. 3–36). New York, NY: New York University Press.

Griffin, D. (1994). *Satire: A critical reintroduction*. Lexington, KY: University Press of Kentucky.

Grosz, E. (1990). Criticism, feminism, and the institution. In S. Harasym (Ed.), *The post-colonial critic: Interviews, strategies, dialogues* (pp. 1–16). New York, NY: Routledge.

Gupta, A., & Ferguson, J. (1992). Space, identity, and the politics of difference. *Cultural Anthropology, 7*(1), 6–23.

Hasan, M. (2003, April 6). Political satire in modern India. *The Hindu*. Retrieved from http://www.hindu.com/thehindu/lr/2003/04/06/stories/2003040600010100.htm

Havens, T. (2005). Globalization and the generic transformation of telenovelas. In G. R. Edgerton & B. G. Rose (Eds.), *Thinking outside the box: A contemporary television genre reader* (pp. 271–292). Lexington, KY: The University Press of Kentucky.

Hutcheon, L. (1985). *A theory of parody: The teachings of twentieth century art forms*. New York, NY: Methuen, Inc.

Jameson, F. (1998). Notes on globalization as a philosophical issue. In F. Jameson & M. Miyoshi (Eds.), *The cultures of globalization* (pp. 54–77). Durham, NC: Duke University Press.

Kellner, D. (2002). Theorizing globalization. *Sociological Theory, 20*(3), 285–305.

Kohli-Khandekar, V. (2006). *The Indian media business* (Vol. 2). New Delhi, India: Sage Publications.

Kraidy, M. (2002). Hybridity in cultural globalization. *Communication Theory, 12*(3), 316–339.

Kraidy, M. (2005). *Hybridity or the cultural logic of globalization*. Philadelphia, PA: Temple University Press.

Kraidy, M. (2008). Reality TV and multiple Arab modernities: A theoretical exploration. *Middle East Journal of Culture and Communication, 1*, 49–59.

Kraidy, M. (2009). Reality television, gender, and authenticity in Saudi Arabia. *Journal of Communication, 59*, 345–366.

Kumar, S. (2005). Innovation, imitation, and hybridity in Indian television. In G. R. Edgerton & B. G. Rose (Eds.), *Thinking outside the box: A contemporary television genre reader*. Lexington, KY: The University Press of Kentucky.

Kumar, S. (2006). *Gandhi meets primetime: Globalization and nationalism in Indian television*. Urbana, IL: University of Illinois Press.

Miller, T. (2005). *Anti-Americanism and popular culture*. Anti-Americanism Working Papers. Budapest, Hungary: Central European University.

Moran, A. (1998). *Copycat TV: Globalization, program formats and cultural identity*. Ann Arbor, MI: University of Michigan.

Naim, C. M. (1995). Popular jokes and political history: The case of Akbar, Birbal and Mulla Do-Pyaza. *Economic and Political Weekly, 30*(24), 1456–1464.

Parameswaran, R. (2009, Fall). Moral dilemmas of an immoral nation: Gender, sexuality, and journalism in page 3. *The Image of the Journalist in Popular Culture Journal, 1*, 70–104.

Pieterse, J. N. (1994). Globalization as hybridization. *International Sociology, 9*(2). Reprinted in M. G. Durham & D. Kellner (Eds.), *Media and culture studies: Keyworks* (pp. 658–680). Malden, MA: Blackwell Publishing.

Punathambekar, A. (2010). Reality TV and participatory culture in India. *Popular Communication, 8*(4), 241–255.

Rajagopal, A. (2001). *Politics after television*. UK [city?]: Cambridge University Press.

Robertson, R. (1994). Globalization or glocalisation? *The Journal of International Communication, 1*(1), 33–52.

Sanghvi, V. (2011, September 9). News TV: Tripping on TRP. *The Hindustan Times*. Retrieved from http://blogs.hindustantimes.com/medium-term/2011/09/09/news-tv-tripping-on-trp/

Schiller, H. (1992). *Mass communication and American empire*. Boulder, CO: Westview Press.

Schwartz, S. L. (2004). *Performing the divine in India*. New York, NY: New York University Press.

Sonntag, S. K. (2009). The changing global-local linguistic landscape in India. *English language education in South Asia* (pp. 29–39). India, New Delhi: Cambridge University Press.

Sonwalkar, P. (2002). Murdochization of the Indian press: From by-line to bottom-line. *Media, Culture & Society, 24*(6), 821–834.

Spivak, G. C. (1990). Interviews, strategies, dialogues. In S. Harasym (Ed.), *The post-colonial critic: Interviews, strategies, dialogues*. New York, NY: Routledge.

Straubhar, J. (2006). (Re)asserting national television and national identity against the global, regional, and local levels of world television. In M. G. Durham & D. Kellner (Eds.), *Media and culture studies: Keyworks* (pp. 681–702). Malden, MA: Blackwell Publishing.

Sunder Rajan, R. (1992). *The lie of the land: English literary studies in India USA*. New Delhi: Oxford University Press.

Tomlinson, J. (1991). *Cultural imperialism: A critical introduction*. Baltimore, MD: John Hopkins University Press.

Thussu, D. K. (1999). Privatizing the airwaves: The impact of globalization on broadcasting in India. *Media Culture and Society*, *21*(1), 125–131.

Thussu, D. K. (2007). The ''Murdochization'' of news? The case of Star TV in India. *Media Culture and Society*, *29*(4), 593–611.

Vatsyayan, K. (1996). *Bharata: The Natyasastra*. New Delhi, India: Sahitya Akademi Press.

Satire in the Holy Wonderland: The Comic Framing of Arab Leaders in Israel

Limor Shifman

This article traces the depiction of Arab leaders in televised Israeli satire during the last two decades. First, I discuss the construction of Yasser Arafat's image in the popular show *Hartzufim* (1996–2000), claiming that his polysemic framing as an Arab-Jew served both the emotional needs of Jewish-Israelis in a bewildering era of transformations and the commercial interests of the show's producers. I then examine the depiction of other Arab leaders in *Eretz Nehederet* (2003–present), highlighting the continuous dominance of the "Israelification" framing strategy as a mode of hegemonic cooptation. Yet, in contemporary entertainment-driven media environment, this framing of Arab leaders tends to be de-politicized and fantasy-anchored, rather than news-anchored.

In theory, Israel should be a great place for political satire. It may be a cliché to say that political reality is often far more surprising, intriguing, and unpredictable than anything a satirist could come up with, but when it comes to the Holy Land this is probably the case. Packed with a mindboggling array of contradictions and involved in a ceaseless conflict with its Arab neighbors, Israel is always either on the verge of a crisis, or in the midst of one. Yet when it comes to televised satire, the offerings are surprisingly limited. So far, only three prominent satirical shows have been aired in Israel: *Nikui Rosh* ("Head Cleaning"; 1974–1976), *Hartzufim* ("Crappy/Cheeky Faces"; 1996–2000), and *Eretz Nehederet* ("What a Wonderful Country"; 2003–present).[1]

This article focuses on the two latter programs, probing them in light of the dramatic political, cultural, and social transformations that Israel has undergone in the last two decades. Two intertwined realms of change set the background for this expedition, the first of which relates to the political economy of Israeli media. While *Nikui Rush* was broadcast in an era of single-channel, national, public service-based television, *Hartzufim* and *Eretz Nehederet* emerged into, and were shaped by, a new commercially driven media ecology. In this environment, entertaining the audience to draw high ratings became a central logic underpinning all genres, including satire.

---

[1]This simplified shortlist consists of very popular shows that focused mainly on *political* satire: many other comic shows that incorporated some satirical elements have been broadcast in Israel over the years, as well as some purely satirical shows that were not as successful as the ones listed here.

A second transformation relates to the Israeli-Palestinian conflict and its representation on television. Following the Oslo accords of 1993, the ban on inclusion of Palestinian voices in Israeli media was removed. Since then, Palestinian representatives (both ordinary people and politicians) have been featured regularly on Israeli screens, and the trend continued even after the renewal of violence during the Al-Aqsa Intifada of 2000–2005 (Liebes & Kampf, 2009; Liebes, Kampf, & Blum-Kulka, 2008). This mediated deluge of Arab representatives—often framed in softer and more positive light than in the past—has not skipped satire. If in the veteran *Nikui Rush* Arab characters appeared rarely (mostly to criticize Israeli racism), since the mid-1990s Palestinian and other Arab leaders have become an integral component of Israeli televised satire.

The presentation of enemy leaders in comedy and satire is intriguing because it potentially spans a broad range of ideological meanings. On one end of the spectrum, we can find extreme racist humor denigrating the "other" and re-enforcing feelings of superiority among the in-group. Yet humor about the enemy may also bear an opposite meaning in which the other becomes an object of identification and the dominant in-group is criticized. In what follows, I trace the comic depiction of Arab leaders on commercial television in Israel during the last two decades, asking *how are Arab leaders constructed by Israeli satire, and what is the ideological meaning of these representations?*

The article opens with a telegraphic account of Israeli televised humor about Arabs in the precommercial era. I then describe the changing Israeli media landscape of the 1990s, moving on to analyze the depiction of the Palestinian leader Yasser Arafat in the *Hartzufim* puppet-based show. I claim that the hegemonic framing strategy of "Israelification" used to depict Arafat, as well as his polysemic construction, served both emotional and commercial needs. In the second part of the article I explore how other Arab leaders are depicted in the contemporary show *Eretz Nehederet,* highlighting the continuous dominance of the "Israelification" framing strategy as a mode of hegemonic cooptation. Yet the framing of Arab politicians in *Eretz Nehederet* veers away from the news to the realm of de-politicized fantasy, a transition I ascribe to political and commercial forces working in tandem. This leads to a concluding reflection on the ideological function of satire in contemporary Israeli commercial media.

COMIC REPRESENTATIONS OF ARABS IN 1980s ISRAEL

The Israeli-Arab conflict, raging for more than 100 years, is one of the most intractable conflicts of our times. Of the numerous aspects of this multifaceted and traumatic conflict, I focus here on a rather narrow one—comic representation of Arabs on Israeli television. The roots of this humorous framing can be traced back to the early days of Jewish settlement in what is present-day Israel. Settlers' attitudes towards Arabs were marked by a blend of admiration and condescension: they were conceived, on the one hand, as courageous, chivalrous, and close to the land (thus resembling biblical Jews), yet on the other, were looked down upon as primitive and culturally inferior (Even-Zohar, 1980). Following the eruption of clashes between Jews and Arabs in the 1920s, this dualistic approach migrated into the stereotypes of the "good" and the "bad" Arab. The "good Arab" served the Zionist vision; the "bad Arab" opposed and threatened it. This dichotomous mode of presentation was prevalent in Israeli theater, cinema, and literature until the late 1960s.

Processes of critical self-reflection following the Yom Kippur (1973) and Lebanon (1982) wars, as well as the first Intifada (1987), led to a challenging of previous stereotypical modes of representation of Arabs in theater and cinema (Urian, 1997). Comic sketches, however, continued to portray Arabs mainly according to the "good Arab" stereotype. These sketches, presented on Israeli television and stage since the mid-1980s, transformed the Arab from a potential threat to an object of ridicule.[2] A prominent attribute of the "good Arab" sketch was its portrayal of Arabs with a composite of Arab and Jewish-Israeli traits. Arabs in these sketches spoke fluent Hebrew, were interested in popular Israeli culture, and were well-versed in local politics. In many senses, this mode of depiction can be interpreted as a mode of hegemonic cooptation (Gramsci, 1971) in which the ruling class maintains its power by assimilating potentially dangerous ideas in remolded forms.

In 1980s Israel, this process of cooptation did not include any reference to Arab leaders—only "ordinary" Arabs were featured in televised humor. The single prominent appearance of an Arab leader on Israeli televised comedy prior to the Oslo Accords took place during the first Gulf War in 1991, when Israel was under rocket attack from Iraq. A stream of vernacular jokes, stickers, and caricatures mocking Saddam Hussein was followed by the dictator's impersonation on the popular skit show *Ha-Olam Ha-Erev* ("The World Tonight"). Saddam was depicted as a paradigmatic "bad Arab": a ruthless and insane dictator, whose conditions for withdrawing from Kuwait included, for instance, placing young American women as servants in every single Iraqi household. The comic exaggeration in Saddam's portrayal turned the great demon to a ludicrous butt, offering some comfort and relief in a time of great anxiety (Shifman, 2008).

The scarce comic representation of Arabs on Israeli television of the 1980s can be attributed both to the marginality of Arabs in televised news in an era marked by continued violence and hostility, and to the minor place of comedy in the programming of Israel's single channel. This state of affairs, however, was altered with the advent of two transitions seeded in 1993, a year that carried with it dreams of a new Middle East and a new media environment.

1990s ISRAEL: TELEVISED SATIRE IN A NEW MEDIASCAPE

Until the 1990s, Israel had only one television channel. Funded mainly by compulsory fees paid by the public, this BBC-like station was particularly rich in educational and patriotic content. Yet a combination of political, economic, and social shifts, which may be crudely charted as underpinned by individualization and privatization, led to legislative changes and the eventual launch of the commercial "Channel 2" in November 1993. The new channel shortly became the most popular in the country, defining new norms in the Israeli media landscape. A flow of entertainment-based genres swamped the small screen, bringing the epoch of "infotainment" to Israeli primetime (Liebes, 2003). One of the most prominent changes brought about by Channel 2 was an increase in the variety and number of original Hebrew-language comedy and satire shows, which were considered ratings magnets. While some non-political sketch shows were

---

[2]The practice of using humor to cope with a perceived ethnic or racial threat is not unique to Israel, of course. In the American context, for instance, the Sambo comic stereotype has been extensively analyzed as helping whites cope with repressed feelings of fear and intimidation while maintaining their sense of control (Ely, 1991).

reasonably popular, it took more than two years and an extremely traumatic moment for the first successful Israeli commercial satire to emerge.

The Oslo Accords between Israel and the Palestinians, signed in 1993, generated a heated debate in Israel: alongside enthusiastic supporters, an increasingly vocal series of protests was held in various settings by the political right-wing. On November 4, 1995, Prime Minister Yitzhak Rabin was assassinated by Yigal Amir, a young Israeli Jew from the radical right whose goal was to stop the piece process (Wolfsfeld, 2004). The assassination and subsequent elections, won by the candidate of the right-wing Likud Party, Benjamin (Bibi) Netanyahu, and not Shimon Peres, Rabin's natural successor, had a decisive impact on Israel's televised satire. While between 1993 and 1994 the farcical and nonsense-oriented humor shown on Channel 2 had been born from a momentary feeling of relief after the Oslo Accords, Rabin's assassination was a wake-up call for satirists (Shifman, 2008). Producers and creators of comedy, most on the political left, felt they had been too complacent before the assassination. Israeli televised satire blossomed; even programs that had not been especially critical adopted a more biting tone. Within this environment, *Hartzufim* ("Crappy/Cheeky Faces") stood out as the most successful satire of the late 1990s.

Modeled after the British puppet-based show *Spitting Image*,[3] *Hartzufim* was imported in an era marked by dramatic changes in political communication. The deep social processes of Americanization, liberalization, and individualization that had energized the changes in the Israeli mediascape also penetrated the political sphere. A steady decline in party membership eventually led to institutional processes of political personalization, followed by media coverage increasingly slanted towards individual politicians (Rahat & Sheafer, 2007). Reflecting this new epoch, *Hartzufim* focused on people and personalities rather than issues and ideologies. If the standard bearer of 1970s satire, the sketch-based *Nikui Rosh*, had dealt with the economy, education, and security, *Hartzufim* focused on Yasser (Arafat), Bibi (Netanyahu), and Dan (Meridor). Most politicians were depicted as uni-dimensional characters: one was presented as a weak kitten, another as Napoleon, and a third as a prostitute. In this sense, *Hartzufim* integrated perfectly with the image-based world of advertising surrounding it. While commercials were selling clear images of products, the *Hartzufim* marketed clear images of politicians.

Ratings showed that the Israeli public was enthusiastic about consuming the images the *Hartzufim* was selling. The program penetrated the very heart of Israeli public and political discourse in the late 1990s. The influence on the political system ascribed to it was enormous, from making and breaking the careers of individual politicians to bringing down the government. Two political figures were considered to have been the most affected by the program: Dan Meridor and Yasser Arafat. In the case of Meridor, who served as the Minister of Finance in the government formed by Benjamin Netanyahu after the 1996 elections, *Hartzufim* was credited with having contributed to his dramatic plunge in popularity and eventual resignation. In contrast, the

---

[3] *Hartzufim* was based on a format that was utterly new to Israel but quite popular across the globe: puppet-based satire. The trademark of this genre is the use of grotesque "latex puppets of well-known figures and characters, both fictional and real" (Meinhof & Smith, 2000, p. 43). The visual representation of these famous figures varied across shows. For instance, the successful French program, *The Bebette Show* (1984–1995), used *Muppet Show* puppets to capture a "zoo full of political beasts," starring Kermit the Frog as President Mitterand (Collovald & Neveu, 1999, p. 341). A different visual representation system was adapted in the British *Spitting Image* (1984–1996), which, as its name ironically hints, focused on caricaturized versions of politicians and other celebrities.

alleged influence of the *Hartzufim* on Palestinian leader Yasser Arafat's image was utterly positive: many commentators claimed that Arafat's growing popularity among the Jewish population in the late 1990s could be attributed to the show. In what follows, however, I will cast some doubt on this prevalent interpretation.

DEPICTING YASSER ARAFAT ON *HARTZUFIM*

The mid-1990s were characterized by a dramatic transformation in the way Yasser Arafat was framed and conceived in Israel. For countless years, the Palestinian leader had been presented in Israeli media as a bloodthirsty terrorist determined to destroy Israel. He was scorned and demonized, portrayed as "the Nazi in the bunker" or the "two-legged beast." But mutual recognition between Israel and the PLO in the Oslo Accords brought about an utterly new media discourse about Arafat. Almost overnight, this leader turned from an "enemy" and "terrorist" into a "friend" and "leader" who signed the "peace between the brave" (Mandelzis, 2003).

Arafat's puppet debuted on the show during its first season, and a poll conducted by the broadcasting authority found that it quickly became the show's most popular puppet (Rot-Cohen, 2001). The results of the poll, wrote Ehud Asheri,

> reflected first and foremost the undeniable contribution of the *Hartzufim* to the dramatic change that took place in Arafat's image among the Israeli public. The man with the hirsute face, the great demon, so recently public enemy number one, went through an accelerated process of exoneration, was formally absorbed into the legitimate Israeli political system, and is today accepted as an integral part of our lives, much like the *hartzuf* image that was designed for him: a mischievous, smiling, likeable, crafty, but harmless character who reminds us more than anything of the stereotype of the cunning Jew who knows how to get by. (1996, p. 3)

Asheri's article represented a prevalent interpretation in the late 1990s, according to which *Hartzufim* legitimized the Palestinian leader in the eyes of the Jewish-Israeli public. Nevertheless, my close reading of the sketches featuring Arafat between 1996 and 2000 reveals that the positive image ascribed to Arafat's puppet was only part of a more complex framing. The central framing strategy evident in these sketches is the depiction of Arafat as an *Arab-Jew*. Alongside his trademark keffiyeh, the *rais* is constructed through an assortment of Jewish-Israeli signifiers: he speaks fluent Hebrew, conducts close and warm relations with Israeli politicians, and is intimately familiar with Jewish traditions such as the festive Passover *seder* dinner. This juxtaposition produces a comic effect explainable by incongruity theories of humor, according to which humor derives from an unexpected encounter between two different spheres or elements (Billig, 2005). In addition, Arafat's character is constructed as one that can be laughed at out of superiority: he is feminine, his voice is weak, and he tends to stutter. Arafat's puppet can thus be analyzed as a demonstration of hegemonic cooptation, in which the "other" is remolded to fit in with familiar schemes.

However, a closer look at the skits reveals a gap between the softened *image* of Arafat and his actual *behavior*. While the image is that of a nonthreatening, feminine old man, his actions within the narratives reveal destructive intentions. The intimidating elements usually only become manifest at the very end of the sketches, when he threatens to carry out terror attacks. For instance, in one of the sketches, after both major political parties refuse to take Arafat on board their election airlifts (flights chartered to bring Israeli expatriates to the voting polls), Arafat suggests he will "take Sabena," a reference to the 1972 terrorist hijacking of a Sabena flight.

Arafat's puppet thus consolidated for the first time in the history of Israeli pop culture the two contrasting hegemonic frames described earlier as the "good Arab" and "bad Arab." These veteran framings were incarnated in two more specific images highly relevant to Arafat's mediated image: the politician/statesman versus the terrorist. The superimposition of these contrasting frames into one puppet, I assert, served both the emotional needs of the Jewish-Israeli audience and the commercial interests of the show's creators.

The construction of Arafat as a comic hero combining both positive and negative traits may have addressed the discomfort and dissonance generated by the swift transformation in Arafat's public status in Israel after Oslo. This dual framing allowed bewildered Israelis to laugh *at* Arafat as well as *with* him, enabling them to hold on to old views and embrace new ones at the very same time. Thus, contrary to the claim that the popularity of Arafat's puppet among Jewish Israelis was derived from its positive traits, I assert that its success was the result of the combination of negative and positive elements the puppet embodied. Weirdly enough, the consolidation of two hegemonic stereotypes of Arabs as good and bad into one character offered a new and somewhat subversive look, as it framed an individual Arab as a complex and multifaceted human being.

This mode of depiction, however, did not serve emotional needs alone; it may also have served commercial ones. According to a series of polls conducted between 1994 and 1997 by the Tami Steinem Center for Peace Research, both perceptions of Arafat as a statesman and as a terrorist were prevalent in the Jewish-Israeli population of the time.[4] The polls recorded some fluctuations following dramatic events of these years, which were marked by both suicide bomb attacks against Israeli civilians and continuous peace negotiations. Following Fiske (1987), I thus argue that the polysemic construction of Arafat as both a politician and a potential threat served the commercial purposes of the show, allowing various groups to interpret the program differently, each according to their own identity needs. As early as 1974, Vidmar and Rokeach showed that when faced with a polysemic character (in their case, Archie Bunker), people see in it what they want to see. Arafat's puppet allowed similar freedom of interpretation: Those who perceived him as a terrorist could have found validation for their views in many sketches, as could those who perceived him mainly as a leader. In this sense, *Hartzufim* was satire catering to all tastes. At that point, the blend between satire and commercial TV had not yet reached its peak—that happened only in the third millennium.

"IT'S OKAY, YOU CAN SPEAK HEBREW": ARAB LEADERS ON *ERETZ NEHEDERET*

Israeli Interviewer: It's nice to discover you're so up-to-date on our cultural scene.
Arab Interviewee: I am not that up-to-date in culture; I prefer your television. Let's play "Which Survivor contestant do you most resemble?" (Bashar al-Assad's character in an early appearance on *Eretz Nehederet*)

---

[4]The complete set of polls can be found at the Tami Steinmetz Center for Peace Research: http://www.tau.ac.il/peace/.

The most popular satirical program in Israel for the last decade has been *Eretz Nehederet* ("What a Wonderful Country"). Debuting in 2003, the show has been a jewel in Israel's ratings crown, hooking audiences of varied backgrounds. Aired weekly, *Eretz Nehederet* is constructed as a parody newscast in which a straight-faced host tries to navigate his way through a minefield of wacky interviewees, an array of politicians and pop-culture celebrities imitated by comedians. Featuring actors rather than puppets, the show has been described as having certain elements in common with both *The Daily Show* and *Saturday Night Live*, but also as being less sophisticated and more vulgar than these two older American programs (Tsfati, Tukachinsky, & Peri, 2009). *Eretz Nehederet* is regarded as prominent not only as a source of entertainment but also as a source of political information and evaluation of politicians, particularly by young people (Balmas, 2008). However, the show has also drawn severe criticism: some commentators claim that it leans towards popular entertainment, neglecting its satirical "mission," while others, largely right-wing settlers, object to the show's critical portrayal of Jewish settlers as a violent and somewhat insane group.

Eretz Nehederet has been broadcast in an era characterized by a series of negative developments in the Israeli-Arab conflict. Three months after *Hartzufim*'s last episode in June 2000, the Al-Aqsa Intifada broke out. A supporter of the widespread violence, Arafat was once again transformed—this time from partner to enemy—and was depicted as such in Israeli media until his death in 2004. The second Lebanon war (2006) and the war in Gaza (2009) marked an era of continuous bloodshed. Yet somewhat surprisingly, Liebes and Kampf (2009) found that even though violence increased, the depiction of Palestinians in Israeli media became more varied and positive in the third millennium, continuing the openness characterizing the representation of Palestinians since the initiation of the Oslo peace process.

In contrast to the standstill in the peace process, Israeli television kept moving ahead at full speed. A second national commercial channel was launched in 2002, operating alongside a plethora of cable and satellite-based channels that emerged in the late 1990s. Fierce competition between these various commercial players over the small Israeli market led to budget cuts in domestic programming production, affecting genres with higher production values, such as drama and documentaries (Shamir, 2007). In this new environment, heavily dominated by reality and quiz shows, the lines between politics and entertainment, fiction and reality, authenticity and fakeness have become more blurred than ever. The so-called postmodern era has finally conquered the Holy Land.

Transformations in both spheres—the political and the cultural—are well reflected in the way Arab leaders are framed in *Eretz Nehederet*. Since its launch, many Arab leaders have been emulated in the show, including Saddam Hussein, Hassan Nasrallah, Bashar al-Assad, Muammar Gaddafi, and Muhammad Abu Tir (from Hamas). Interestingly, those imitated most often were Israel's most extreme and bitter enemies, mainly dictators depicted in Israeli media as terrorists. The more moderate leaders (in particular Arafat's successor, Abu Mazen), were rarely imitated.[5]

---

[5]This falls in line with the findings of Balmas, Sheafer, and Wolfsfeld (2011), according to which Hamas representatives appeared much more frequently than Fatah representatives in Israeli news in the aftermath of the 2006 Gaza elections which brought Hamas to power. It also echoes the process described by Wolfsfeld (2004), according to which Israeli media tends to focus on the concrete, specific and immediate threats of terror associated with the Hamas rather than on the more abstract, general and distant discourse related to peace.

In all these cases, the same pattern of Israelification takes place, incorporating three main dimensions: linguistic, social, and cultural. The linguistic aspect is the most simple and straight-forward: Not only do all the Arab leaders in the show speak fluent Hebrew, but they also have virtuosic control of contemporary Israeli slang (albeit with an Arab accent). Thus, for instance, in Saddam Hussein's first appearance, the interviewer addresses him in English, but Saddam quickly assures him, "It's okay, you can speak Hebrew." Interestingly, when American leaders such as George W. Bush and Barack Obama are mimicked on the show, they do not speak Hebrew—they speak in English, accompanied by Hebrew subtitles. Moreover, the linguistic differences between American and Israeli politicians are often accompanied by cultural clashes and misunderstandings, particularly in relation to the peace process.

Surprisingly, such clashes do not characterize relations between Arab leaders and Israeli politicians on the show; in fact, their relationships are depicted as utterly harmonious. While the host attempts to ask serious news-related questions, his Arab interviewees drift into issues such as consumerism and popular culture. The Israeli politicians impersonated in the show seem quite happy with these topic shifts and make perfect partners for vibrant discussions about food, hairstyles, and getting high in Amsterdam. In some cases, the Arab leaders mediate childish fights between Israeli politicians; in others, they take part in carnivalesque panels involving showbiz celebrities and politicians. For instance, in one recent skit, Muammar Gaddafi forms a dictator support group that includes his "colleague" Bashar al-Assad, but also the mayor of Tel Aviv, the domineering mother of a famous model, and a hugely popular Israeli pop lyricist. The fiercest criticism in this sketch and others seems to be directed not at the Arab leaders, but against representatives of Israeli popular culture, mainly the lyricist and the shallow and commercialized field of contemporary Oriental music he represents.

The main process underpinning the encounter between Jewish and Arab leaders on the show can thus be described as de-politicization. Religious, political, and ethnic-based disputes are put aside in these meetings, conveniently replaced by more light-hearted and consensual issues. This mass-mediated fictional form of encounter echoes what happens in face-to-face real-life contact between Jews and Arabs. Studies have found that for Israeli Jews, the successful encounter with Arabs is very often one in which Arabs are de-politicized and their national identity, aspirations, and claims of injustice and discrimination are excluded from the discussion. This idealized de-politicized Jewish-Arab dialogue often focuses on folkloristic topics (food, ceremonies) and on the similarities between Jews and Arabs as human beings (Maoz, 2004, 2011).

In *Eretz Nehederet*, however, the strongest common denominator between Arabs and Jews relates not to the general human condition, but rather to their contemporary role as consumers of goods and popular culture. What marks the Arab leaders as part of the imagined Israeli community is not their perfect Hebrew or their communication skills, but their deep interest in Israeli popular culture and commercial television: Hassan Nasrallah is desperate to star on the Israeli equivalent of *American Idol*; Bashar al-Assad is particularly knowledgeable about Israeli commercials; and Muammar Gaddafi, in a glamorous golden robe, co-hosts a lifestyle fashion show. They comment on programs, actors, producers, and brands, proving to be extremely knowledgeable about Israeli football, music, cinema, and an assortment of TV genres.

Television thus becomes the main point of reference of *Eretz Nehederet*, the focal point of the world, the mode through which politicians from both sides experience themselves and their environment. This deep reliance on mediated images may be interpreted in two ways. First, one might read it as criticism of a highly commercialized postmodern environment in which instant celebrities are at least as important as word leaders. Contrary to a show like *The Colbert Report* that contests fundamental aspects of right-wing political communication in the postmodern age (Baym, 2007), criticism in *Eretz Nehederet* seems to focus on the shallowness of postmodern popular culture.

Yet a second interpretation of the program would suggest that alongside its manifest criticism of postmodern culture, the show's mechanisms of representation seem to blend perfectly into it. The main pleasure *Eretz Nehederet* offers is that of identifying one familiar televised framing playfully juxtaposed with another. In this sense, the show seems to reflect what Meinhof and Smith—in their work on *Spitting Image* (2000, p. 57)—refer to as "TV pastiche," that is, television based on a pleasure of "intertextual recognition of 'life as seen on TV'" rather than on satirical commentaries on political processes. Interestingly, this depiction is less relevant to the Israeli show actually based on *Spitting Image*'s puppet format, *Hartzufim*, which focused much more on politics than on popular culture.

Eretz Nehederet, in contrast, is immersed in popular culture as much as in politics. Intertextuality in the show relates not only to other programs, but also to *Eretz Nehederet* itself. Thus, in the course of their re-appearances on the show, each of the Arab leaders becomes more and more self-referential to his own comic image and gestures, gradually turning into a simulacrum (Baudrillard, 1983) not of his news-based image, but of his *Eretz Nehederet*-based persona. Thus, for instance, television viewers learn to expect that any interview with Hamas leader Abu-Tir will eventually include a moment in which Abu-Tir hints that the host is gay. This comic gesture becomes an integral part of Abu-Tir's construction—part of the unwritten pleasurable contract between the show and its audience. This contract, as unfolded below, has little to do with the way Abu-Tir is portrayed in the news.

FROM NEWS-ANCHORED TO FANTASY-ANCHORED SATIRE

In this final section, I wish to reexamine the ways in which *Eretz Nehederet* and *Hartzufim* frame Arab leaders in relation to what I tag "news-anchored" and "fantasy-anchored" modes of news parody. While in practice news-anchored and fantasy-anchored modes of satire are importantly intertwined, feeding off each other in multifaceted ways, I attempt to disentangle them here for analytical purposes. News parody programs, by definition, relate to news, yet the nature of the relationship between news and parody may vary greatly. At the *news-anchored* end of the axis we find programs that relate to televised news on at least four levels: (1) they imitate the newscast format, (2) they criticize it (as well as the workings of mass media in general), (3) they relate to people and events that appear in the news (and thus may provide "hard" political information), and, finally, (4) they criticize the political acts of public figures appearing in the news. This fourth layer of criticism, it may be argued, is what turns news parody into political satire. In other words, news-anchored satirical parody such as *The Daily Show* and *The Colbert Report* criticizes not only the format of the news, but also the actions of its protagonists (Baym, 2005, 2007; Bennett, 2007; Gray, Jones, & Thompson, 2009).

But news parody is not merely a reflection of the news. By its nature, it is based on distortion, playfulness, and the addition of new elements to those documented in news. In some shows these new elements become so prevalent that they constitute what I term *fantasy-anchored* news parodies. Such parodies imitate the *format* of the news and relate to the *people* who appear in the news, but do not offer news-related political criticism (as is similarly the case on *Saturday Night Live*'s "Weekend Update" newscast, as observed by Day and Thompson in this special issue). In other words: fantasy-anchored satire presents news-related actors in a de-politicized manner.

Eretz Nehederet is rife with examples of fantasy-based satire, particularly when it comes to the depiction of Arab leaders. In such appearances, the host gives occasional news-related hints, but the characters themselves are just not interested in talking politics. Most of these sketches thus drift far away from the news to trance parties (Abu Tir), conspicuous consumption (Gaddafi), and, of course, television and reality shows (Nasrallah). A striking example is a sketch featuring the Libyan leader Muammar Gaddafi as a camp, shopping-obsessed weirdo, visiting Israel so he can spend money in the local malls.

"Fantasy" assumes two meanings in this satirical context. The first refers to *fiction;* that is, however loosely one may treat the terms truth and objectivity, it is quite clear that the portrayal of Muammar Gaddafi as an effeminate wacko buying dresses at the Israeli branch of Zara is fictional. "Fiction" relates in this sketch not only to the *setting* of the mall but also to the *cluster of personal attributes* that is relevant to the functioning of a certain political figure in the public sphere and is featured in the news. Thus, while the skit was based on Gaddafi's extravagant lifestyle, it is still far-removed from his political attributes highlighted in the news.[6]

Yet in the context of the Arab-Israeli conflict, fantasy might bear a second meaning: that of *wishful thinking.* After many years of bloodshed, such portrayals of Arab leaders may reflect a deep-seated craving to lead normal, non-political lives, where small trivial details are far more important than ideological or religious disputes. But since such mundane details are linked in the show mainly to consumption, this fantasy seems to echo the dream of hegemonic capitalism as much as it relates to the utopian new Middle East.

One other explanation for the de-politicized framing of Arab leaders on *Eretz Nehederet* relates to the political views of the show's production team. Given their explicit dovish left-wing orientation, the show's creators had to walk a fine line in constructing Arab leaders. On one hand, portraying them according to racial stereotypes of Arabs as stupid or primitive—similar to frames offered on right-wing-oriented Israeli television and Internet-based shows—was unacceptable; on the other, a complex political framing of leaders engaged in terrorist acts or direct attacks on Israel would probably have been rejected by the general Israeli audience. The de-politicized prism thus renders the portrayal of Arab leaders in a somewhat positive and "softened" light. In some cases, they are presented as better politicians than their Israeli counterparts, who tend to be portrayed in a more news-based and critical manner. Yet since the depiction of Arab leaders is rarely related to the news, the potential influence of this mode of presentation on Israeli viewers remains enigmatic.

In contrast to *Eretz Nehederet*, news parody as a genre was a much smaller component of *Hartzufim*: only a few minutes of each episode were framed as a studio-based newscast. Most of the show was made up of sketches placing politicians in varied settings, spanning bars and bedrooms, theater stages and meeting rooms, airports and kitchens. Yet ironically, when it came to the construction of Arab leaders, *Hartzufim* was much more news-anchored than *Eretz Nehederet*. Even when the skits were located in markedly nonpolitical arenas, such as dance floors, they were

---

[6]It should be noted that the news, in Israel and elsewhere, has itself undergone processes of de-politization and personalization (Rahat & Sheafer, 2007; Thussu, 2007; Wolfsfeld, 2004), yet *Eretz Nehederet*'s satire on Arab leaders seems to have taken this trend one step deeper into fantasyland.

always tied to political events and they evaluated leaders according to their political conducts, as reported in the news. For instance, the skit in which Arafat tries to join the election-time airlift is packed with information about political players, relationships, and power struggles.

How can we account for this transition from news-anchored to fantasy-anchored satire? By way of conclusion, I wish to offer two explanations: the first relates to the state of Israel, the second to the state of television. As discussed above, *Hartzufim* debuted in an era of high hopes about the peace process. However, the eruption of the Al-Aqsa Intifada in 2000, as well as a series of further violent outbreaks throughout the decade, marked an era of growing despair. In such a state of standstill and absence of real negotiations, the need for fantasy may have increased. Satire thus seems to follow the trend that Liebes and Kampf (2007) describe as "routinizing terror": the unrelenting multi-victim terrorist attacks on Israel in that era did not bring about a linear escalation in the intensity of media coverage of this issue, but rather were accompanied by escapist genres such as soap operas and lifestyle shows.

The second explanation is simpler and relates to the political economy of media production and consumption. Fantasy-anchored news parodies may be almost worthless in terms of political knowledge and democratic deliberation, but they seem to be good news for business, for two main reasons. First, such satire is so distant from reality that it is less prone to draw fire or disengage viewers. How can one feel outraged about a skit portraying Nasrallah as an ambitious candidate on *Survivor*? And second, in the case of *Erez Nehederet*, fantasy-anchored satire is often based on intertextual hints at other shows broadcast on Channel 2, thus highlighting their centrality and promoting them. While this journey from Holy Land to wonderland has probably been pleasant and amusing to its viewers, it raises a number of questions about the function of satire in the Israeli commercial context.[7]

If the main difference between *Hartzufim* and *Eretz Nehederet* relates to their reliance on the news, their most striking common denominator is the Israelification of Arab leaders. In both shows Arabs are portrayed as immersed in Israeli language, culture, and politics. They speak fluent Hebrew, serve as mediators among Israeli politicians, and never forget to watch local television. Thus, Arab leaders are transformed from existential threats to comic butts who are not that different from the average Israeli viewer. While this strategy may have helped in reducing the menace posed by enemies, it seems to keep televised satire about Arab leaders within the safe realm of consensus.

REFERENCES

Asheri, A. (1996, December 31). The Hartzufim regime. *Haaretz*, D3 [Hebrew].

Balmas, M. (2008). Competing messages: The effects of the satire program "Eretz Nehederet", compared to the effects of news programs on leaders images in the elections of 2006. (Unpublished master's thesis). Jerusalem, Israel, The Hebrew University.

Balmas, M., Sheafer, T., & Wolfsfeld, G. (2011). When foreign political actors matter: Press performance during political crises. Paper presented at the *Annual Meeting of the American Political Science Association (APSA)*, Seattle, WA.

Bennett, W. L. (2007). Relief in hard times: A defense of Jon Stewart's comedy in an age of media cynicism. *Critical Studies in Media Communication, 24*, 278–283.

---

[7]It is important to note that since the size of the Israeli market is so small, a commercial television show will not survive if it addresses only a small portion of the population. In other words, mainstreaming seems to be vital for the sustainability of Israeli commercial satire.

Baudrillard, J. (1983). *Simulations*. (P. Foss, P. Patton, & P. Beitchman, Trans.). New York, NY: Semiotext(e).

Baym, G. (2005). The Daily Show: Discursive integration and the reinvention of political journalism. *Political Communication*, 22(3), 259–276.

Baym, G. (2007). Representation and the politics of play: Stephen Colbert's "Better Know a District." *Political Communication*, 24(4), 1–18.

Billig, M. (2005). *Laughter and ridicule: Toward a social critique of humour*. London, England: Sage.

Collovald, A., & Neveu, E. (1999). Political satire on French television. *Modern & Contemporary*, 7(3), 339–349.

Ely, M. (1991). *The adventures of Amos 'n' Andy: A social history of an American phenomenon*. New York, NY: The Free Press.

Even-Zohar, I. (1980). The growth and consolidation of a local and native Hebrew culture in Israel, 1882–1948. *Catedra*, 16, 163–195 [Hebrew].

Fiske, J. (1987). *Television culture*. London, England: Methuen.

Gray, J., Jones, J. P., & Thompson, E. (2009). The state of satire, the satire of state. In J. Gray, J. P. Jones & E. Thompson (Eds.), *Satire TV: Politics and comedy in the post- network era* (pp. 3–36). New York, NY: New York University Press.

Gramsci, A. (1971). *Selections from the prison notebooks* (Q. Hoare & G. Nowell Smith, Eds.). London, England: Lawrence and Wishart.

Liebes, T. (2003). *American dreams, Hebrew subtitles: Globalization from the receiving end*. Cresskill, NJ: Hampton Press.

Liebes, T., & Kampf, Z. (2009). From black and white to shades of gray: Palestinians in the Israeli media during the Second Intifada. *International Journal of Press/Politics*, 14(4), 434–453.

Liebes, T., & Kampf, Z. (2007). Routinizing terror: Media coverage and public practices, Israel 1996–2004. *The Harvard International Journal of Press/Politics*, 12(1), 108–116.

Liebes, T., Kampf, Z., & Blum-Kulka, S. (2008). Saddam on CBS and Arafat on IBA: Addressing the enemy on television. *Political Communication*, 25(3), 311–329.

Maoz, I. (2004). Coexistence is in the eye of the beholder: Evaluating intergroup encounter interventions between Jews and Arabs in Israel. *Journal of Social Issues*, 60, 404–418.

Maoz, I. (2011). Does contact work in protracted asymmetrical conflict? Appraising 20 years of reconciliation-aimed encounters between Israeli Jews and Palestinians. *Journal of Peace Research*, 48(1), 115–125.

Meinhof, U. H., & Smith, J. (2000). Spitting Image: TV genre and intertextuality. In U. H. Meinhof & J. Smith (Eds.), *Intertextuality and the media: From genre to everyday life*. Manchester, England: Manchester University Press.

Mandelzis, L. (2003). The changing image of the enemy in the news discourse of Israeli newspapers, 1993–1994. *Conflict & Communication online* 2(1). Retrieved from http://www.cco.regener-online.de/2003_1/pdf_2003_1/mandelzis.pdf

Rahat, G., & Sheafer, T. (2007). The personalization(s) of politics: Israel 1949–2003. *Political Communication*, 24(1), 65–80.

Rot-Cohen, O. (2001). The emergence of televised political satire in Israel between the 1970s and 1990s. (Unpublished MA thesis). Ramat Gan, Israel, Bar Ilan University [Hebrew].

Shamir, J. (2007). Quality assessment of television programs in Israel: Can viewers recognize production value? *Journal of Applied Communication Research*, 35(3), 320–341.

Shifman, L. (2008). *Televised humor and social cleavages in Israel, 1968–2000*. Jerusalem, Israel: Hebrew University Magnes Press [Hebrew].

Thussu, D. K. (2007). *News as entertainment: The rise of global infotainment*. London, England: Sage.

Tsfati, Y., Tukachinsky, R., & Peri, Y. (2009). Exposure to news, political comedy, and entertainment talk shows: Concern about security and political mistrust. *International Journal of Public Opinion Research*, 21(4), 399–423.

Urian, D. (1997). *The Arab in Israeli drama and theatre*. Amsterdam, the Netherlands: Harwood.

Vidmar, N., & Rokeach, M. (1974). Archie Bunker's bigatory: A study in selective perception and exposure. *Journal of Communication*, 24, 36–47.

Wolfsfeld, G. (2004). *Media and the path to peace*. Cambridge, England: Cambridge University Press.

Out of Control: Palestinian News Satire and Government Power in the Age of Social Media

Matt Sienkiewicz

This article analyzes the Palestinian sketch comedy show *Watan Ala Watar*, placing the groundbreaking program in the context of theories of satire, government control, and popular resistance. Detailing the show's tumultuous relationship with the Palestinian Authority, the article argues that despite publicly supporting *Watan Ala Watar* so as to create the impression of a liberal media regime, the government ultimately could not accept the existence of uncensored political comedy. However, the article shows that through the use of new media, the program has continued to have an impact despite the government's refusal to put it on air.

SATIRE TV: LIBERATOR OR PROTECTOR OF THE STATUS QUO?

Describing the potential for comedy in places of conflict, scholar Majken Jul Sorenson (2008) observes that "political humor needs some incongruity and absurdity in order to thrive—if things are as the politicians say they are, then there is almost nothing on which to build satire, parody, and irony" (p. 174). In the Palestinian territories, incongruity and absurdity are in abundance. Few politicians, Arab or Israeli, are thought capable of even knowing how things really are, let alone communicating such complexities. Every city has two names (one Hebrew, one Arabic) and a contested history. Roads are opened and closed at the discretion of an Israeli occupation that needs not explain its actions. Perhaps most incongruous of all, the collective hopes of the Palestinian people are bound up in a "peace process" that, for the past few decades, has produced neither peace nor shown signs of actually being in process. It is for these reasons that the Palestinian political satire program *Watan Ala Watar*, first produced for 2009's Ramadan season, has never lacked for content. There have always been ample targets for such a show, but only recently have political and industrial circumstances opened the Palestinian territories to such satire. In this article, I outline the historical changes that have made *Watan Ala Watar* possible and consider the meaning of both the show's immediate success and its ultimate demise.

Over the past decade, both scholars and pundits have engaged in a discourse regarding the liberating powers of televised political satire (Baym, 2010; Day, 2011; Jones, 2010). A common trend, particularly within American debates on the topic, has been the positioning of television news satires such as *The Daily Show with Jon Stewart* and *The Colbert Report* as antidotes to increasingly superficial and undemocratic movements in both governments and the media. Able to take aim simultaneously at politicians and the people who report on them, such programs hold a unique vantage point from which to expose the extent to which citizens are removed from the powerful institutions that shape their daily lives.

Writing for the *New York Times* online, Amber Day (2010) summarizes this perspective by noting that Stewart and Colbert "tap into a very real desire among the public to see a different kind of political discussion taking place: one not scripted and stage-managed by spin-doctors." By making fun of both the form and content of the news, satirical programs are thought to create a space in which hegemonic powers can be questioned and modes of apparent common sense can be challenged. In the introduction to their volume *Satire TV*, Gray, Jones, and Thompson (2009) take this notion further, claiming that satiric, current events-oriented comedy is essentially connected to the desire for political freedom. Citing the genre's appeal across cultures and time, they argue that political satire remains "historically persistent" as a result of "societal and individual *needs* for such forms of expression" (p. 15).

However, a specter haunts this celebration. Mainstream media, no matter how biting its political satire, is always produced under the auspices of institutions engrained in the power structures being critiqued. Viacom, a media giant that spent $560,000 lobbying the government in 1998, produces both *The Daily Show* and *Colbert Report* (Murphy, 2008, p. 2). *That Was The Week That Was* may have skewered British politicians, but it did so on behalf of the government that made its existence possible. Scholar, author, and public intellectual Umberto Eco (1984) put forth a powerful articulation of this concern in his critique of the supposedly freeing nature of the carnival. Whereas theorists such as Bakhtin (1984) celebrate the ways that carnival skits and play acting cause "the hierarchy of the cosmos [to be] reversed" (p. 364), Eco sees a conservative superstructure at work. He argues that "carnival can only exist as an *authorized* transgression," restricted in time and scope. He directly indicts contemporary television satire by adding that "if the ancient, religious carnival was limited in time, the modern mass-carnival is limited in space: it is reserved for certain places, certain streets, or framed by the television screen" (1984, p. 6). He notes that "comedy and carnival are not instances of real transgressions: on the contrary, they represent paramount examples of law reinforcement. They remind us of the existence of the rule" (p. 6). To paraphrase Emma Goldman's cynicism about voting, the follower of Eco might argue that if satire changed anything, they'd make it illegal.[1]

By analyzing the Palestinian program *Watan Ala Watar* in this article, I consider a situation in which a government has struggled conspicuously to keep control over political comedy, ultimately learning that in the world of contemporary media and social networking, news satire is not nearly as "contained" as Eco once presumed it to be. The Palestinian territories are perhaps the single place on Earth in which notions of control, freedom, civility, and sovereignty are most contested. Subject to both an unrelenting Israeli military occupation and the often repressive proto-national Palestinian Authority (PA), Palestinians, perhaps more than anyone, are in need of the liberating powers of satire. In 2009, they received such an opportunity with the premier of *Watan Ala Watar* ("Country Hanging by a Thread")[2], a political and news satire program that

---

[1] Goldman's original statement, "If voting changed anything, they'd make it illegal," is undocumented and attributed to others as well.

[2] English translations of the show's title vary heavily, with *Country on a String* being the most prevalent. However, I believe "hanging by a thread" better conveys the original meaning.

marked a new direction for the PA-controlled broadcasting outlet Palestine TV. Viewers previously accustomed to long-winded speeches by government ministers and news reports in which the leading political party, Fatah, always came out ahead, suddenly saw actors mocking long-exalted institutions and individuals. For example, shortly after Palestine TV covered the sixth Fatah party convention, which took 20 years after the fifth, *Watan Ala Watar* broadcasted the "seventh convention, live" from the year 2059 (Ezzedine, 2009). In a place in which every day of political stagnancy is associated with lost opportunities for national sovereignty, it is noteworthy that such an attack was disseminated with a government logo embedded on the screen.

This article chronicles the circumstances by which *Watan Ala Watar* arose, recounts the local and national reactions to the show, and considers the government's complex relationship with the program and its producers. What began as a loving embrace between government and critic ultimately became a battle over control. In writing this history, I argue that the Palestinian Authority originally embraced *Watan Ala Watar* in order to advance its reputation as a liberal democracy via association with the wider celebrations of political satire. Additionally, I show that when the government attempted to censor the show, fearful of the political impact it might have in the midst of the 2011 "Arab Spring" revolutions, it found that globalization and social media had elevated the program to a place beyond its control.

PALESTINIAN SATIRE, GOVERNMENT CONTROL, AND THE BIRTH OF *WATAN ALA WATAR*

To discuss the liberating nature of satire in the Palestinian Territories,[3] it is necessary to clarify the complex and evolving targets towards which such biting humor is aimed. It may be surprising that while *Watan Ala Watar* occasionally takes aim at the Israeli occupation, the majority of its episodes are geared towards internal Palestinian critique. Head writer and star Imad Farajin describes this as a sign of progress and evidence of free speech in an age during which Israel plays no direct role in media originating in areas under PA control (Rafiq, 2010). However, as one might expect, Palestinian satire has a long and vibrant tradition, the majority of which takes aim at the occupying forces that have controlled Palestinian life for centuries.

Perhaps the earliest systematic description of Palestinian satire comes from a 1968 report by the Iraqi Ministry of Culture entitled "Poetry of Resistance in Occupied Palestine" (Hijjawi, 2009). The report, completed just a year after the West Bank and Gaza Strip were united under Israeli military occupation, describes a fundamental break in Palestinian poetry away from "the traditional poetic forms" and toward "modern techniques" more appropriate for expressing the needs of resistance (p. 7). Cited among these is satire. The report describes this new aspect of Palestinian art as a tool by which to regain control. Through poetic satire:

> The enemy and the henchmen are ridiculed and the acts of suppression are expressed with bitter irony. This trend expresses a lively and an unconquerable spirit which considers all happenings as an

---

[3]I use this term to describe the West Bank and Gaza Strip, both under Israeli military control but having been given over to limited Palestinian Authority after the Oslo Accords of 1993. *Watan Ala Watar* has been produced exclusively in the West Bank, as Gaza has been under the political control of the opposition Hamas party since 2007 and therefore cut off from the West Bank in most ways.

ephemeral and transitional condition which sooner or later must and will be changed and put back to normality.

Palestinians of course had need for comedic satire prior to the era of occupation. Slyomovics (1991, p. 22) argues that "to praise or vilify a ruler has traditionally been the role of the Arab storyteller," suggesting that satire's entry into Palestinian arts draws on ancient roots. Nonetheless, the Iraqi report powerfully establishes the tradition of using satire as an element of resistance that stretches back at least to the onset of Israeli occupation and continues to this day through *Watan Ala Watar*.

Palestinian scholar Sharif Kanaana (1990) has provided the most sustained analysis of Palestinian political humor. His work focuses primarily on the period surrounding the first *intifada* (uprising against Israeli occupation) and thus describes the time period before Palestinians were allowed *any* form of electronic broadcasting. Kanaana argues that during this time, a distinct category of "intifada humor" coalesced in the form of jokes that would circulate throughout the Palestinian territories (p. 231). During this crucial moment, Kanaana suggests, joke-making shifted away from self-deprecating humor and towards an empowering comedy based on mocking occupiers and asserting Palestinian agency. This brand of humor served the traditional role of the Carnivalesque, inverting power structures and asserting that "there is a deeper reality behind the surface" that undermines notions of Israeli superiority (p. 234). *Watan Ala Watar* aims to create a similar funhouse mirror effect. But, provocatively, it does so by inverting the gaze of its humor, aiming it largely at internal Palestinian concerns. Show producer Sami al-Jabber, in an article in the *Christian Science Monitor*, argues that this shift results from a reduction of political tensions in the West Bank since the end of the second *intifada* in 2001. "[The] withdrawal of Israeli forces from West Bank," he notes, led to a "kind of a normal situation. This gives us a chance to say things" about internal problems (Mitnick, 2009).

However, well before the situation Jabber describes, Palestinians first needed to gain the right to produce any media whatsoever. In 1993, the signing of the Oslo Accords gave the newly formed Palestinian Authority control, for the first time, over part of the broadcast spectrum. In 1995 the PA signed into law the Palestinian Press Law, a document liberal in letter but more complex in practice. As Jamal (2000) argues, a combination of vague language and political intimidation encouraged most media outlets to engage in self-censorship (p. 500). According to local broadcasters, as recently as 2005 the PA was forcibly censoring television output, occasionally calling small local stations and demanding they immediately stop what they were airing (Ghaneim, personal communication, April 6, 2010). This, combined with the government's total control of the only national broadcasting outline, Palestine TV, made a program such as *Watan Ala Watar* unthinkable until recently.

This is not to say, however, that Palestinian satire was absent in the early years of the Palestinian Authority. Operating outside of the Palestinian territories, Elia Sulieman, a Palestinian citizen of Israel, cultivated a unique brand of political comedy that perhaps helped pave the way for *Watan Ala Watar*'s style. Sulieman developed a subtle, artistic style of political comedy based on disjointed sketches that mirror what Slyomovics (1991) describes as Palestinian art's tendency to mirror the "fragmented, open-ended" Palestinian topography that results from the presence of Israeli occupation (p. 20).

In a famous scene from the film *Divine Intervention*, Sulieman destroys an Israeli tank with the flick of a peach pit. Praising this brief mini-narrative, Dabashi (2006) argues that "rarely in the history of cinema has a cinematic will to resist and subvert power so joyously dismantled the entire machinery of a state apparatus" (p. 135). Although *Watan Ala Watar* does not have the same artistic ambitions as the Cannes Jury Prize-winning Sulieman, the show does occasionally invoke a similar brand of stark, simple comic imagery. For example, one episode features a report on a travel agency that gives "tours" of Jerusalem that merely include the opportunity for West Bank residents to look through a telescope slid through a hole in the "separation barrier" dividing cities such as Ramallah and Bethlehem from Arab East Jerusalem. Unable to cross the military checkpoint that divides the land, this is the best the agency can offer. Though perhaps less technically impressive or viscerally cathartic than Sulieman's exploding tank, the absurd image of *Watan*'s telescope affixed to the imposing, impersonal gray barrier is similar in spirit.

Though working within this comedic tradition, *Watan Ala Watar* would never have existed without major recent changes in the politics and media system of the Palestinian territories. For one, the rapid adoption of satellite television throughout the Middle East has fundamentally changed viewer expectations for television content, creating a demand for new kinds of programming. A technology reserved for the rich throughout most of the 1990s, by the mid-2000s many Arab countries featured over 90% satellite ownership, with even straggler nations such as Egypt and Morocco approaching 50% (Sakr, 2007, p. 1). This invasion of foreign, Arabic language programming had a profound effect on governments that previously held a tight grip on the airwaves. Early (2002, p. 330) argues that the satellite revolution forced the Syrian government to significantly loosen its restrictions on television content. This included an embrace of political satire that sparked important public discussions about government and history. According to Early, satellite television and the internet "knelled the death toll of censorship" in the Middle East, as producers were able to circumvent government control by approaching alternative outlets (p. 332).

However, in the Palestinian territories, things were never so simple. Television producers need not only an outlet for broadcast but also the resources to create consistent, high quality content. As Gertz and Khleifi (2008) note, the Palestinian film industry "does not exist in any organized, consistent sense," an observation that pertains to television as well (p. 33). Through the mid-2000s, the only reliable producers of Palestinian television were the PA's Palestine TV and the opposition Hamas party's Al-Aqsa TV. Neither of these was interested in underwriting a program anywhere near as controversial as *Watan Ala Watar*. However, throughout the 2000s, two major changes took place alongside the growth of satellite TV and the internet. First, a small but not insignificant alternative broadcaster emerged in 2003 in the form of the Ma'an Network, an institution funded by Western sources, including the US State Department, that brought together local commercial stations with the aim of providing an alternative to government television (Sienkiewicz, 2010, pp. 3–14). Though Ma'an's presence remained relatively small, the existence of a local producer making Palestinian comedies and dramas certainly provided Palestine TV with motivation to expand its programming repertoire. Ultimately, however, it took a major political event to finally make *Watan Ala Watar* possible.

Starting with its creation in 1995, Palestine TV had been based in Gaza City. In the aftermath of the brutal 2007 Palestinian Civil War through which Hamas seized control of the Gaza Strip, the PA moved its broadcasting headquarters to Ramallah and, in doing, made major personnel shifts at the top of the organization. A policy liberalization followed, with new station head Yasser Abed Rabbo encouraging a changed brand of programming that, for the first time, allowed independent Palestinian producers to create series for Palestine TV. Rabbo consciously wished to improve Palestine TV's international and local image, perhaps with a secondary goal of removing the American ban on funding the station that was instituted in 1998 due to accusations that it "engaged in a campaign to restrict free press and promote violent propaganda [. . .] and undermine all the United States seeks to achieve in the Middle East" (Congressional Record, 1998, p. 19323). *Watan Ala Watar* has become a key part in this campaign, as evidenced by Rabbo's appearances in international news stories about the show, where he cites it as evidence of Palestine TV's new strategy of "adding not only more comedy but also more serious open political programs" (Odeh, 2009).

Watan Ala Watar

In a blog post from September 2009, the satellite network Current TV's website linked to a *Time Magazine* report on *Watan Ala Watar*, framing the video with the question "Is this the Palestinian Daily Show?" (Current TV, 2009). American journalists particularly have been fond of the analogy and its insinuation of far-reaching, politically liberal satire. Public Radio International's Matthew Bell invoked the comparison in both positive and negative senses, noting that the program's taboo-breaking content parallels American comedy expectations while, "in terms of production value," the show is "a far cry from *Saturday Night Live* or *The Daily Show*" (The World, 2010). This latter point is certainly the case. Adapted originally from a stage production entitled *Gaza . . . Ramallah,* which satirically took on the notion of *tatbiyeh* (Palestinian normalization with Israel) (Hass, 2008), *Watan Ala Watar* is a bare bones program that often employs a single camera, long-take aesthetic more reminiscent of 1950s' American comedy shows than the graphic-heavy fare of *The Daily Show* or *Colbert.*

Watan Ala Watar premiered in 2009 during the Ramadan season, a time when Muslim families often sit down to watch television during or after the traditional *iftar* meal that breaks each day's fast. As Kraidy and Khalil (2009, p. 100) note, during Ramadan, Arab broadcasters put forth their "very best" programs and expend the "lion's share of their yearly budget." Even still, *Watan Ala Watar* was produced on a shoestring budget cobbled together from government money and a small sponsorship from the local cellular company Jawwal (Massou, personal communication, November 8, 2010). Nonetheless, *Watan Ala Watar* delivered to Palestine TV what might have been its first ratings triumph. By the show's second season in 2010, Palestine TV came in second among the local audience, losing only to regional powerhouse MBC and beating out major international outlets including Al Jazeera. *Watan Ala Watar* led the way for this unprecedented success, pulling in an estimated 41% of the Palestinian audience (Ma'an News Agency, 2010).

With regards to content, the comparisons to *The Daily Show* are not unfounded. On occasion, the program directly presents itself as news. In one such sketch, the satire simultaneously takes on the foibles of both Palestine TV's news department and the politicians it reports on. In the episode, star and head writer Imad Farajin plays the host of Palestine TV news. He fails to properly identify himself, instead telling the audience they are watching Al Aqsa TV, the station of Hamas and an utter anathema to Palestine TV's management. The news producer acts unprofessionally as well, yelling off screen and arguing with the host. Equipment breaks and the host stumbles through his lines. Whereas programs such as *The Colbert Report* take aim at contemporary media by lampooning its use of technology or graphics as a substitute for real information, *Watan Ala Watar* here takes an opposite tact, exaggerating Palestine TV's lack of resources in order to put into doubt the quality of its news output. At this point the sketch turns to the content of Palestinian politics, as the host sarcastically notes that a major political figure whose career might be put in jeopardy if a new vote were to occur is "in no hurry" to organize the next election. When things get particularly bad, the scene cuts, apropos of nothing, to a nationalistic music video often used as filler for Palestine TV throughout the day. The moment simultaneously mocks Palestine TV's conventions and the means by which the outlet, controlled by the Palestinian Authority, might be prone to glossing over or avoiding difficult questions.

In another episode produced in the mode of "fake news," US President Barack Obama, played by Khaled Massou, enters Ramallah. In the sketch, Obama shakes hands with Palestine TV chief and PA minister Yasser Abed Rabbo and remarks, rather hilariously, that he was late because he was unaware there would be Israeli checkpoints to go through. The sketch thus poignantly mocks America's ignorance of life in the Palestinian territories. A similar production approach is employed in the scene described above, in which Palestinian President Mahmoud Abbas holds the seventh Fatah conference 500 years too late. Though produced with an austere budget, the episode nonetheless attempts to mimic Palestine TV's coverage of political conferences, engaging a dual level of humor that attacks both politicians and media institutions at once.

The majority of *Watan Ala Watar*'s sketches, however, involve the lampooning of Palestinian figures or culture at large. They employ a wide range of visual strategies, from the news parodies described above to scenes staged in a simple, theatrical fashion. Topics such as religion and sexuality, generally treated in only the most serious of manners, are unprecedentedly played with and mocked. The show also crosses a cultural redline in directly attacking individuals, the source of much censorship in the earlier stages of Palestinian television. Local broadcasters report that in the early 2000s they could criticize institutions with relative impunity but were often shut down as soon as they mentioned names (Ghaneim, personal communication, April 6, 2010). *Watan Ala Watar* goes much further, including a famous episode in which Hamas leader Ishmael Haniyeh flirts with a Lebanese pop singer, making lewd sexual remarks that directly attack his pious image. On the other side of the political aisle, the show also mocked former Fatah intelligence chief Tawfiq Tirawi, who, in response, defended the show's right to exist but took great exception to "criticizing people by name" (Rafiq, 2010).

APPLAUSE AND COMPLAINTS

Internationally, the original response to *Watan Ala Watar* was surprised admiration. Outlets ranging from America's National Public Radio to *Time Magazine* to *The Guardian* and Agence France-Presse (AFP) reported on the program in glowing terms. A common theme in this Western discourse was the notion that the show provided unique opportunities for Palestinians, both in terms of freedom of speech and the chance to laugh despite presumably unhappy conditions. A *Time.com* video report declared that *Watan Ala Watar* showed that political satire had the ability to make people laugh *"even* in Palestine" (Time.com, 2010, emphasis in original). The report goes on to note that Palestine is "a place where there is usually little room to criticize." AFP took this notion a step further, ending its report with a quote from Yasser Abed Rabbo boldly claiming that after years of censorship, *Watan Ala Watar* provided evidence of a "high level of media freedom" that modeled the Palestinian desire for political freedom (Ezzedine, 2009). This quote would ultimately come to represent a moment of extreme government hypocrisy when the show was shut down. A final trend found throughout Western reviews of the program was the level of government approval the show enjoyed. Major PA figures made themselves available for comment on the program, almost invariably displaying a good-natured appreciation for the show even when it satirized their own party. Rabbo appeared in many of the reports and often spoke on behalf of president Mahmoud Abbas to AFP in praise of the program. This lead YNet, a major Israeli news website, to reprint the AFP story with a photo of Abbas captioned simply with "Abbas. Glowing Review" (YNet, 2009). This discourse echoes in pan-Arabic reporting on the show as well, a point particularly emphasized in an Al Jazeera (Arabic) report in which longtime PA minister Saeb Erekat praises the program's ability to hold people like himself accountable (aljazeerachannel, 2009). As will be shown further in the discussion of the government's domestic response to the program, it is quite clear that the Palestinian Authority aimed to enhance its reputation through embrace of the program.

Within the Palestinian media, response to the program was decidedly more mixed. The show's popularity was universally acknowledged, as was its unique place in the history of Palestinian media. The Palestine News Network issued a report after the first airing of the program declaring that *Watan Ala Watar* had sparked unprecedented debate by crossing "red-lines" and remarked that the producers were "flooded with calls" from people wanting to make suggestions and talk more about the program (Shayeb, 2009). However, the show also raised a variety of commentators' ire. In particular, members of the Hamas movement were adamantly opposed to the program, with the party's media ministry declaring the show "Israeli propaganda" due to its criticism of Palestinian culture (Rafiq, 2010). They were not alone in demanding its cancellation. The *Al Watan Voice* newspaper attacked the program, saying that by its second season in 2010, it had become illogical, inartistic, and had resorted to "abusing Palestinian society" (Abu Allan, 2010). Even some members of Fatah, the political party responsible for the show's broadcast on Palestine TV, voiced displeasure, as former minister of parliament Adli Sadeq (2009) wrote an editorial decrying the program's crass nature and describing its content as "ridiculously idiotic."

Palestinian governmental sources, however, went to considerable lengths to associate with the show despite its harsh criticism of Fatah leaders. In an interview with the Ma'an News Agency, Yasser Abed Rabbo claimed that President Mahmoud Abbas had postponed a meeting in Jordan in order to catch the episode about the extremely delayed seventh Fatah conference (Ma'an News Agency, 2009, June 9). Prime Minister Salaam Fayyad held a special reception for the show's cast, praising the program's efforts to involve more people in political debate (Ma'an News Agency, 2009, September 15). Perhaps most strikingly, the PA's minister of Women's Affairs provided *Watan Ala Watar* with an official government commendation, leading to a widely disseminated photo in which the cast stands, smiling, next to President Mahmoud Abbas (Ma'an News Agency, 2010, October 4). This image, along with the awards, commendations, and exaggerated praise, marked a concerted effort by the government to claim the program as its own, thus giving the impression that elites not only were in on the joke but also were giving the people a great gift by supporting *Watan Ala Watar*.

GOVERNMENTAL CONTROL AND ONLINE CHAOS

The love affair ended rather abruptly, however. On February 27, 2011, in the midst of the many revolutions that constituted the "Arab Spring," Imad Farajin posted a new picture to *Watan Ala*

Watar's Facebook account, bringing it to the attention of the more than 30,000 users who "like" the show's page. The photo featured Farajin and co-star Manal Awwad, the former dressed as a cartoonish version of Libyan dictator Muhammar Gaddafi, complete with Kit-Kat wrappers and crushed Coca-Cola cans standing in for the self-awarded medals that decorate the Colonel's real-life uniform. Over the course of the next week he added more photos, building anticipation for the show. On March 2, he changed the "status" on his personal page to "Gaddafi episode, this Thursday, 8 pm, Palestine TV." The show, however, did not air. The next day, Farajin apologized to his fans, posting this note: "Sorry, Palestine TV prevented the broadcast of the Gaddafi episode, Imad Farajin." The *Watan Ala Watar* page filled with comments, including accusations of political repression, demands that Farajin find a new station to broadcast the show, and a sense of anger typified by one user's charge that "the people demand the end of Palestine TV's (current) management" (Zidane, 2011). Farajin then disappeared from Facebook for a few days, an unusual period of online silence that prompted speculation among his fans, including one who made a post questioning whether he may have been imprisoned for defying government orders.

Farajin was not under arrest, but he was in the midst of a contentious public relations battle with his government and broadcasting partner. On March 5, *Dar Al Hayat*, a major pan-Arabic newspaper, printed a story on the situation in which Farajin revealed that Palestine TV had refused to air the sketch and previously had rejected a script involving a satiric representation of deposed Egyptian leader Hosni Mubarak. Farajin accused Palestine TV of putting politics before the interests of its people and rejected the official explanation that the sketch had been banned due to concerns over the treatment of Palestinians living in Libya. He announced the end of the show, saying that he, Khaled Massou, and Manal Awad would go on a live comedy tour until he could find an alternative broadcasting outlet that would ensure he would never face similar censorship (Zidane, 2011).

Having, he thought, officially broken away from Palestine TV, Farajin posted the controversial episode on YouTube, making it available across the globe. It is a strange sketch, featuring a "Palestinian Gaddafi" who gives a Gaddafi-style speech altered primarily by replacing Libyan references with Palestinian ones. Gaddafi is presented as insane, a notion common to satire across the world at the time, particularly on *The Daily Show* (McGlynn, 2011). Although the perpetually vulnerable position of the Palestinian people and government must be taken into account, it is unclear how the sketch might be dangerous, except insofar as it pushed the line up to which Palestine TV was sanctioning the mockery of leaders. In any case, the episode, like all of *Watan Ala Watar*'s efforts, was immediately popular among the Palestinian population. Within weeks, various repostings of the episode accrued more than 100,000 views. The story then began to grow and reproduce itself, as internet traffic motivated outlets such as MBC, Al Jazeera, *The Wall Street Journal*, and Agence Presse-France to write about the censorship. Social and mainstream media coalesced, driving ever increasing attention to the story and, presumably, destroying much of the good will the Palestinian Authority had originally accrued by supporting *Watan Ala Watar*. Palestine TV changed its position. It agreed to air the episode and Farajin returned to the show, having gained a considerable amount of positive exposure from the controversy. Palestine TV agreed never to censor another episode.

This promise, however, lasted only a scant few weeks. Sixteen days into the 2011 Ramadan season, Palestinian Authority Attorney General Ahmad Mughani demanded that Palestine TV cease airing the program for good. The ruling was based on a little-used piece of Jordanian legislation dating back to before Israel's occupation of the West Bank that provides the government "the right to take proper legal action under the article that talks about slander against the authority" (Abukhatar, 2011). According to Farajin (personal communication, December 6, 2010), there was never any specific accusation levied at *Watan Ala Watar*; the program was simply pulled from the schedule without so much as a phone call to the creators.

Importantly, the 2011 season of the show was not different in any significant fashion from its previous iterations. According to Farajin, it was not his show but Arab politics that had fundamentally shifted. He attests that *Watan Ala Watar* was an unintended victim of the success of the Arab Spring revolts of 2011. Speaking to the Abu Dhabi based *The National*, Farajin argued that the popular uprisings in Syria and Egypt had turned the government fearful, making previously acceptable jokes off limits (Naylor, 2011). Once more, Farajin took to the web, rousing widespread support for his cause and garnering the attention of a variety of major international news outlets. This time, however, *Watan Ala Watar*'s enemies also took to the virtual battlefield, hacking into the show's Facebook page and deleting 40,000 followers (Warner, 2011).

And yet, despite these efforts, the program still circulates widely on YouTube and other video-sharing sites, a constant reminder of the ways in which the Palestinian Authority believes it must restrict freedom in order to remain in power. It is unclear if Farajin will be able to resurrect the show in any form that would allow for new episodes. However, having made a name for himself both online and off, his satiric approach to the Palestinian condition has been firmly entrenched into the cultural lives of thousands of Palestinians.

UNBOUNDED SATIRE IN THE DIGITAL AGE

At first blush, the unfortunate demise of *Watan Ala Watar* may seem to reinforce the skeptical position regarding satire as an agent of social upheaval taken by Umberto Eco, Herbert Marcuse (1972), and others. In discussing the political efficacy of comedy, Eco (1984) uses ironic scare quotes when writing the phrase "comic 'freedom'" (p. 1). In doing so, he implies that even the most apparently subversive comedy takes place within the prevalent hegemonic order. Thus, he contends that such moments of satire are allowed only insofar as they maintain the preexisting order by releasing public tension and desire for change. These moments of comic inversion, during which elites are made to be fools and the common man gets to laugh at his social superior, are always clearly demarcated, so as to reinforce the notion that, when it ends, things must return to normal. When the carnival is over, the fact that the peasants had comically switched roles with the royalty has served only to entrench the roles to which everyone will be returning.

In the case of *Watan Ala Watar*, the Palestinian Authority did everything in its power not only to encourage a limited space in which long-established standards of media decorum could be broken but also to make sure that the world knew it was doing so. Associating itself with the rapidly growing trend of international news satire, the PA worked to benefit from the people's need to see the absurd world in which they live poked and prodded in the public sphere. It attempted to frame the series in a variety of ways, handing out awards and praise at every turn. By having the writers of a program famous for inverting the system pose at the end of each season for gleeful photos with the men who control this system, the PA stated boldly that such inversions were temporary and all in good fun. In many ways, the PA's strategy here mirrored the system of "managed critique" that Goldman (1982) identifies in American commercial television. In the case of programs that present outside viewpoints on reality, such as *Mork and Mindy*, Goldman contends that, through careful narrative crafting, "the momentary introduction of doubt concerning the status quo" is used to reaffirm "established forms of conventional morality tempered by the reformist wisdom of an idealist ideology of liberal humanism" (p. 368). With its ceremonies and press statements, the PA attempted to bind *Watan Ala Watar* in a meta-narrative in which the show's specific critiques were secondary to the fact that the program was allowed to critique at all.

And yet, during the heart of the Arab Spring, when attention was more focused than ever on the freedoms that Arab governments do and do not allow their citizens, the PA decided that even this was too much. First, they balked at the show making fun of Muhammar Gaddafi, perhaps in fear of losing Arab support at a time when the outcome of the Libyan revolution remained much in doubt. Then, after Gaddafi and other Arab elites had fallen, the PA decided they could not be in the business of endorsing the breakdown of established political order, even when the transgression occurred in the realm of comedy. As Woods (2000) argues, the collapse of one taboo has a tendency to produce a slippery slope in which other similar taboos are soon broken. No longer confident in their ability to bind *Watan Ala Watar* in the manner Eco describes, the PA chose to cut it off completely for fear of setting off a chain reaction that could lead to upheaval.

The PA has found, however, that the contemporary mediasphere works very much against the boundedness that Eco sees as necessary for comedy to maintain its essentially conservative nature. *Watan Ala Watar* would not stay neatly framed by the screen when it did air and, more importantly, it could not be controlled even when it did not. Social networking, combined with the growing tendency of people to share videos and news stories across internet platforms, introduced a fundamentally new situation that comedy pessimists such as Eco could never have anticipated. It took government support for *Watan Ala Watar* to come into being, but once it did it was simply a matter of time before the show shook loose of its bounds, using YouTube and Facebook as a means of spreading (an admittedly minor) revolution against Palestine TV.

It is possible to understand the show ultimately as having been effectively reigned in, as it appears unlikely that Farajin will have the ability to finance another season without governmental help. However, *Watan Ala Watar* must be understood as a fundamental success in two important ways. On the one hand, the program will live on online, remaining an inspiration for people in Palestine and beyond who might choose to use comedy in an effort to change their political lives. The widespread coverage of the show's cancellation in fact ensured an audience far more global than it ever could have achieved otherwise. Along similar lines, the program's web presence has made Farajin a figure of popular dissent far different from any previously seen in Palestinian politics. Perhaps more importantly, however, *Watan Ala Watar*'s turbulent life cycle becomes an almost perfect piece of anti-government satire in and of itself. The speed at which the Palestinian government went from fawning over the program to killing it is its own form of dark comedy, something that Farajin himself would be proud to have written. At its best, satire exposes the hypocrisy and double standards employed to maintain the social status quo. If nothing else, the rise and fall of *Watan Ala Watar* has forcefully served this very purpose.

REFERENCES

AbuAllan, M. (2010, August 14). Watan ala watar. *Al Watan Voice*. Retrieved from http://www.alwatanvoice.com/arabic/news/2010/08/14/152792.html

Abukhater, M. (2011, August 10). West Bank: Not everyone's laughing at Palestinian TV Comedy. *LA Times*. Retrieved from http://latimesblogs.latimes.com/babylonbeyond/2011/08/west-bank-palestinian-tv-show-frightens-officials.html

aljazeerachannel. (2009, September 18). Watan ala watar, Palestinian satire. Retrieved from http://www.youtube.com/watch?v=iepD_zr6PtU&feature=fvsr

Bakhtin, M. M. (1984). *Rabeleis and his world*. Bloomington, IN: Indiana University Press.

Baym, G. (2010). *From Cronkite to Colbert: The evolution of broadcast news*. Boulder, CO: Paradigm.

Current TV. (2009, September 22). Is this the Palestinian daily show? Current.com. Retrieved from http://current.com/items/90995857_is-this-the-palestinian-daily-show.htm

Dabashi, H. (2006). In praise of frivolity: On the cinema of Elia Suleiman. In H. Dabashi (Ed.), *Dreams of a nation* (pp. 131–162). London, England: Verso.

Day, A. (2011). *Satire and dissent: Interventions in contemporary political debate*. Bloomington, IN: Indiana University Press.

Day, A. (2010, October 28). Satirist telling the truth. *New York Times*. Retrieved from http://www.nytimes.com/roomfordebate/2010/10/28/when-does-a-fake-political-rally-turn- real/satirists-telling-the-truth

Early, E. (2002). Syrian television drama: Permitted political discourse. In D. L. Bowen & E. Early (Eds.), *Everyday life in the Muslim Middle East* (pp. 322–334). Bloomington, IN: Indiana University Press.

Eco, U. (1984). The frames of comic freedom. In T. Sebeok (Ed.), *Carnival!* (pp. 1–9). New York, NY: Mouton.

Ezzedine, H. (2009, September 10). Palestinian tv satire targets politics for first time. *The Daily News Egypt*. Retrieved from http://www.thedailynewsegypt.com/palestinian-tv-satire-targets-politics-for-first-time.html

Gertz, N., & Khleifi, G. (2008) *Palestinian cinema*. Bloomington, IN: Indiana University Press.

Goldman, S. (1982). Hegemony and managed critique in prime-time television: A critical reading of *"Mork and Mindy."* *Theory and Society, 11*(3), 363–388.

Gray, J., Jones, J. P., & Thompson, E. (2009). The state of satire, the satire of state. In J. Gray, J. P. Jones, & E. Thompson (Eds.), *Satire TV: Politics and comedy in the post-network era* (pp. 3–36). New York, NY: NYU Press.

Hass, A. (2008, December 25). Gazan humor in ramallah. *Haaretz.com*. Retrieved from http://www.haaretz.com/print-edition/opinion/gazan-humor-in-ramallah-1.260202

Hijjawi, S. (2009). *Poetry of resistance in occupied Palestine*. Retrieved from www.sulafahijjawi.ps/PoetryOfResistance_Sulafa_Hijjawi.pdf

Jamal, A. (2000). State-formation, the media and the prospects of democracy in Palestine. *Media, Culture and Society, 22*, 497–505.

Jones, J. P. (2010). *Entertaining politics: Satiric television and political engagement*. Lanham, MD: Rowman & Littlefield Publishers.

Kanaana, S. (1990). Humor of the Palestinian "intifada." *Journal of Folklore Research, 27*(3), 231–240.

Kraidy, M., & Khalil, J. (2009). *Arab television industries*. London, England: British Film Institute.

Ma'an News Agency. (2009, June 9). Watan a watar ironically promises to convene 7th fatah conference 500 years from now. Retrieved from http://www.maannews.net/arb/ViewDetails.aspx?ID=223825&MARK=%D9%88%D8%B7%D9%86

Ma'an News Agency. (2009, September 15). Upon receiving stars of Watan Ala Watar- Fayyad ministries pay tribute. Retrieved from http://www.maannews.net/arb/ViewDetails.aspx?ID=226109&MARK=%D9%88%D8%B7%D9%86

Ma'an News Agency. (2010, September 24). Poll: MBC most watched station, followed by Palestine TV. Retrieved from http://www.maannews.net/arb/ViewDetails.aspx?ID=317526&MARK=%D9%88%D8%B7%D9%86

Ma'an News Agency. (2010, October 4). Ministry of women's affairs hosts cast of watan ala watar. Retrieved from http://www.maannews.net/arb/ViewDetails.aspx?ID=229672&MARK=%D9%88%D8%B7%D9%86

Marcuse, H. (1972). *Counterrevolution and revolt*. Boston, MA: Beacon.

McGlynn, K. (2011, March 5). Jon Stewart takes on Muammar Gaddafi's insane behavior. [Web log message]. Retrieved from http://www.huffingtonpost.com/2011/03/03/jon-stewart-takes-libya-gaddafi_n_830706.html

Mitnick, J. (2009, September 25). Palestinian tv airs daring satire. *The Christian Science Monitor Online*. Retrieved from http://www.csmonitor.com/World/Middle-East/2009/0925/p09s01-wome.html

Mitnick, J. (2011, March 6). Palestinian authority pulls program lampooning Gadhafi. *The Wall Street Journal Online*, Retrieved from http://online.wsj.com/article/SB10001424052748703362804576184592661574896.html

Murphy, K. (2008). Clerk of the House of Representatives, Legislative Resource Center. Lobbying report. Washington, DC: Viacom International Services, Inc. Retrieved from http://www.google.com/url?sa=t&source=web&cd=3&ved=0CCcQFjAC&http%3A%2F%2Fsoprweb.senate.gov%2Findex.cfm%3Fevent%3DgetFilingDetails%26filingID%3DE5214665-9BD3-446C-BB87-6F3AA8BA1BDC&rct=j&q=viacom%20lobby%20report%20pdf&ei=fwgCTsXMF8ev0AHajcG2Dg&usg=AFQjCNFmkFv0vqA_ihIA4paoJNw4nrhTlQ&sig2=Vfm8nSW2AciCH9tVF5ObiA&cad=rja

Naylor, H. (2011, August 22). Palestinian official halts TV series, calls it "harmful" to society. *The National*. Retrieved from http://www.thenational.ae/news/worldwide/palestinian-official-halts-tv-series-calls-it-harmful-to-society

Odeh, N. (Producer). (2009). Palestinian satire making waves. Retrieved from http://english.aljazeera.net/news/middleeast/2009/09/200992745558974962.html

Rafiq, S. (2010, August 24). Provocative television satire raises ire of some Palestinians. *JMCC.org*. Retrieved from http://www.jmcc.org/news.aspx?id=1555

Sadeq, A. (2009, March 20). Watan ala watar. *Palpress.co.uk*. Retrieved from http://www.palpress.co.uk/arabic/?action=detail&id=1483

Sakr, N. (2007). *Arab television today*. London, England: I.B. Tauris.

Shayeb, J. (2009, August 29). Watan ala water: Bold drama the crosses red lines. *Palestine News Network*. Retrieved from http://arabic.pnn.ps/index.php?option=com_content&task=view&id=62157

Sienkiewicz, M. (2010). Hard questions: Public goods and the political economy of the new Palestinian televisual public sphere. *The Velvet Light Trap*, 66, 3–14.

Slyomovics, S. (1991). "To put one's fingers in the bleeding wound": Palestinian theatre under Israeli censorship. *Drama Review*, 35(2), 18–38.

Sorensen, M. J. (2008). Humor as a serious strategy of nonviolent resistance to oppression. *Peace & Change*, 33(2), 167–191.

Time.com. (2010). TV comedy eases Palestinian tensions. Retrieved from http://www.time.com/time/video/player/0,32068,40963186001_1925148,00.html/

United States Congress. (1998). Congressional record. Washington, DC: Government Printing Office.

Warner, J. (2011, September 3). The "Saturday Night Live" of the West Bank. *Salon*. Retrieved from http://mobile.salon.com/politics/feature/2011/09/03/palestinetv

Woods, J. (2000). Slippery slopes and collapsing taboos. *Argumentation*, 14, 107–134.

The World. (2010, September 10). Palestinian tv show skewers leaders. [Web log message]. Retrieved from http://www.theworld.org/2010/09/palestinian-tv-show-skewers-leaders/

YNet. (2009, December 9). Palestinian tv satire targets politics for 1st time. *YNetnews.com*. Retrieved from http://www.ynetnews.com/articles/0,7340,L-3775570,00.html

Zidane, B. (2011, March 5). Comedy episode about Gaddafi prevented on "Watan Ala Watar." *Dar Al Hayat*. Retrieved from http://international.daralhayat.com/internationalarticle/240726

The Geopolitics of *Parazit*, the Iranian Televisual Sphere, and the Global Infrastructure of Political Humor

Mehdi Semati

This article examines *Parazit*, a weekly Persian-language satiric news program that is often called the Iranian *Daily Show*. Although funded by the United States and circulated via an integrated global communication infrastructure to the dismay of the Iranian government, *Parazit* has become a popular program in Iran. After discussing the geopolitical context of *Parazit*, the article considers the form and content of the show in terms of global intertextuality, its techniques of satire, and the political orientation of *Parazit*'s creators. Additionally, it argues the interviews on *Parazit* and the show itself exemplify globally inflected discursive integration, with noteworthy ramifications for the Iranian political culture.

On Thursday, January 20, 2011, *The Daily Show with Jon Stewart* (*TDS*) hosted two guests: Kambiz Hosseini and Saman Arbabi, co-creators of *Parazit*, a weekly 30-minute Persian-language satirical news program that is seen by Iranians the world over. The show and its creators have received much publicity in the Western press (Bahrampour, 2011; Brown, 2011). *Parazit* is often described in the Western media as "the Iranian *Daily Show*" (e.g., Bahrampour, 2011). Although it started as a 10-minute segment on Voice of America (VOA) in May 2008, it was expanded into a 30-minute program in March 2009.

During the interview when the hosts of *Parazit* appeared on *TDS*, Kambiz Hosseini told Jon Stewart, "We're getting everything from you. You're the prophet." Stewart was flattered by the compliment and commented on the connections between their shows by issuing a compliment of his own: "You're like our show but with real guts. I am proud to be considered in the fraternity of humorists you guys are in. And I am honored to have you on the show and I am humbled by it."

Parazit reaches its audiences inside Iran primarily via satellite television, which tends to be the medium of choice for families and older viewers. YouTube and Facebook are also used, although mostly by younger audiences. *Parazit* is undoubtedly a popular program in Iran. According to Bahrampour (2011), "Although VOA doesn't know how many people watch *Parazit*, posts on the show's Facebook page were viewed more than 17 million times last month and its YouTube channel generates 45,000 hits weekly." The page for *Parzit* on Facebook is "liked" by

559,531 individuals (as of July 20, 2011). As Bahrampour (2011) reports, "fans circulate boot-legged DVDs of the latest episodes and imitate the clothing and expressions of the program's creators."

In its short existence, *Parazit* has become an important venue for Iranian expats and those in exile in various fields to engage in a televisual interaction that is new to Iranian political culture. The guests have included journalists (e.g., Masoud Behnood, Maziyar Bahari), rappers (e.g., Shahin Najafi), rockers (e.g., Hypernova front man "king Raam"), women's rights activists (e.g., Shadi Sadr), human rights activists (e.g., Hadi Ghaemi, executive director, Campaign for the Human Rights in Iran), and prominent politicians in Iranian politics (e.g., Abolhasan Bani-sadr, the first President of Iran after the revolution). Even diplomats have tried to use the venue in order to address Iranian people and politicians. When Alan Eyre, the Persian-speaking spokesperson for the US State Department was a guest on *Parazit*, he explained that although Hillary Clinton, the US Secretary of State, had to cancel her appearance on the show, she will be on the show one day soon.

On the day Hosseini and Arbabi appeared on *TDS*, Jon Stewart introduced the guests as "the co-creators of America's [sic], the co-creators of Voice of America's *Parazit*, a satirical news show that broadcasts in Iran." This brief description in the introduction by the host points to some noteworthy differences that exist between these two shows. Among these differences are two points that frame the argument in this article.

First, whereas *TDS* was created for profit motives by a television network that belongs to a transnational media corporation, *Parazit* was created for VOA, which is an official external broadcast entity funded by the federal government of the United States. Although it might be lost on the average viewer of *TDS*, the admission at the outset by Jon Stewart that the program belongs to VOA is important insofar as it inadvertently acknowledges the geopolitical context that has made *Parazit* a possibility.

Second, the statement by Jon Stewart that the show "broadcasts in Iran" points to another important difference between these programs. Whereas *TDS* is made within the United States for the domestic as well as transnational audiences, *Parazit*, which originates in Washington, D.C., is not allowed by the Iranian government to be seen on Iranian national media and is only viewed by audiences through illegal means. Satire here is considered truly subversive, especially because the text is beamed into Iran from outside via global communication technologies.

The mere presence of Kambiz Hosseini and Saman Arbabi as the hosts of Parazit, a minimally funded and minimally staffed Persian-language show on a free-to-air satellite channel, on *TDS*, with its rich inventory of elite guests, reveals an asymmetry that can only be explained by the (cultural) politics of global media. What is more, such a meeting of the hosts of *Parazit* who express great admiration for Jon Stewart on the show and their warm reception by Jon Stewart point to global intertextuality as the condition of possibility for *Parazit*. Since the show could legitimately be described as a part of the popular culture of Iran even though it originates in Washington, D.C., with the funding of the US government, and is distributed via digital media technologies, we can claim that global intertextuality is a feature of the global popular culture, which is made possible by a global digital infrastructure, and is shaped by the politics of global popular culture.

In order to discuss the geopolitics of *Parazit* and the global intertextuality that has enabled the creators of the show to produce and circulate it transnationally, this article addresses the following topics. In the first section I address the geopolitical context of the show by discussing the politics of external broadcasting and the internal socio-political context of its reception in Iran. In the second section, I address some of the formal features of *Parazit*—the way its content is organized—and make some observations on the similarities and differences between *Parazit* and *TDS* (although I will make observations on similarities and differences throughout the paper). In the third section I discuss the interviews on *Parazit*. Drawing from the works by Baym (2005, 2007), I argue these interviews exemplify globally inflected discursive integration, created in the context of an integrated global communication infrastructure. In the concluding section, I address the importance of the show for the socio-political context of its reception in Iran.

GEOPOLITICS OF EXTERNAL BROADCASTING *PARAZIT* IN IRAN

The word "parazit" in Persian means "static."[1] The creators of the show and the Western press are usually quick to point out that this choice in naming the show as *Parazit* refers to the Islamic Republic's attempt to jam the signals of foreign broadcasters in Iran. As I will explain below, it is true that the government of Iran attempts to jam signals of satellite networks that are broadcast to Iran by foreign governments, be they Persian-language or foreign-language channels. However, we need to consider the larger context in which "entertainment" is deployed for political ends.

VOA is a government-funded body that has its origins in the broadcasting activities of the United States as a part of its larger efforts during WWII. Established in 1942, VOA was a part of the Office of War Information. Its purported role was to explain the American government's war objectives and postwar activities. Along with other taxpayer-funded external broadcasting entities, VOA became a tool for the US government in its Cold War with the Soviet Union. Radio Free Europe, which broadcast programming into Eastern European countries under the influence of the Soviet Union, and Radio Liberty, which directed its broadcasting services directly into the Soviet Union, were among other broadcasting entities that were part of the geopolitics of the Cold War era. Although the bipolar world of the Cold War is gone, many of the tools that were used to dismantle the Soviet Union ideologically are still at work for the United States government, now under the control of the State Department.

Parazit as satire can be conceptualized as a tool for geopolitical influence in the context of the adversarial relationship between the Islamic Republic and the United States. The 1979 revolution that overthrew the American-backed monarchy and ushered in an Islamic Republic transformed Iran as a staunch alley of the United States into one of its most formidable adversaries in the Middle East. The US Congress approved funding for the VOA to start broadcasting in Persian in 2003. Persian News Network (PNN) was launched in 2007. As McMahon (2010) reports, "VOA today receives about $10 million to run PNN with 83 fulltime staff" (p. 27). The ascendency of neoconservatives and the pursuit of an aggressive posture towards Iran during George W. Bush's presidency, captured infamously by Bush's branding of Iran as a member of the "axis of evil," is the larger context for the expenditure of resources in the form of "public diplomacy." In pursuing public diplomacy to reach out to Iranian people, President Barack Obama has used YouTube to deliver good wishes for Persian New Year to Iranians. Outlets such as PNN are created to achieve foreign policy objectives by communicating the views of the United States to people and

---

[1] All translations are author's unless otherwise indicated.

audiences inside the target countries. Broadcast and online activities by VOA and other foreign entities are part of this context. Here the instrumentalization of culture by the United States at the service of geopolitics is a structural factor that has made the creation of *Parazit* a reality. In turn, the Islamic Republic views all cultural and political programming beamed into Iran through this lens of a new Cold War waged against its interests (see Semati, 2010a).

It is no surprise, therefore, that the Iranian government does its best to jam satellite signals (to cause parazit), preventing its population from receiving what it conveniently labels "cultural assault" or "soft war." If the United States uses broadcasting for geopolitical influence, then such an instrumentalization of culture is reciprocated by the Iranian government as it refers to cultural forms such as *Parazit* as instruments of "soft war."

The appeal to the notion of "soft war" reflects an implicit recognition by the Iranian state of the precarious internal socio-political context in which it finds itself. Externally, after the debacle in Iraq, the Islamic Republic feels confident that no military action will be taken against its interests. Internally, after witnessing the loss of public support and legitimacy in the wake of the disputed presidential election of 2009, the state has adopted a zero tolerance policy toward any expression of dissent. In this context, the real challenge for the state is to win the hearts and minds of its citizens. The Iranian government is arguably more sensitive about a program such as *Parazit* precisely because it addresses politics in the form of entertainment. As I will argue below, by representing an ordinary citizen's view of power, by giving expression to the public's displeasure with power, the satiric news program is more threatening to a state that is fast losing legitimacy.

Although the Iranian government tries to control and monitor access to media content for political reasons, it finds itself overwhelmed by media that are difficult to contain. Satellite television, blogs, online social media (e.g., Facebook), internet (e.g., YouTube), underground culture (e.g., rap and rock), and other digital media frustrate the government as it tries to limit access to information and culture (see Alikhah, 2008; Semati, 2008a, 2008b, 2009). Using various media, Iranians often contest the media hegemony of the state via circulation of images, songs, jokes, and poems that constitute counter narratives and oppositional discourses (Semati, 2010b). In short, Iran is an information-rich environment with an educated and sophisticated population that has learned how to ignore propaganda and ideological posturing that is the hallmark of the state-run media (see Semati, 2007).

Parazit arrived in Iran in both this highly contested digital media environment, and an equally contested political environment. The show expanded into a 30-minute program in March 2009, in the context of the 2009 campaigns for presidency, the disputed election, and its bloody aftermath. Although the fan base seems to mainly comprise people who have no sympathy for the Iranian government, I contacted individuals who I know are supporters of the government in order to gauge the reaction of the supporters of the Iranian regime. Their clearly expressed disdain for the show indicates they watch the show, or are aware of its content and the explicit criticisms of the regime.[2] One of these young supporters of the regime went as far as to give me a lecture about how I should not "waste" my time and academic training ("*ham-e dars-khondanha*") on such a frivolous show and that I cannot call what I am doing regarding this show research ("*tahgheegh-e elmi*") because he thinks the show is junk television ("*chert*"). It is clear from such

---

[2] I made phone calls and sent messages via e-mail and Facebook.

a reaction that the show is a thorn in the side of the conservatives. As US public broadcasting has reported:

> In fact, the government has taken notice, even producing its own state-run anti-*Parazit* program. It uses similar techniques, sometimes even clips from the show itself, while reminding viewers that *Parazit* is supported by the U.S. government and branding its two creators spies. (Brown, 2011)

In short, *Parazit* has made its presence known inside Iran and outside (judging from YouTube and Facebook presence, and the appearance of its hosts on *TDS*). In the next section, I discuss some of the formal features of the show and the way its content is organized.

Parazit: Form and Content

Political humor takes aim at "officialdom" (Schutz, 1977) or more broadly at "the powerful" (Jones, 2010). Satire "not only offers meaningful political critique but also encourages viewers to play with politics, to examine it" instead of simply accepting it as "information" or as "truth" (Gray, Jones, & Thompson, 2009, p. 11). Satire's "calling card is the ability to produce social scorn or damning indictments through playful means and, in the process, transform the aggressive act of ridicule into the more socially acceptable act of rendering something ridiculous" (pp. 12–13). Satire as an art form is not new to Iranian political culture (see Dabashi, 2008; Neshat & Nodjoumi, 2008). *Parazit*, however, as a text that comes from outside to poke power in the eyes in Iran is a new phenomenon.

Much has been made of the inspiration that *TDS* has provided *Parazit*. The comparison to *TDS* is not without merit. Some formal features of *Parazit* reflect Hosseini's claim that "we're getting everything from you." In this section, after commenting on the host of the show and his sidekick, I draw attention to some of these similarities and differences, which are best explained analytically in terms of global intertextuality. I first address some formal features of the show that reflect global intertextuality. Next, in drawing a sharper contrast to *TDS*, I demonstrate how the source of humor is not in professional writing of jokes (as practiced on *TDS*) but in creating juxtapositions to highlight absurd elements in Iranian politics. Third, I demonstrate another difference that exists between these two shows: creators of *Parazit* wear their politics on their sleeves. Although for the purpose my presentation I will focus on one episode of *Parazit* (third season, episode 14, broadcast on July 15, 2011), I draw from my exposure to the show over the past two years.

As far as the hosts of the show are concerned, *Parazit* is unlike any traditional programs that Iranian audiences have seen before. Hosseini and Arbabi are younger than traditional hosts of news programs. As Bahrampour (2011) puts it, "Most Persian News Network programming is made up of straight news and commentary. The hosts are older than Hosseini and Arbabi and generally don't go on camera in Sex Pistols T-shirts, nose rings, and green-and-black-painted fingernails." They tend to speak an informal, direct, and conversational Persian. They want to present the "news" in a language with which ordinary audiences can identify. As Arbabi says in their interview with PBS, "reporting the news has been repetitive. So we turn it into how we would talk about it as if we're talking to you right now or we're sitting at a bar." This is what Jones (2010) characterizes as talking about politics and news from an "outsider's perspective," or as a form of "authentic talk"—viewers find such a way of talking about politics closer to their experience of politics and of talking about news and politics.

Hosseini's discourse is free of *ta'arof*, a politeness system in interpersonal interactional situations in Persian culture that is antithetical to direct speech (see Beeman, 1976). Their delivery is improvised and playful but passionate and sincere. In an interview with the host of *On the Media*, Hosseini (2011a) speaks about anger: "We use dark humor and angry dark comedy because for me growing up in Iran, I felt a lot of suppression. That caused a lot of anger, not only for me, for my, my generation." He says that, "Even though we are angry and we are a product of a revolution that we had nothing to do with, we're trying to manage to control this anger and try to talk to, to Islamic Republic government and say, dude, what you are doing to us is not right and we need our freedom back." As Test (1991) has argued, satire transforms natural human emotions such as anger, contempt, and indignation into artistic expressions with political power. During their appearance on *TDS*, Jon Stewart speaks about "the heart of" and "the passion in" *Parazit*. What the show might lack in the professionalism of *TDS*, it makes up for it in passion and the seriousness of the subject of its comedy.

Among the formal intertextual features of the show is a segment tilted "The good, the bad, and the ugly." This is not unlike what Keith Olbermann called "The Worst Person in the World" on his show *Countdown*. In another intertextual element of the show, Hosseini, following Keith Olbermann on *Countdown*, throws the papers on which he had written questions up in the air or towards the camera. The global intertextuality here is evident in the borrowing of ideas and formal features from other broadcast news programs. During this segment Hosseini chooses people from Iranian politics and society and labels them as the good, the bad, and the ugly. In another intertextual element of the show, the intro to the segment is accompanied by the soundtrack from the famous "spaghetti Western" the segment is named after. In the particular episode I consider here, the people of Kurdistan were chosen as "good" because, according to Hosseini, they went on strike "to protest terrorism by the Islamic Republic." Moral police, the division of police in Iran that tries to enforce moral codes (e.g., observing codes for women's attire), were chosen as bad because "in order to pay their rent" they have chosen an occupation that entails harassing women on the streets. The personality chosen for "ugly" was the Minister of Health because, according to Hosseini, even though the condition of health-related issues in Iran has deteriorated, the Minister has not resigned from her position. Such a targeting of the "officialdom" is a feature of political humor (Schutz, 1977).

Unlike *TDS*, the source of humor in *Parazit* is not so much in professional writing of jokes as much as it is in pointing out the absurd elements in Iranian politics through a juxtaposition of "common sense" and officials' views of the world. Hosseini's comments are meant to be an average person's common sense reaction to the absurdities of politics in Iran in a stark juxtaposition. In political satire, juxtaposition is a generic element that casts the "presumptions and pretensions of the politicians" against the "intuitions and instincts of the commonplace" (Street, 2001, p. 69). A segment of the show features a series of video clips of officials, public figures, television personalities on state-run TV, and politicians in Iran who have issued statements that are either absurd intrinsically or patently out of touch with the reality of people's lives in Iran. The segment provides a treasure trove of comedy. Clerics are among the frequent targets of the segment and the show as a whole. That they provide a great deal of comedy for the show is easy to understand: they are in power and their profession entails a great deal of talking (preaching). In this day and age, religious speech in the public sphere meant as either rules for living or for political calculations is fundamentally amusing if not comical. It is in this segment that Arbabi plays his role as sidekick. He occasionally makes a face, a gesture, or an observation as a comic reply to Hosseini for emphasizing absurdity.

In this episode, the segment includes statements from lesser-known clerics, segments from state-run television, the Minister of Health, and more prominent clerics. The statements by lesser-known clerics address proper "Islamic" clothing and dangers of new and novel ways of observing religious days. The comedy here lies not in what Hosseini says but in the performance of these clerics (one is a very entertaining public speaker) or the absurd statements made by them. For example, a man on state-run television is shown to be associating high heel shoes with genies and the design on t-shirts with being put under a spell. After this statement, Hosseini asks the audience the following question: "Do I even need to spend energy to write comedy?" Obviously not!

In another clip we see a woman on state-run television, with some authority presumably, talking about conceiving children on different nights of the week. She says, for example, if a child is conceived on a Thursday night, the child will be a scientist. If a child is conceived on a Monday night, God is very satisfied. If a child is conceived on a Tuesday night, the child will cultivate martyrdom. Here Hosseini implies that state-run television thinks audiences are stupid. For the word stupid he uses a word that he needs to look up in the dictionary. He asks his sidekick for a dictionary, and here we see an example of the occasional use of props on the show. Again, the comedy is not so much in what Hosseini says, but in the clips he has chosen to show, in creating juxtaposition that captures the absurdities of Iranian politics. Here satire has the ability to express the public's displeasure with power as it represents an ordinary person's view of those in power (see Gray et al., 2009).

Parazit's creators, unlike *TDS*, wear their politics on their sleeves. The opening sequence with graphics and high-octane rock music in the background starts with these words: "*azadi* (freedom), *edalat* (justice), *demokracee* (democracy), *barabari* (equality), *jame-e madani* (civil society) . . . who has the answers? Who, me? [says Hosseini], Who him? [says Arbabi, the sidekick]." The difference with *TDS* in the opening sequence is this explicit reference to moral and political high ground. The opening sequence then dissolves into a shot of the host behind his desk, while the transition simulates static and signal interference (as in parazit or signal jamming).

In the segment that follows the opening sequence, the host introduces himself. In this episode, Hosseini introduces the show in the following manner: "I am Kambiz Hosseini. Our guest for this week is Hossein Alizadeh [an Iranian diplomat who resigned from his post in Finland in protest]. . . . This is *Parazit*." From there he goes on to describe the show in a riff that satirizes a famous speech by Ayatollah Khomeini [the leader of the 1979 revolution]: "This is a show that will install a government; this is a show that will install a government with the help of the people . . . " The riff abruptly ends with the sound of canned applause, emphasizing the satiric intent. Hosseini continues, "This is a show that in the next 30 minutes will tickle the foundation of power on behalf of the children of revolution." Although delivered in a tongue-in-cheek fashion, the reference to moral and political high ground is much more explicit than *TDS* would ever make.

Interviews on *Parazit*: New Televisual Interaction, Iranian Style

To the extent that broadcasting in Iran has always been a business of the state, Iranians are not used to seeing their leaders interrogated, mocked, or satirized openly and directly. It should be pointed out that IRIB airs popular talk shows (often with audiences calling in their questions) that include questioning of public figures in sports and popular culture. These shows include *Haft* (Seven), *Sandalee Dagh* (Hot Seat), and *Navad* (Ninety). However, with the advent of satellite television and external broadcasting by exile groups and other more credible sources (e.g., BBC Persian TV), Iranians have been exposed to criticism of their rulers. In a society such as Iran where the state tries to monopolize the means of political expression, all cultural forms tend to become politicized. What is unique about *Parazit* is that Iranians are seeing an entertainment television program that directly and explicitly engages in satire of the state and Iranian politicians from abroad.

One way to approach interviews on a show such as *Parazit* is to compare them to traditional journalistic interviews that have been a staple of public affairs programming on television. Traditionally, such interviews have been viewed as components of the public sphere (in the Habermasian sense) in that they have a democratic function by "soliciting statements of official policy, holding officials accountable for their actions, and managing the parameters of public debate" (Clayman & Heritage, 2002, p. 2). The critics of such a view argue that the assumption of a rational-critical discourse at the heart of a Habermasian notion of public sphere does not hold when we consider the dynamics of television as a medium. Pels (2003), for example, suggests that "televisual mediation" entails emphasis on stylistics and aesthetics at the expense of critical-rationalist addressing of politics. DeLuca and Peeples (2002), to take another example, argue that television puts "a premium on images over words, emotion over rationality, speed over reflection, distraction over deliberation" (p. 133).

Against these approaches, Baym (2007) argues that the complexity and transformations of the televisual sphere compel us to rethink an easy denigration of television. Technological developments, niche targeting of audiences, and recognition of multicultural diversity have led to a rethinking of our assumptions about content, genre, and textual forms. Baym (2005) has labeled these developments and the emerging context as "discursive integration," which he defines as "a way of speaking about, understanding, and acting within the world defined by the permeability of form and the fluidity of content" (p. 262). Broadcast news in this context is subject to such transformations. As Baym (2005) argues, "Discourses of news, politics, entertainment, and marketing have grown deeply inseparable; the languages and practices of each have lost their distinctiveness and are being melded into previously unimagined combinations" (p. 262). Traditional approaches to the journalistic interview, which made a differentiation between it and the entertainment-oriented interview, no longer suffice.

Jones (2010) and Gray et al. (2009) count a number of technological developments in the televisual sphere as important structural changes that opened a space for the emergence of *TDS*. These have included the proliferation of mechanisms and platforms for production and distribution of content that facilitated the rise of cable television with niche marketing and narrowcasting. The space for the emergence of *Parazit* was also created by the same set of technological developments writ large at the global level. Satellite television, internet, social networking sites, and other digital media clearly helped carve a space for *Parazit*. The "permeability of form and the fluidity of content," especially one that is globally inflected, is not possible without the technological agency at the global level.

Jon Stewart's interviews on *TDS*, Baym (2007) argues, exemplify this discursive integration. On the one hand, they resemble the traditional late night television chat shows where guests plug their latest offerings and engage in light-hearted talk. On the other, high-level officials from the political class frequently appear on the show where they face Jon Stewart with his probing questions. Stewart's interviews "rework the rules of news and celebrity interviewing to produce a novel form of televisual interaction that blends postmodern stylistics with a modernist ethos of rational-critical dialogue" (p. 93). In "redefining the speech situation," the interviews on *TDS* "fuse chat style and public affairs content to create a multi-faceted form of televisual speech that transcends the divide between news and entertainment and rational discourse and aesthetic spectacle" (pp. 99–100). As a postmodern cultural form, Jon Stewart's interviews "are shaped by discursive border-crossing, the interweaving of interpersonal chat, rational-critical argument, marketing, and of course, humor" (p. 103).

Like *TDS*, the interviews on *Parazit* combine elements of news and celebrity interviewing (although over time the interviews have become more somber as the roster of guests has increasingly included politically oriented individuals). The influence of Jon Stewart on Hosseini is apparent. In an interview with Radio Farda, Hosseini is asked if someone like Stewart provides him a model to emulate. He says, "I personally like Jon Stewart a lot. I used to watch him on his show on MTV in the 1980s." Hosseini (2011b) claims that although they do not try to imitate him, "we somehow are following down a path that he has traveled." In many ways Hosseini addresses political issues with a critical-rationalist approach, yet he does so within the field of "postmodern" play where stylistics and spectacle are par for the course.

What is more striking about Hosseini's interviews is that they are devoid of *ta'arof*. In her reporting, Bahrampour (2010) makes the following observation: "Persian culture, with its elaborate politeness rituals, is, after all, the furthest thing from the directness of Jon Stewart." She quotes Hosseini: "You have a half-hour [interview] with these people and the whole time the journalist is going, 'Oh, I'm sorry . . . Can I get you something? . . . If you don't mind, I want to ask you this.' . . . No–I just sit in front of people and say, 'What the fuck?'" I believe this dispensing with the politeness of Persian culture is a necessity in a speech situation where the interviewer intends to take up the persona of a critical-rationalist muckraker (i.e., Jon Stewart).[3]

The person interviewed for the episode I have been discussing is Hossein Alizadeh, a diplomat who resigned his post in Finland. Hosseini's introduction and his characterization of the former diplomat leave no doubt about his political views. He introduces the guest as a diplomat who relinquished his position in the Islamic Republic as a protest against the events that took place in Iran after the disputed presidential election of 2009. He finishes his introduction by saying that this diplomat "quit his post and joined the protest movement of the people of Iran." He adds, Alizadeh is "a diplomat who could not longer take the bullying of a dictator."

In a move that clearly distinguishes *Parazit* from *TDS* and establishes how the creators of the show see it as a platform to reach Iranians, at the end of his interviews Hosseini gives one minute to his guests to address the audiences of the show. While some guests have chosen to address young people in Iran (e.g., Bani-Sadr), others have chosen to address Iranian officials (e.g., Hossein Alizadeh). In one case, the guest decided to observe one minute of silence in honor of those killed or those who are in prison in Iran (Maziar Bahari).

---

[3]There are a few Persian-language news programs beamed into Iran which display a directness absent in news programs in Iran. For example, Enayat Fani, the host of *In Other Words* (*be ebarat-e deegar*) on BBC Persian TV, asks tough questions of his guests. However, his program offers traditional journalistic interviews.

Hosseini's questions are unusually blunt and devoid of politeness. During this interview, he only makes two attempts at humorous questions. Most questions are serious, direct, and lead the interviewee and the audience toward a particular political orientation. His questions regarding Alizadeh's political affiliation are meant to disclose Alizadeh's political trajectory and his eventual disillusionment with the Islamic Republic and its leaders. Moreover, the progression of these questions leads to a questioning of a bedrock principle of the Islamic Republic (*velayat-e faqih*, or rule of the jurist) and the Supreme Leader of the Islamic Republic.

This is where one could make an argument that what differentiates Jon Stewart from Hosseini is while the former maintains a good degree of political impartiality the latter wears his politics on his sleeves. In their interview with Bahrampour (2010), Arbabi, after making a reference to "a lot of sad news coming out of Iran," says: "We have to walk a fine line. We come from that generation of kids who got up in Iran and protested the government. We share their politics, so we echo their voice." Yet one has to submit that it is difficult to maintain impartiality in the face of an authoritarian political structure. However, a common complaint by political elites about *Parazit* (and Hosseini by extension) is that by finding the most absurd elements in the Islamic Republic, the show, from a safe distance, either takes cheap shots or creates a straw man argument.

Perhaps this is where other differences between Jon Stewart and Hosseini become discernible. Jon Stewart is a professional comedian, and Hosseini has no such background. Whereas *TDS* has a team of writers and researchers, *Parazit* does not have a wealth of resources and much of the comedy on the show seems improvised and rather amateurish. While Jon Stewart's professionalism and credibility in conducting interviews is impeccable, Hosseini struggles to be funny and a good interviewer. This lack of professionalism sometimes leads to exchanges that are rather offensive. To give an example, when he hosted Shadi Sadr, a prominent women's rights activist, on *Parazit*, he asked the following questions: "Are you a feminist? What is a feminist? Some say women are either beautiful or feminist. You are a beautiful woman in my opinion, how did you become a feminist?" If this is humor, it appeals to the chauvinist tendencies in Iranian political culture. It is debatable if a sarcastic tone in delivering these lines, to the extent that one could be detected, would lead to a questioning of such tendencies, a questioning that is the trademark of successful satire and political humor.

In summary, the interviews on *Parazit* clearly embody both postmodern stylistics and a modernist ethos of rational-critical dialogue. Hosseini's approach is direct and unapologetic. His interviews are more partisan compared to Jon Stewart's, although it is difficult not to be partisan when dealing with an authoritarian government. However, the interviews and the show are not as professional as what one finds on *TDS*. If the show does not display the same degree of professionalism as *TDS*, and admittedly we should not expect it to, it displays a passion that transcends politics and entertainment.

CONCLUSIONS: *PARAZIT* AND THE DEMOCRATIC IMAGINARY IN IRAN

Parazit has become a popular text with a global circulation in a short period. The space created for the emergence of the show can be delineated from the arguments of this article. The geopolitical developments have played their role. The funding by the US government for VOA, in the context of the ongoing adversarial relationship that utilizes international broadcasting as a tool of "public diplomacy" is another element that contributed to the formation of that space. Another element is the governing political structure in Iran that does not tolerate dissenting opinion in its broadcasting services. *TDS*, as a cultural form admired by Hosseini and Arbabi, also contributed to the formation of this space. Various digital media technologies that facilitated the production and distribution of content transnationally (which led Stewart to see *Parazit* "on the web") are the enabling infrastructure of this new space. We should also include the lack of competition that created the space for the emergence of the show. The internal political conditions, and the global reactions to them, also contributed to this formation: the presidential election of 2009, its disputed outcome, and its bloody aftermath have raised the profile of Iranians and their struggle for democracy globally. *Parazit* owes much of the publicity and the credibility it has garnered to that globally mediated profile and the politics of its rise. That is to say, *Parazit* has become a higher profile show because a Western constituency finds its politics and its discourse in sync with its own political and cultural sensibility.

The popularity of *Parazit* in Iran reflects another reality in Iranian society. The televisual sphere in Iran that is created by the state is packed with discourses that try to reproduce an ideological consensus in accordance with the state's vision of an "Islamic" culture. These efforts by the Islamic Republic are not unlike the efforts by modern political parties in the West that try to cultivate trust in their political "brands." The techniques of branding in the world of politics are borrowed from the domain of business and commercial activities (Street, 2006). In Western societies, where citizens enjoy various degrees of freedom of expression, they have opportunities to disrupt the transmission and dissemination of the hegemony of branding messages. Warner (2007) has argued that "*The Daily Show with Jon Stewart* 'jams' the seamless transmission of the dominant brand messages by parodying the news media's unproblematic dissemination of the dominant brand, broadcasting dissident political messages that can open up space for questioning and critique" (p. 17). "Culture jammers" give the established media and those who promote branding techniques to sell their brand a taste of their own medicine (e.g., using counter narratives and images to confront the hegemonic images and discourses). Here *TDS* is viewed as a "political culture jammer" that uses parody and satire to "disseminate dissident interpretations of current political events," and jam the transmission of dominant political brand messages (p. 19).

This view of *TDS*'s communicative contribution as "jamming" is instructive in explaining the political function of *Parazit* in Iranian political culture. To return to the meaning of the word *parazit* itself, the noun *parazit* means static. When it is used as a verb (*parazit andakhtan*) it means disrupting. To the extent that the machinations of the Islamic Republic in creating and promoting their ideological consensus is an enormous undertaking in the vast field of media and culture, these images and discourses are bound to be contradictory, leaky, and in some instances absurd. This feature of (news) media communication in Iran presents *Parazit* and Hosseini the opportunity to be political culture jammers in a field that offers them plenty of targets.

Every commentator that has made a reference to the meaning of the word *parazit* has discussed it as the effort of the state to jam the signals of this and other shows like it. However, the significance of the show for political culture in Iran is better understood if we explain the word *parazit* in a way that means it is Hosseini, Arbabi, and their show doing the jamming. In an interview with VOA on the idea and the birth of the show Hosseini conceptualizes the show as *parazit* in this sense (Hosseini, 2009). Regardless of the level of professionalism exercised by Hosseini and *Parazit*, the show is ultimately a positive development in Iranian political culture in that it contributes toward a democratic imaginary wherein citizens have the rights to satirize and even ridicule their rulers.

REFERENCES

Alikhah, F. (2008). The politics of satellite television in Iran. In M. Semati (Ed.), *Media, culture, and society in Iran: Living with globalization and the Islamic state* (pp. 94–110). London, England: Routledge.

Bahrampour, T. (2011). Iranian daily show, meet "The Daily Show." *Washington Post*. Retrieved from http://www. washingtonpost.com/wp-dyn/content/story/2011/01/21/ST2011012103765.html?sid=ST2011012103765

Baym, G. (2007). Crafting new communicative models in the televisual sphere: Political interviews on *The Daily Show*. *The Communication Review*, *10*(2), 93–115.

Baym, G. (2005) *The Daily Show*: Discursive integration and the reinvention of political journalism. *Political Communication*, *22*(3), 259–276.

Beeman, W. (1976). Status, style and strategy in Iranian interaction. *Anthropological Linguistics*, *18*(7), 305–322.

Brown, J. (2011, February 28). For Iranian TV viewers, Parazit offers reprieve from static, PBS Newshour. Retrieved from http://www.pbs.org/newshour/bb/world/jan-june11/parazit_02-28.html

Clayman, S., & Heritage, J. (2002). *The news interview: Journalists and public figures on the air*. New York, NY: Cambridge University Press.

Dabashi, H. (2008). Ardeshir Mohassess, Etcetera. In S. Neshat & N. Nodjoumi (Eds.), *Ardeshir Mohassess: Art and satire in Iran* (pp. 17–29). New York, NY: Asia Society and Museum.

DeLuca, M., & Peeples, J. (2002). From public sphere to public screen: Democracy, activism, and the "violence" of Seattle. *Critical Studies in Media Communication*, *19*(2), 125–151.

Gray, J., Jones, J., & Thompson, E. (2009). The state of satire, and satire of the state. In J. Gray, J. Jones, & E. Thompson (Eds.), *Satire TV: Politics and comedy in the post-network era* (pp. 3–36). New York, NY: NYU Press.

Hosseini, K. (2009). "Where were *Parazit* born?" Retrieved from http://www.youtube.com/watch?v= kLcX9iTpvy8&playnext=1&list=PLF7FE4FFA4336374A

Hosseini, K. (2011a). Satire Iranian-American style [Interview *On the Media*]. Retrieved from http://www.onthemedia. org/2011/jan/14/political-satire-iranian-american-style/transcript/

Hosseini, K. (2011b). *Parazit*: Comedy with dangerous enemy. [Interview with Radio Farda in Persian]. Retrieved from http://www.radiofarda.com/content/f3_parazit_interview/2300223.html

Jones, J. (2010). *Entertaining politics: Satiric television and political engagement* (2nd ed.). New York, NY: Rowman & Littlefield.

McMahon, R. (2010, October). U.S.-funded media and the "soft war" in Iran. *Foreign Service Journal*, 26–30.

Neshat, S., & Nodjoumi, N. (2008). *Ardeshir Mohassess: Art and satire in Iran*. New York, NY: Asia Society and Museum.

Pels, D. (2003). Aesthetic representation and political style: Re-balancing identity and difference in media democracy. In J. Corner & D. Pels (Eds.), *Media and restyling of politics: Consumerism, celebrity and cynicism* (pp. 41–66). Thousand Oaks, CA: Sage.

Schutz, C. E. (1977). *Political humor: From Aristophanes to Sam Ervin*. London, England: Associated University Presses.

Semati, M. (2007). Media, the state, and the pro-democracy movement in Iran. In I. A. Blankson & P. D. Murphy (Eds.), *Globalization and media transformation in new and emerging democracies* (pp. 143–160). Albany, NY: SUNY Press.

Semati, M. (2008a). Living with globalization and the Islamic state: An introduction to media, culture, and society in Iran. In M. Semati (Ed.), *Media, culture, and society in Iran: Living with globalization and the Islamic state* (pp. 1–13). London, England: Routledge.

Semati, M. (Ed.). (2008b). *Media, culture, and society in Iran: Living with globalization and the Islamic state*. London, England: Routledge.

Semati, M. (2009). Communication, media, and popular culture in post-revolutionary Iran. *The Middle East Institute viewpoints*. Retrieved from http://www.payvand.com/news/09/feb/1146.html

Semati, M. (2010a). Islamophobia, culture and race in the age of Empire. *Cultural Studies*, *24*(2), 256–275.

Semati, M. (2010b).Alternative cultural sphere and media in Iran. In J. Downing (Ed.), *The Sage international encyclopedia of social movement media* (pp. 365–367). Thousand Oaks, CA: Sage.

Street, J. (2006). The celebrity politician: Political style and popular culture. In P. D. Marshall (Ed.), *The celebrity culture reader* (pp. 359–370). New York, NY: Routledge.

Street, J. (2001). *Mass media, politics, and democracy*. London, England: Palgrave.

Test, G. (1991). *Satire: Spirit and art*. Tampa, FL: University of South Florida Press.

Warner, J. (2007). Political culture jamming: The dissident humor of *The Daily Show With Jon Stewart*. *Popular Communication*, *5*(1), 17–36.

The Witty Seven: Late Socialist-Capitalist Satire in Hungary

Anikó Imre

This article adopts the comparative framework proposed by anthropologists Dominic Boyer and Alexei Yurchak (2010), who establish a "family resemblance" between the aesthetics and ideological contexts of contemporary Western political satire and a late socialist Russian and Eastern European mode of irony defined by overidentification with its satirized object or idea. I discuss the long-running Hungarian postsocialist satirical talk show *Heti Hetes* as a linchpin between late socialist and late capitalist forms of political satire. The program bears the characteristics and legacies of both and reveals unexpected similarities between public discourses otherwise radically separated into two different political systems during the Cold War. *Heti Hetes* provides the ground for a multilevel analysis, which accounts for the national specificities of a long legacy of political cabaret as well as the shared regional circumstances of late socialism. The broadest goal of the article is to draw up the global historical trajectory of contemporary Western television satire.

American television finally embraced satire in the postnetwork era. Humor had tended to take less critical and negative forms on television until the late 1970s; more critical forms of social satire had been carried by print journalism and comic books. The three large television networks preferred safer, more mainstream forms of comedy that attracted advertisers and the largest possible audience shares. After decades of broadcasting given to least objectionable programming and nonoffensive, mainstream forms of comedy, satire has transformed from a rare mode of expression on the periphery of television into a genre that encompasses TV-land. The history of this shift has been well explored: it has been enabled by a changing technological infrastructure that allowed for a large number of channels to deliver diversified programming via cable and satellite, widespread access to digital technologies of production and distribution, and the conglomeration and integration of ownership over multiple media platforms (Baym, 2005; Gray, Jones, & Thompson, 2009).

The establishment of Comedy Central in the United States as a distinct brand among Viacom's assets has been a milestone in this narrative. Ironically, the channel's two flagship comedy news shows, *The Daily Show with Jon Stewart* and *The Colbert Report*, have galvanized political participation and civic interest to an extent far beyond what even their hosts would admit. Rather than simply offering humorous commentary on what would be assumed to remain authentic, "real" news, "fake" news has taken over what has remained of the service to provide reliable information about matters of public interest. The amount of audience trust placed in these late night news comedies reveals a corresponding erosion of trust in network news and other traditional news sources.

By all accounts, this migration of trust from authentic to fake news is happening on a global scale. The changes that have brought it about are also symptoms of a globally converging media world—beginning with the transnational expansion of Comedy Central itself. This collection is itself an effort to understand the popularity of comedy news in the context of transnational media change.

The global synchronicity of media change was my founding assumption when I began searching the Hungarian television scene for programs comparable to *The Daily Show* and *The Colbert Report*. *Heti hetes*, or "The Weekly Seven" (a pun based on the fact that the words "seven" and "week" both mean "hét" in Hungarian), seemed to confirm my assumption. A weekly, hour-long news comedy show that has successfully run on the Hungarian commercial channel RTL Klub since 1999, it was modeled after the German RTL's format *Sieben Tage, sieben Köpfe*, or "Seven Days, Seven Heads." Both programs have a host read short news bites from the past week on which a panel of six celebrities comment in a humorous, often satirical fashion, including short, preprepared skits or musical numbers. Some of the six guests are permanent members of the team, while others are one-time or returning guests. Much like Comedy Central's satirical news shows or Bill Maher's *Politically Incorrect* (1993–2002) and *Real Time* (2003–present), to which *Heti hetes* is more similar in format, the program targets absurdities in politics and public life, which range from the silliest to the most politically charged.

The more I watched and learned about the program, however, the more evident it became that its similarity to American late-night comedy news was superficial. While the format is indeed new and thus could be attributed to the globalization and commercialization of postsocialist television industries, the program's longstanding success has more to do with Hungarian audiences' already existing affinity with the genre of political satire. The show draws on a strong tradition of political comedy, whose roots reach back to early-20th-century stage cabaret, and which continued on state-controlled radio and television throughout the socialist period. This recognition also shed light on why the satirical modes engaged by Jon Stewart and Stephen Colbert were so familiar to me. The way in which they provide a crucial outlet through laughter for public frustration with political smokescreens and talking points triggers memories of the period of late socialism, the 1970s and 1980s. This was a time of "political thawing" in most Soviet-ruled countries, which marked a transition from total state control and censorship over the media to limited freedom of speech that allowed criticism to seep in through humor.

The analogy I established in my moment of personal epiphany is confirmed by anthropologists Dominic Boyer and Alexei Yurchak (2010), who go as far as claiming that late socialist media in Eastern Europe anticipates late night television news satire in the United States. They establish a "family resemblance" between the aesthetics and ideological context of contemporary political satire worldwide, including *The Daily Show*, *The Colbert Report*, *The Yes Men*, *The Onion*, *South Park*, faux documentary shows such as *The Office*, *CNNN* in Australia, Sacha Baron Cohen's satirical performances on *Da Ali G Show* on the one hand, and a mode of parodic overidentification they identify by the Russian term *stiob* on the other. They define *stiob* as an ironic aesthetic that thrived in late-Soviet socialism and "differed from sarcasm, cynicism, derision or any of the more familiar genres of absurd humor" in that it "required such a degree of *overidentification* with the object, person, or idea at which [it] was directed that it was often impossible to tell whether it was a form of sincere support, subtle ridicule, or a peculiar mixture of the two" (p. 5).

This analogy has far-reaching implications for understanding the historical trajectory and political significance of television satire in a transnational framework. It brings up the sticky question of just what "free" late capitalist media today have in common with late socialist, centralized, "freedom-deprived" media. This question is not invalidated by the obvious differences between the two, such as the fragmentation of the viewing public into multiple niche audiences as opposed to a supposedly homogeneous national audience, the different degrees in the freedom of the press, and the differences between entertainment-centered programming targeting consumers and the educational-enlightening rationalism of late socialist media targeting citizens. Boyer and Yurchak (2010) claim that key to the analogy between the discursive and ideological contexts of late socialism and "late liberalism" is the highly monopolized conditions of discourse production in both cases. The monopolization of media production, the formalization of political discourse within the news media through party, state and corporate talking points and political theater, the increasing emphasis on modes of performance across media outlets at the expense of substantive and critical analysis or even an attempt at factuality, are not mere coincidental resemblances between late socialist and late capitalist conditions. They argue that the collapse of communism and the disappearance of the ideological threat that had previously propped up the self-righteousness of capitalist media during the Cold War have substantially contributed to the erosion of public trust in the news since the fall of communism.

In the past two decades, late capitalist media, diplomacy, and trade have had to justify themselves through self-persuasive, repetitive references to the absolute freedoms guaranteed by the holy market, including personal liberties and the self-explanatory "Western lifestyle," which is often collapsed into human life and democracy (Boyer & Yurchak, 2010). The loss of an absolute ideological enemy such as the Soviet Empire has created a nonrelational, universal mantra, a kind of dogma not unlike the Marxist-Leninist tenets obsessively repeated by socialist propaganda. Within the United States, this increasingly self-referential, self-justifying, performative discourse has become absurd in the face of the grim realities of corporate wars and deepening economic crisis during the Bush years. Political satire has only voiced and amplified the meta-commentary generated by the gap of absurdity that has opened up between rhetoric and reality.

What follows is that the analogy between the two situations that have legitimated eerily similar forms of satirical discourse is necessary to explore in order to draw up the *global* historical trajectory of contemporary Western television satire. Conversely, rather than a new phenomenon transplanted into postsocialism by victorious capitalism, a program such as *Heti hetes* is a linchpin between late socialist and late capitalist forms of political satire. As a show that bears the characteristics and legacies of both, it provides excellent ground for a critical comparison. Unfolding such a large-scale comparison from a specific program also makes it possible to conduct the analysis at several different, interlocking levels. I begin with the shared regional features of late socialist political satire, including snapshots of examples that also embody national specificities. Then I discuss *Heti hetes* in the specific context of Hungarian political cabaret and satire, explaining how its success with audiences is embedded in a century-long tradition of political cabaret. I frame the entire discussion within the historical project that sets in analogy socialist and postsocialist television satire.

LATE SOCIALIST POLITICAL SATIRE

Television satire is a "posttrust" lens on politics, permeated by suspicion about authority. It gains particular legitimacy "when historical reality presents periods of social and political rupture (such as culture wars, hot wars, and unpopular leaders) or mind-numbing manufactured realities (such as celebrity culture, media spin, and news management)." In these times, "satire becomes a potent means for enunciating critiques and asserting unsettling truths that audiences may need or want to hear" (Gray et al., 2009, p. 15). In the Eastern European region, the entire period of socialism, and arguably the entire 20th century, was a long series of ruptures and upheavals. Satire has been an indispensable filter for public discourse. It is one in a range of "negative" or "dark" modes of expression often associated with arts in the region. These include dark humor, the grotesque, and the absurd, manifest in the work of artists from Gogol through Ionescu to Makavejev. The late socialist period of the 1970s–1980s gave rise to a regionwide flourishing of satire in socialist media. By then, principles of a utopian Marxist-Leninist social transformation had lost much of their legitimacy. However, the clichés of political communication continued to be repeated, rigidifying into their own parodies. The form of communication called *stiob* in Russian simply amplified these parodies through playing back to the regime its own vacuous linguistic and audiovisual performances.

In the United States, despite the corruption of the epistemological certainty of television news, the very notion of "fake news" still presupposes the existence of "real news," at least as a lost ideal projected into the past. In the Eastern European region and the Soviet Union, ever since television grew into a mass medium during the 1950s–1960s, television news never even pretended to be ideologically neutral. It was deployed under state and Soviet control as a means of propaganda: heavily censored, filtered, and formalized, it was to support the principles of socialism and educate socialist citizens. In both cases, satire is used as a mode to amplify the absurdity of monologic news, which seeks to establish through repetition the very epistemological certainty it claims as its basis. By replaying the echoes that reverberate in the self-referential chamber of "serious" news, satire creates a dialogic discourse in the Bakhtinian sense in which multiple, simultaneous voices play against one another (Baym, 2005, p. 266; Day, 2009).

Boyer and Yurchak (2010) identify some major underlying structural similarities between the two situations. The first of these is the centralization of media ownership and control. In the United States and much of the world today, despite multiplying media outlets and the democratizing potential of the internet, the gradual retreat of the state from media regulation has effectively unified the sources of information in very few, very powerful hands. The concentration of ownership has also led to increased commercialization. Instead of being a public service, as it has been considered in the dominant tradition of European television, news gathering and sharing primarily serve purposes of entertainment for profit (Baym, 2005, p. 261). Expensive foreign correspondents, time-consuming fact checking, and thorough analysis have fallen victim to the fragmentation and commodification of deregulated news production.

It was also a centralized, hierarchical infrastructure that consolidated the news in the Soviet empire into highly standardized and censored messages. Not unlike Rupert Murdoch's News Corporation, this was a multitiered empire, where national news media were continually checked to make sure they adhered to the rhetoric of socialism set forth by Moscow. While national media in the different countries demonstrated varying degrees of openness toward and sometimes even entered into collaboration with Western news services, the ultimate power over the flow of information was condensed in the highest party echelons. Boyer (2003) describes how, in East Germany (GDR), standardized language was essential to disseminating information from Berlin to regional media centers, which then rerouted party messages to the district-level party offices that placed the news in print and electronic media. In the GDR, as elsewhere, the socialist citizen would wake up every morning to read the exact same headlines in the exact same formulation in every paper. News was provided by the single national information service, in this case the Allgemeine Deutsche Nachrichtendienst; press photos were supplied by the national news photo service, and journalist training was centralized at Karl Marx University in Leipzig. Long-time General Secretary Erich Honecker personally reviewed and revised headlined news on a daily basis. In a similar vein, through the 1960s, Hungarian State Television and Radio had a single, powerful director trusted by party authorities, who also hand-picked the institutions' department heads and even reporters according to the candidates' ideological convictions and class backgrounds rather than their preparation or talents. The agitational-propaganda department, the ideological arm of the party, had the final say over the content and form of the news (Zalán, 1966).

The daily experience of centralized news is not unlike that of the coordinated daily talking points repeated by conservative news outlets in the United States, from talk radio to Fox News. Watching the documentary *Outfoxed: Rupert Murdoch's War on Journalism* (Greenwald, 2004), one feels an eerie *déjà-vu*: The film foregrounds the strategic repetition of rhetorical formulas and carefully crafted daily messages on Fox News, which are often communicated through memos and guidelines by Murdoch and his trusted delegates. As former Fox News reporters explain, some with their faces blocked out or voices altered, the news is skewed to reflect News Corporation's conservative spirit and at times Murdoch's own political convictions, such as his devotion to Ronald Reagan. As Geoffrey Baym remarks, against the background of the partisan spin and highly standardized format that defines "real" news, Jon Stewart's comedic discussions with his guests strike one as "honest" and "normal" (2005, p. 272).

In both cases, the economic and political centralization of the structure of news reporting thus produces a highly reiterative, performative rhetoric, whose goal is to solidify the very reality it creates. The scale of this development is brilliantly demonstrated by Charlie Brooker on his BBC 4 program *Newswipe*, in a parody skit entitled "How to Report the News."[1] Brooker assumes a reporter's familiar, phony voice and persona to narrate and demonstrate the clichés that secure the "authenticity" of a news story, from "a lackluster establishing shot of a significant location" to "lazy and pointless vox pops" by people in the street. This faithful adherence to the formula produces a perfectly passable news segment despite the lack of reported content. In a similar vein, Jon Stewart often does not need to do more than isolate and replay fragments of what he calls the political theater of "real" news. It is the operation of this theater that he interrupted in his (in)famous 2004 appearance on *Crossfire*, where he broke the character he was assigned and refused to be Tucker Carlson's "clown." *The Daily Show* frequently offers montages that juxtapose utterances of the same political talking points in the news media to foreground their coordinated orchestration, as in conservative politicians' and news media's strategic use of the euphemisms "job creators" instead of "rich people" and "climate change" instead of

---

[1] See http://www.youtube.com/watch?v=aHun58mz3vI.

"global warming." Colbert takes the performance a step further, and even closer to *stiob*, when he channels the persona of conservative talk show host Bill O'Reilly.

In comparison, one may argue that socialist news, at least in the early decades of socialism, was actually more sincere than contemporary late capitalist news. In the GDR, for instance, the language of the news was the result of a careful calculation of social engineering, whose goal was to change collective consciousness. This project, Boyer argues, while obviously a part of the larger scheme of international socialism, also revived the 19th-century German cultural bourgeoisie's desire to create a national consciousness among all the peoples who shared the German language as their main connection to one another. Socialist media was to complete the paradoxical project of manufacturing the *Volk* on whose preexistence the entire concept of a national consciousness was based. The language of socialist news was designed with the noble intention to unite the referential precision of socialist philosophers such as Lenin and Marx with the poetic quality of Goethe. The result, however, was neither; rather it was a kind of *Funktionärsdeutsch*, whose repetitive efforts to approximate a monologic ideal only created indeterminacy and polysemy. The effect was "like listening to reports from another planet," as one of Boyer's former East German interviewees put it (Boyer, 2003, p. 523).

By the 1970s and 1980s, even in relatively oppressive countries such as the Soviet Union, this distancing effect moved from the margins into the center of political discourse. In the Soviet Union, *stiob* sensibility emerged in the context of what Boyer and Yurchak calls "hypernormalization," when the structure of late Soviet authoritative discourse gradually became more formalized and self-referential (Boyer & Yurchak, 2008). The ironic sensibility was as an expression of skepticism about political rhetoric in general and not necessarily in opposition to socialist propaganda. Much like *The Colbert Report*, it was successful as an outlet because it followed the official rhetoric so precisely that it was often hard to detect the parodic intent. *Stiob* was thus a most effective popular coping strategy, especially since direct confrontation would have been easily recognized and neutralized by the state. Overidentification had the additional advantage that one could reject some misguided socialist practices without having to reject the idea of communism as a whole (Boyer, 2003; Boyer & Yurchak, 2008).

One notorious instance of late socialist satire was Russian provocateur Sergei Kuryokhin's posing as a historian on the May 17, 1991, episode of the popular cultural-historical television program "The Fifth Wheel" *(Piatoe koleso)*. He gave a long lecture that supposedly revealed some previously unknown facts about Lenin, such as that he and his followers were eager consumers of certain hallucinogenic mushrooms found in Russian forests, which altered their personalities and effectively turned them into mushrooms. Since Kuryokhin's performance reproduced the rhetoric and form of authoritative televisual discourse so faithfully, the "mushroom hoax" caused temporary confusion even among educated audiences. The effect was similar to the elaborate anti-corporate hoaxes committed by "The Yes Men," to Charlie Brooker's "How to Report the News," and to Colbert's faithful performance of Bill O'Reilly (Boyer & Yurchak, 2010).

This way of defamiliarizing Soviet-style rhetoric was widely exercised within the region, by the pop music group *AVIA* in the Soviet Union, the Orange Alternative *(Pomarańczowa Alternatywa)* movement in Poland, the literary and music performances of Dmitri Prigov, the highly ritualized daily life of the artistic group Mit'ki, the performances of "man-dog" Oleg Kulik, and the work of East Berlin's Prenzlauer Berg artists, among others (Boyer & Yurchak, 2010). Perhaps best known among these performances are those of the Russian Necrorealist collective and the originally Yugoslavian artist-political group Neue Slowenische Kunst (NSK), both of which have continued their activities into the post-Cold War decades. The groups' main strategy is to reproduce both communist and capitalist rhetoric to excess, which isolates and critiques the shared discursive and political elements between the two. NSK was established in Slovenia in 1984. The music group Laibach has been the most famous "department" of NSK, ever since their first public appearance on the Slovenian cultural-political TV magazine *TV Tednik* ("TV Weekly") in 1983, where they wore military uniforms and used a quote from Hitler as their inspiration for what became their "Nazi-Kunst." They later adopted a quote from Stalin as their slogan: "We, LAIBACH, are the engineers of human souls." In 1992, NSK created their own "State in Time," a global state without a territory that issues its own passport to anyone who applies and opens embassies and consulates wherever they are invited (Kovačević, 2008). In a gesture worthy of Stephen Colbert, they also developed a practice named "NSK Garda," whereby they hire local army personnel to guard the NSK flag in the countries they visit. This reproduction of a standard nationalistic ritual through interchangeable props and in the service of a fictional, deterritorialized state foregrounds the fact that nation-states are secured by patriotic rituals of violence (Kovačević, 2008).

The Hungarian program *Heti hetes* also owes a great deal to the satirical sensibility of late socialism. However, it also shows a deep continuity with a much older, national tradition of political cabaret. This legacy compels a more subtle analysis, which foregrounds the crucial importance of different national traditions for the formation and circulation of satirical humor. At the same time, the program also bears the effects of profound postsocialist media change in the past two decades, which makes it a prime example of a historical transition and convergence between socialist and capitalist political satire.

HUNGARIAN POLITICAL CABARET AND *HETI HETES*

György Ónodi, the creator of *Heti hetes*, said in a recent video interview: "They tried to make the same program in Poland, but canceled it after four episodes. This is a Hungarian program; it's Hungarian political cabaret. The way the *chanson* is French, this kind of political cabaret is ours" ("Az utolsó"). Let me put in historical relief the implications of this statement.

In socialist Hungary, political thawing began relatively early, shortly after the failed 1956 anti-Soviet revolution, when János Kádár began his 30-year authoritarian reign as Secretary General of the socialist party. Television, which became a mass medium around this time, almost immediately adapted political humor from Hungarian Radio, which had itself absorbed the legacy of stage cabaret. The first Hungarian-language cabaret, The Bonbonier, opened in Budapest in 1907 (Apats, 2007). From the beginning, cabaret meant something very different from the term's French original: Rather than a variety show with light entertainment and lewd jokes, it elevated political satire to the level of a serious public forum. Cabaret was a progressive space, where comedians directly responded to current political events with wit and courage. The best writers of the time wrote and performed on stage, many of them former journalists for whom journalism and political satire were two sides of the same coin. At the end of World War I, there were about 30 cabarets in Budapest. By the end of World War II, there were about 50, despite increasing anti-Semitism and, after 1939, mass deportations, which devastated the cabaret since most comedians were Jewish (Rick, 2008). It was in these years that performers assembled a rhetorical toolkit that bypassed the ears of the pro-German police and was to be deployed successfully during socialism. These strategies included slips of the tongue, playing dumb, ambiguity and double language, and performances of overidentification.

After the devastation of the war, theaters needed to be rebuilt. The first cabaret reopened as early as 1945, followed by many others. For a few years, until communist dictatorship took power, there seemed to be a true opportunity to turn political humor into the language of a broad public sphere, widening its niche, cosmopolitan appeal beyond the capitol. The forced communist takeover in 1949 squashed such hopes and planted mistrust against the government again. Censorship became dogmatic; it struck down on political satire and banned political cabaret. It was considered by the party leadership a self-serving, cynical bourgeois pastime, which had no place in the communist society of the future (Alpár, 2011). Cabaret could be banned but not silenced, however. It simply applied the forms of *stiob* overidentification as early as the 1950s–1960s that Soviet political humor was to take in the 1970s–1980s. Comedians of the time, first on stage and radio and increasingly on television, demonstrated excessive rhetorical loyalty to party requirements of behavior and thinking. They memorized revolutionary slogans and songs, pointed out the moral corruption of capitalism with zeal, and celebrated factory workers for their productivity. They did so while winking at the audience, who well understood the parodic intent of such extreme performances (Faragó, 1984).

The post-1956 thawing, in anticipation of what was to happen in more dictatorial countries of the Soviet bloc a decade or so later, reestablished the "man of the street," or the Budapest petit-bourgeois of the original political cabaret, as its comedic hero, with unspoken Party approval. By the 1970s, the performative leverage afforded to comedians expanded to openly poking fun at socialist bureaucracy, the deceitfulness of official news, or the shortage of consumer products. Comedian Géza Hofi embodied the voice of late socialist political cabaret, probably the most liberal of its kind in the region. His New Year's Eve comedy standup TV specials were eagerly awaited as media events and national celebrations, and continue to be fondly remembered as the golden standard of political cabaret.

However, the more of socialism's weaknesses satirists were allowed to point out, the less it all mattered. Increasing freedom of expression went along with satire's decreasing subversive edge. Instead of censoring or even opposing criticism, the regime increasingly adopted a policy of tolerance towards it, where socialist rhetoric still prevailed but the boundaries of censorship became elastic. The Party's willingness to embrace its critics and laugh at its own shortcomings effectively coopted its intellectual opposition.

Perhaps this state of ambivalence is where the parallel with contemporary political satire is most noticeable. By the mid-1980s, political satire descended into self-serving "joking around" for the most part. This was also an indication that the political and economic transition toward capitalism had been well underway in late socialist Hungary in the heart of state-controlled television. The era associated with the height of political humor in the region was routinely assessed by Hungarian critics of the 1980s as a state of decline and irrelevance (Csepeli, 1984; Faragó, 1984; Kristóf, 1980). *Heti hetes*, although a product of a much diversified television landscape, carries the sense of decline and ambivalence from late socialism into neoliberal capitalism. It is to be examined, precisely, as a model for a successful conversion of a national and regional legacy of political humor on television into postsocialist, global circumstances.

The German show *Sieben Tage, sieben Köpfe*, which inspired creator Ónodi and his team, ran on RTL on Friday nights from 1996 to 2005. The program featured presenter Jochen Busse, five permanent celebrities, and one revolving guest, typically from the world of comedy. The German show was eventually canceled due to low ratings when it transpired that a team of writers produced the jokes to be delivered by the celebrities, as is also customary with American comedy programs. My recent informal survey among German academics rang no bells whatsoever when I mentioned the show in 2011. This is hardly the case with *Heti hetes*, which has received consistently high ratings in Hungary since it was launched in September of 1999. In 2001 it earned the Kamera Hungaria audience award in the "Most Popular TV Show" category. It has stayed among the 25 most watched Hungarian programs and earned an audience share of 32–35% ("Heti nézettség" 2010). This has been so despite its late starting time of 9:50 p.m. on Sunday night and the fact that RTL's rival channel, TV2, has made targeted efforts to lure viewers away from the program in the same time slot ("Verebest" 2010).

No one can accuse the show of being overly scripted, which is one important reason for its endurance. Its ad-lib quality was evident when original host Jenő Csiszár opened the very first program with an unwieldy sentence punctuated by awkward pauses, which he eventually brought to a close by declaring that he was not sure what exactly would happen on the new show. One of the celebrity guests interrupted the cringe-worthy silence, "It seems that we'll mostly embarrass ourselves." This opened the floodgate of funny banter that has since marked the program's dynamic.

Permanent *Hetes* member János Gálvölgyi speculated on the show's longevity in a recent interview: "The key to its success, I think, if we remove all the forced explanations, is that people are simply interested in the seven guys who sit there; they are interested in what these guys have to say about the world" (Apats, 2011). Audience responses, especially in online discussions, also suggest that loyalty to the show is mostly due the long-standing popularity of its guests. Besides the basic requirement of wit, most of the seven participants combine respectable status as public personalities with distinguished careers in some form of performance, which, in some cases, go back to the beginning of socialist television. Gálvölgyi is typical in this regard. He was launched to fame as a parodist on the 1968 national television talent show *Ki Mit Tud*, a lavish annual event on a socialist television otherwise fairly deprived of entertainment programming. He has been a fixture of TV comedy ever since, while also sustaining a career as a stage actor. His own humorous weekly half-hour television show, *The Gálvölgyi Show*, has been on the air since 1991, first on the national broadcaster MTV and since 1998 on RTL Klub. Along with three other permanent *Hetes* members, he was a frequent guest on the radio program *Rádiókabaré KFT*, whose regular segment "*A hónap hírei*" ("News of the Month") anticipated the dynamic of *Heti hetes*.

Similar to Gálvölgyi, all permanent members and most of the revolving guests on the show represent the most visible and witty segment of the intellectual elite. In a small nation-state such as Hungary, such an elite is thoroughly interconnected. Since they are constantly in the public eye, they also enjoy an unprecedented degree of intimacy with their national audience, one solidified in previous eras of precarious political comedy. This has major consequences that are peculiar to the program and its national context. One is that the guests can afford to behave like family members or old friends, whose interaction involves a great deal of teasing and personal digressions. For instance, Imre Bajor is constantly reminded of his baldness and Tivadar Farkasházy of his speech impediment. Such digressions often take up much of the airtime and become the main attraction of the show, to the extent that it is hard for the host to reel in the jokes or even to get through the brief news articles that structure the program. The viewer accustomed to the strict professionalism of American programming would be stunned by the loose structure and personal tone of the show. But it is precisely this leisurely spontaneity and intimacy of the discussion that makes the audience connect with the Seven. On the January 31, 2011, program, the microphones had technical difficulties. While the show is taped on Fridays following a Thursday night meeting among the guests, the final broadcast of this program included the bit where the technician came in to fix the microphones, while the guests involved him in joking conversation. On the January 2, 2011, program, the host, László Jáksó, interrupted his own monologue to turn to someone in the studio audience who was apparently eating crackers from a rattling bag. Far from being irritated by the incident, Jáksó noted it was "cute" that viewers would feel comfortable enough to snack, and asked them to share their crackers with the panel members. This, of course, launched a domino of subsequent jokes.

There is another side to the very familiarity that gives the show its distinctive character among the many other comedic programs that have sprung up since the end of socialism. In online discussions, viewers often criticize the fact that most of the Seven are men well over 50, unattractive, and repetitive.[2] In response, the producers have made efforts to refresh the panel by younger faces, most notably by adding András Hajós as a permanent panelist in 2004, the same year that the original host, Csiszár, was replaced by Jáksó. Hajós, a musician-comedian in his early 40s, had established himself as the lead singer of a rock band and has recently become one of the most familiar television faces, having hosted several of his own talk shows, including one on the Hungarian Comedy Central ("Csak egy," 2008).

The single woman among the core panelists is Judit Hernády, a popular actress-singer who has been a regular contributor to television comedy since the 1970s but, like Gálvölgyi, has also garnered a reputation as a serious stage actress. Her presence sets in relief the profound masculinism of the public sphere as it manifests itself on television. The other six guests each embody certain comedic character functions, which no doubt originate in early cabaret: the naïve one, the smartypants, the clown, the vulgar type, the sophisticated cosmopolitan, the tolerant one. Hernády is first and foremost "the woman." As the only woman, she assumes the responsibility of representing all women with diligence: When the discussion becomes explicitly sexist, she comments from "the" female perspective. It is her "natural" lot and duty to talk about the personal sphere of the nuclear family. She is the only one on the panel who willingly and often speaks about herself as a parent, evoking her daughter so frequently that she is almost a virtual character on the show.

At the same time, as a respectable artist, she has also earned the right to sit at the boys' table. This exempts her from having to perform Riviere's classic female masquerade; it is not a coincidence that she is not a stereotypically attractive woman but someone known for her deep voice and tall, masculine stature. This puts her in a strange double position. Often the conversation is so testosterone-filled (compared to the much more restrained sexism of US television) that she has no choice but to engage in vulgarity herself—commenting on her own breasts, vagina, or sex life in an objectifying manner. Given Hernády's honorary status as one of the boys, it is less contradictory that Gálvölgyi talks in the interview above about "the seven guys" on the show (Apats, 2011), or that Farkasházy can say about his co-panelists in another interview, "This is my second family. I love these boys" ("Az utolsó," 2010).

---

[2]See http://www.hoxa.hu/?p1=forum_tema&p2=21887&p4=0 and http://www.sg.hu/listazas.php3?id=967998 509&order=reverse&index=1.

This complete blindness to the sexism embedded in the fabric of the show—as in the fabric of public discourse in general—is another constitutive feature of the national intimacy within the expanded national family embodied by the Seven. While the producers have experimented with other female guests, few of them have been as successful at mediating between the two roles (of "the woman" and of "one of the boys") as Hernády. The episode when young Roma singer Ibolya Oláh was a guest has gone down in *Hetes* history as a massive flop, with most reviews blaming Oláh for "freezing up." In fact, as a young Gypsy woman from a small town, she was at several degrees of remove from the old, privileged, white men of the Budapest artist world, whose "national" discourse suddenly revealed itself to be narrow and exclusive. A similar episode featured 30-something visual artist Kriszta Nagy Tereskova as a guest on the January 2, 2011, program. Tereskova, who borrowed her artist's name from the first female astronaut, assumes a public persona that could be described as a critical postfeminism: She performs to excessive perfection the social norms of behavior imposed on women. In the show's tight brotherly environment (and in Hernády's absence that week), she had little opportunity to assert herself, but toward the end of the program she took a meta-stand (reminiscent of Jon Stewart on *Crossfire*) and pointed out how unmercifully the men had laughed at her. She reached out to Hajós, the youngest and presumably most open-minded of them. In response, Hajós explained to her with marked condescension that the program was not a good place for "feminist and ecohysterical" views and proceeded to call her "kitten." Despite this dismissal, this was still a rare moment of self-reflection, when the program's, and by expansion, national political comedy's, underlying gendered rules were forced into articulation.

Another area where the program shows a clear continuity with late socialist and contemporary capitalist satire alike is in its cautious approach to politics. Ónodi takes pains in interviews to reiterate the political neutrality of the program and defend it from accusations of leaning to the left. This tends to come through in a "protesting too much" fashion not unlike Jon Stewart's similar claims to even-handedness ("Hajós Andras," 2004; Kalmár, 2009). Ultimately, however, even the explicitly political discussions tend to be somewhat toothless. Ónodi emphasizes that RTL Klub imposes no censorship on the show, but that it would be unnecessary anyway as he exercises self-censorship to decide what is appropriate (Kalmár, 2009). The seasoned panelists of the program are also well-versed in self-censorship which, in the era of alleged free speech, is applied in two main directions: on the one hand, towards the corporate ship RTL Klub, beholden to ratings and profit, and invested in keeping its viewership as broad as possible in a small country that cannot afford much niche programming. On the other hand, in a country organized along an intimate familiar dynamic, the political and intellectual elites continue to be deeply interconnected. In addition, the political leadership swings widely every four years after state elections, rewriting laws and setting new directions for the future. Much like under socialism, media personalities need to be cautious not to offend if they want to survive election cycles. Moreover, even though RTL Klub is a commercial channel, it is still subject to state regulation, which has recently tightened under the right-wing FIDESZ government's 2010 media law, an attempt to recentralize control over the media and curtail freedom of expression, which caused an international uproar and cast a shadow over the launch of Hungary's six-month European Union presidency in January 2011. On the show, discussion of the law and other controversial steps taken by the FIDESZ government have been couched in subtle satire and a form of double speak that evokes the rhetoric of the 1970s–1980s, when self-censorship replaced official censorship.

An example and historically specific aspect of the panelists' self-censorship is the deep-rooted connection between Jewishness and oppositional humor. While communism put a lid on issues of Jewishness in order to suppress an honest reckoning of Hungary's shameful Nazi alliance, the recent surge of the radical right, enabled by the internet and local television stations such as Echo TV, has mobilized anti-Semitism among other ethnophobic-nationalist discourses in a frightening way, often lashing out at the "unpatriotic-communist-Jewish" messages spread by *Heti hetes*. Understandably, the panelists themselves stay clear of identifying themselves as Jews both on and off the air, in a notable difference from American-Jewish comedians such as Jerry Seinfeld, Larry David, or Jon Stewart.

As a result of the global debt crisis and the crisis of the European Union, nativist nationalism has been successfully mobilized by most postsocialist ruling parties to develop what are best described as neoliberal authoritarianisms. (As a ritual confirmation of its ideological-economic affiliations, the FIDESZ government, led by charismatic semi-dictator Viktor Orbán, recently hosted Condoleezza Rice to erect a bronze statue of Ronald Reagan in Budapest's "Freedom Square" in front of the Parliament Building in the summer of 2011.) Although neoliberal authoritarianism has released an avalanche of word-of-mouth political jokes in the streets of Budapest, public media venues, particularly television, have toned down the critical edge of their humor, especially when it became clear that the Orbán government does not shy away from personal retribution against its opposition. The cooptation, even complicity of public intellectuals with state politics has become glaringly evident in the current situation, not unlike it was in the 1980s. The structural similarity to the compromised situation of US late night political TV comics is also obvious, even though the limits of their criticism are determined by media corporations beholden to advertising, rather than by political parties.

Heti Hetes thus functions as a linchpin through which to foreground surprising structural affinities among late socialist, postsocialist and late capitalist political satire on TV. While I have highlighted the historical trajectory of the program's nationally specific appeal in order to temper sweeping generalizations, my intention is to point to political television comedy as a place where long-held ideological assumptions about television systems, democracy and censorship break down. In particular, a serious comparative study of late socialist and late capitalist television satire renders untenable the enduring Cold War distinctions between free speech and censorship, democracy and dictatorship.

POSTSCRIPT

As I write, the Murdoch empire is being shaken by the British phone hacking scandal that came to light in July 2011. If one needed any more justification for the parallel between the political circumstances that gave rise to satire news in late socialism and contemporary capitalism, this would certainly be it. While "empire" has mostly been used metaphorically to describe News Corporation, the fact that Murdoch and his trusted executives (most notably his heir James) kept much of the celebrity world under secret surveillance, that they spent massive sums of money keeping people silent about this, and that they collaborated with the police and most likely the government draws up even formerly unsuspected similarities with the late Soviet empire's media operations. The international reach of corporate media power is even more extensive than was that of the Kremlin within the Soviet empire.

The analogy that emerges here between late socialist and late capitalist forms of political communication shifts standard explanations of the recent popularity of political satire in the

United States. Television satire is more than an effect of technological change, a marginalized outlet for leftist liberals, or a cynical corporate forum that perpetuates what it criticizes, like *The Simpsons*. It has an unarticulated but formative global dimension: Political television is one of the terrains where the United States' changing position in the world is being processed. The proliferation of satire is a response to the increase in self-referential absurdity into which much political discourse has devolved since the end of the Cold War, which has only intensified since the terrorist attacks of September 11, 2001. In the absence of a global antagonist, US political and news media discourses have had to ground themselves in tautologies that write off socialism as a failure and confirm, through incessant repetition, that neoliberal democracy is the single guarantor of that mysterious, self-explanatory condition, "freedom." This is a mechanism not unlike socialist propaganda's incessant, self-justifying posing as the guarantor of unity, solidarity, equality and, yes, freedom. The growing voice of satire news and political comedy, while always grounded in specific sociohistorical contexts, as Serra Tinic (2009) reminds, inevitably leads us to this larger geopolitical situation, with its unexpected historical parallels. It might even lead us to discover some unintended ethnocentrism within media studies' stubborn US or Western-centrism, and encourage us to revisit socialist media in more depth for its potential lessons.

REFERENCES

Alpár, Á. (2011). A pesti kabaré. Retrieved from http://tbeck.beckground.hu/szinhaz/htm/25.htm

Apats, G. (2011). Gálvölgyi János: A Heti hetes arra jó, hogy ne hülyüljek el. Retrieved from http://www.origo.hu/teve/20110217-interju-galvolgyi-janossal-a-madach-szinhaz-szineszevel-a-galvolgyi-show.html

Apats, G. (2007). Szeszélyes évadok. Retrieved from http://www.origo.hu/teve/20071130-100-eves-a-magyar-kabare-szeszelyes-evszakok-tortenete.html

Az utolsó Heti hetes. (2010, June 12).Video, NOL TV. Retrieved from http://www.noltv.hu/video/2678.html

Baym, G. (2005). *The Daily Show*: Discursive integration and the reinvention of political journalism. *Political Communication, 22,* 259–276.

Boyer, D. (2003). Censorship as vocation: The institutions, practices, and cultural logic of media control in the German Democratic Republic. *Comparative Studies in Society and History, 45,* 511–545.

Boyer, D., & Yurchak, A. (2008, November). Postsocialist studies, cultures of parody and American stiob. *Anthropology News,* 9–10.

Boyer, D., & Yurchak, A. (2010). AMERICAN STIOB: Or, what late-socialist aesthetics of parody reveal about contemporary political culture in the West. *Cultural Anthropology, 25*(2), 179–221.

"Csak egy nap. Bekukucskáltunk a Heti Hetes kulisszái mögé." (2008). Retrieved from http://www.blikk.hu/blikk_csakegynap/20080225/bekukucskaltunk_a_heti_hetes_kulisszai_moge/

Csepeli, G. (1984). A televíziós szórakoztatásról. *Filmvilág, 1,* 59–60. Retrieved from http://filmvilag.hu/xereses_frame.php?cikk_id=6554

Day, A. (2009). And now . . . the news? Mimesis and the real in *The Daily Show*. In J. Gray, J. P. Jones, & E. Thompson (Eds.), *Satire TV: Politics and comedy in the post-network era* (pp. 85–103). New York, NY: New York University Press.

Faragó, M. (1984). Puha humor. *Filmvilág, 9,* 62–63. Retrieved from http://filmvilag.hu/xereses_frame.php?cikk_id=6339

Gray, J., Jones, J., & Thompson, E. (2009). The state of satire, the satire of state. In J. Gray, J. P. Jones, & E. Thompson (Eds.), *Satire TV: Politics and comedy in the post-network era* (pp. 3–36). New York, NY: New York University Press.

Greenwald, R. (Director). (2004). *Outfoxed: Rupert Murdoch's war on journalism* [Documentary]. United States: Carolina Productions.

"Heti nézettség: legyűrte az RTL Klubot a Tv2." (2010, December). Origo. Retrieved from http://www.origo.hu/teve/20101207-legyurte-az-rtl-klubot-a-tv2.html

"Hajós András lesz a Heti hetes új bohóca." (2004, September 1).Velvet Kommandó, Retrieved from http://velvet.hu/celeb/hetihet0901/

Kalmár, C. (2009, September 10). Nem a Heti hetestől várják a választ. *Origo*. Retrieved from |http://www.origo.hu/teve/20090910-nem-a-heti-hetestol-varjak-a-valaszt-onodi-gyorgy.html

Kovačević, N. (2008). Late communist and postcommunist avant-garde aesthetics: Interrogations of community. In C. Muraru (Ed.), *Postcommunism, postmodernism and the global imagination* (pp. 211–230). New York, NY: Columbia University Press.

Kristóf, A. (1980). A kabaré alkonya. *Filmvilág, 1,* 56–57. Retrieved from http://filmvilag.hu/xereses_frame.php?cikk_id=8028

Rick, Z. (2008). A pesti kabarék a II. világháború idején. Retrieved from http://www.mazsike.hu/pesti+kabarek+a+ii+vilaghaboru+idejen.html

Tinic, S. (2009). Speaking "truth" to power? Television satire, *Rick Mercer Report*, and the politics of place and space. In J. Gray, J. P. Jones, & E. Thompson (Eds.), *Satire TV: Politics and comedy in the post-network era* (pp. 167–186). New York, NY: New York University Press.

Verebest is bevetik a Heti hetes ellen. (2010, February 12). Origo. Retrieved from http://www.origo.hu/teve/20100212-verebest-is-bevetik-a-heti-hetes-ellen.html

Zalán, M. (1966). A magyar rádió és televízió belső felépítése és szerkezete. Internal report #753.3, Open Society Archives, Budapest, Hungary.

"The Tattlers' Tattle": Fake News, Linguistic National Intimacy, and New Media in Romania

Alice Bardan

This article analyzes the successful Romanian weekly satire show *Cronica Cârcotaşilor* (*The Tattlers' Tattle*) in the context of the televisual landscape of postsocialist Romania. I argue that given the widespread skepticism toward the unfulfilled promises of the post-socialist transition and the European Union (EU) accession, the show's ability to curb Romanians' disaffection from politics is remarkable. Positioning Romanians as active television viewers and gatekeepers against practices of manipulation and incorrect uses of the Romanian language, the show fosters discursive contestation and activates a desire for political engagement. My discussion introduces the notion of "national linguistic intimacy" to evoke how the show strives to naturalize the affective ties with the national community by reusing the flavor of Romanian comedic and satirical literature and encouraging language play.

Within recent academic debates on postsocialist Central and Eastern Europe, critics frequently emphasize the sharp contrast between the independent press and the politically biased "regime media" that consistently engage in disinformation. When writing about Eastern European media transition, they are apt to link this imputed manipulation of fact to a perception of Eastern European societies as still imbued with precommunist and communist cultural traits that are ultimately inimical to democracy.

Describing Romanian media in particular, critics intimate that there can be no escape from the communist legacy, bemoaning, article after article, that there is little hope for the country to complete a transformation to "true democracy." To be sure, the self-righteous tone and openly racist terminology used to describe Romanian media still needs to be exposed and challenged. The critics' patronizing attitude reveals how many of them are still blinded by the polarized geopolitical divisions that characterize liberal historiography. This ideology is, I contend, problematic, indicative of what some would call "a scare tactic for disciplining citizens into the conviction that there is no alternative to the contemporary late-liberal, capitalist order" (Boyer & Yurchak, 2010, p. 179).

Critics such as Gilbert, Greenberg, Helms, and Jansen (2008) and Dominic Boyer and Alexei Yurchak (2010) provide us with a far more nuanced understanding of the relationship between liberalism and socialism. Without denying the significant institutional differences between late-socialist and late-liberal modes of media and social communication, Boyer and Yurchak convincingly argue that there is "an uncanny family resemblance" (p. 180) between the two, as late liberalism today operates increasingly under discursive and ideological conditions similar to those of late socialism. In other words, political discourse in contemporary US media exhibits tendencies comparable to late socialist hypernormalization, from highly monopolized media production and circulation to ideological consensus in political and economic news analysis.

Writing "against the new Cold War," Alaina Lemon (2008) urges new scholarship on Eastern Europe to "examine 'everyday' life without dismissing its minutiae" (p. 12), refusing to posit the people from the region as passive recipients of "transition" and questioning dominant accounts. Unfortunately, most research and discussions on Eastern European television and media in general tend to follow policy-oriented approaches, suppressing relevant questions on programming content, issues of ideology, and audience (Imre, 2009a, p. 396). They read the national public in an abstract, homogeneous way, privileging questions of media regulation and neglecting to address issues of audience engagement. As critics such as Aniko Imre have pointed out, the emergent processes of globalization and media convergence that are increasingly shifting the attention of media professionals and audiences to interactive new media forms usually tend to remain outside the scope of scholarly investigations.

It is from this perspective that I propose to open up new lines of inquiry on Romanian media. At the center of my investigation is the analysis of the successful Romanian weekly satire show *Cronica Cârcotaşilor* (which translates into English as "The Tattlers' Tattle") in the context of the televisual landscape of post-socialist Romania (the second most populous country in Central Europe). Hosted by Şerban Huidu and Mihai Găinuşă on Prima TV (which was created in 1997 as one of the first commercial television stations in the country), the show deploys humor as a means of establishing social cohesion, while challenging the audience to think about politics in new and imaginative ways. I argue that by eroding the boundary between news and entertainment and by changing the audiences' patterns of consumption, the show significantly broadens engagement with political media content. Indeed, as the numerous responses to the "Tattlers' News" ("Cârco Stiri") posted daily on the show's Facebook page demonstrate, *Cronica Cârcotaşilor* has succeeded in providing an interconnected space of debate around important social and political issues. What is particularly remarkable about the show is that in addition to fostering discursive contestation and activating a certain set of desires for political engagement, it also encourages its fans to imitate the hosts' attitude and style by coining new words and satirical phrases which constantly reinvent and reinvigorate the Romanian language. The show's success needs to be understood in relation to specific geopolitical contingencies and the history of media reception practices in Romania.

I argue for a more complex understanding of fake news shows than the conventional reading of their function as an oppositional mode of critique. In addition, I suggest that by exposing the distortions inherent in the authoritative discourse of Romanian media, *Cronica Cârcotaşilor* does not destabilize the boundaries of the nation but rather facilitates the creation of "national intimacy" (Imre, 2009b) through its ingenious use of language (what I call "linguistic national intimacy"), aiding the formation of a postsocialist public sphere in Romania.

ORIGINS

Cronica Cârcotaşilor is a fake news show that lampoons various celebrities from the current Romanian political, media, and showbiz scene by exposing their hypocrisy, malapropisms, or linguistic stumbles. It is the longest and most successful satire show in the country, still attracting some of the highest ratings on Romanian television. In addition to tracking the latest blunders of politicians and news presenters, *Cronica Cârcotaşilor* also features "Top Ruşinica" ("Hall of Shamy-Shame"), which targets last week's top three TV bloopers; "Tocăniţa de Gazete" ("Newspapers Stew"), which exposes how newspapers distort the news; and interview segments with "Catalin Dezbracatu" ("Catalin the Undressed"), a snobbish character conceived as a parody of Romanian fashion designer Cătălin Botezatu. Like many other global "fake news" shows, the Romanian version intentionally misuses the newscast format, mimicking it and disrupting the dominant political message to make room for competing conversations. Between 2000, when it first aired, and 2010, when it celebrated 10 years of uninterrupted programming, *Cronica* had more than 300 shows, 26,000 bloopers, and 8,500 "memorable" guests caught in embarrassing situations.

Deliberately conceived to sound a cacophony, the title of the show is meant to represent the situation in which Romania—or, as the presenters call it in diminutive, "Românica" ("Teeny-Tiny Romania") or "Românica care" ("Teeny-Tiny Romania who . . . ")—found itself after 1989. Functioning both as a noun and as an adjective in Romanian, "cârcotaş" refers to a "tattler," a fault-finding, cantankerous, or grumpy person. The main source of inspiration for the show is *Striscia la Notizia*, an Italian satirical program of fake news on Berlusconi's Canale 5 (discussed by Constentino in this special issue). In recent years, however, the two hosts have sought to dissociate themselves from any associations with *Striscia*, stressing that they only followed a format with dancing girls and serious things said in a funny way. When in 2010 Canale 5 sued Prima TV for copyright violation (Paleanu, 2010), Huidu and Găinuşă defended themselves by pointing out that they came up with their own version, *Cârcotasii in Europa* ("The Tattlers in Europe"), which they insisted was an "original format for Romania." In defense of his show, Huidu argued that one could as well blame "The Tattlers in Europe" format for having plagiarized other well-known shows produced by Discovery Channel which feature "travelling abroad" formats.

CRONICA CÂRCOTAŞILOR AND FAKE NEWS

In the broadest sense, *Cronica Cârcotaşilor* targets the medium of television itself and what it does to news and the state of political debate in Romania. Şerban Huidu and Mihai Găinuşă position themselves as instruments of "organized rhyme" and of "popular bickering," denouncing the popular TV news for its unprofessional overreliance on "spite, accusations, and scorn" (Istodor, 2003). Blaming local television news media for a host of societal ills, the two satirists lament that Romanians are constantly bombarded with "toxic news" that, on the one hand, is explicitly graphic in its depiction of violence and, on the other hand, is based on "constructive complaints" by a society intensely preoccupied with tattling on others (Bujenita, 2005). From this perspective, their show becomes, as Huidu puts it, a "tattlers' tattle" that draws on the viewers' constant feedback and urges them to "remain vigilant."

The website for the Romanian show (http://cronica.primatv.ro/) enables interactivity with its fans, enhancing active collaboration and participation. The homepage asks viewers to report what they see as embarrassing on TV or radio, to "like" the show on Facebook, and to read the feeds from the Twitter account "Cârcotaşii." The website streams content segments of about 30 minutes each from both the television and radio versions of the show, making them searchable through a well-organized archive. In addition, it features "Cârco Ştiri" ("Tattlers' News"), which provides real, but alternative news, and a section titled "Cronica Newz," which updates the fans on the latest adventures of the show's team.

One example of such "Tattlers' News" posted on the Facebook account is the news tagged as "Bad news for taxi drivers." By clicking on it, one is sent to the show's website, where the wider context of this "bad news" can be explored:

> RATB [Autonomous Transportation in Bucharest] introduces nighttime public transport opportuni-
> ties. One could say they're making it a club. Really, if the traffic lights work at intersections, they
> will even have disco balls, pole-dancing, and perhaps hear *manele* from convertibles passing by. Will
> they eventually introduce happy hour, with discounts?

In this case, the hosts parody the "good news" about public transportation extended during night-time in Bucharest (a piece of news celebrated on the media with the tagline "RATB takes into account its travelers' wishes") by turning it into "fake news" about how poor taxi drivers will have less business at night. The implication is that because fewer people travel during the night, the tram poles will at last be visible. This, in turn, will be enough to create a party atmosphere with the functioning traffic light providing the festive touch. The scenario created by *Cronica* thus pokes fun at the capital's trams and buses, indirectly criticizing the conditions they provide for passengers.

Through examples such as the one above, the Romanian show lays bare the mechanisms by which news reporting is able to mediate the experience of events. In other words, *Cronica* appro-priates an official piece of information and remediates it, furthering its own narrative, "making it strange," or defamiliarizing it. As McKain (2005) has noted, the point is not that the "real news" indexes to comedians in order to gatekeep or to interject instances that are funny, but that despite the façade of benign joking, something more serious is going on.

Speaking about *The Daily Show* on American television, Geoffrey Baym (2005) argues that such shows are no longer simply "fake" but "oppositional news" that reveal the existence of a new kind of journalism enabled by the turn toward convergence culture. In recent years, the critic points out, such shows have been reconceptualized as assemblages of fluid content that is open to reappropriation by an increasingly sophisticated audience. By exploring the borderlines between discursive domains, by making themselves accessible through different media, these shows compel us to reconsider the ways in which we traditionally think about news content, distribution patterns, and its relationship to the audience. As Baym (2009) points out, follow-ing Yochai Benkler, "the driving engine in new media is not so much mass appeal, but rather deep engagement among a narrow and highly committed subset of people [. . .] What begins on television as a moment of critical comment and a moment of public exposure becomes on the Internet a node within a wider network of information and discussion" (p. 149). In this respect, *Cronica Cârcotaşilor* actively reconceptualizes the audience by opening spaces of discussion and exchange where the "cârcommunity," as they call it, can engage in serious political discussion.

Găinuşă interacts with his fans not only on television and radio but also through his books, which are an extension of his writing for the show. Since 2007, he also writes a blog where he demands serious engagement from his fans, addressing them directly. Huidu also constantly updates his own blog, where he discusses Romanian politics, recommends books to readers, or incites his fans to comment on his photos of the most beautiful places in Romania. Often, the show's Facebook updates send the fans to this blog. "Mistreţu'" ("The Wild Boar"), another member of the *Cronica* team who regularly impersonates the president or plays the role of

"Agent Tuzgureanu," a clumsy policeman, engages with the show's fans on his own blog. Last but not least, the fans can discuss the news on the show's forum or upload and comment clips on YouTube.

Such "interactive journalism" (Nip, 2006) demonstrates that the Romanian public is not passive but rather actively engages with the show on a regular basis and through various media platforms. Indeed, as a form of "convergence culture" (Jenkins, 2006), this new type of interaction with Romanian media consumers has indeed altered the logic by which media industries operate and by which media consumers process news and entertainment.[1]

BĂSESCU HITTING A CHILD

During a 2008 speech in Raleigh, North Carolina, President Barak Obama momentarily scratched his cheek with two fingers. Unnoticed by most viewers, this innocent gesture ended up being discussed at great length by an anchor in the MSNBC coverage of the primaries, who speculated that Obama clandestinely made an inappropriate gesture of "flip-off" directed at Hillary Clinton, his rival. When showing a clip with an MSNBC anchor reporting "news" that Obama made an unfortunate gesture that "some think it's a flip-off. You can judge," Jon Stewart, the famous host of *The Daily Show*, "clapped his hands and exclaimed: 'Obama gave Hillary the finger? She thinks? But she is going to let us judge!'" (Boyer & Yurchak, 2010, p. 210).

In a similar situation, during a speech given when he was running for a second term, Romanian president Traian Băsescu was "caught on tape hitting a child" as he kneeled to pick up a piece of paper that a woman who was pushing through the crowd was desperately trying to give him. Initially reported in the newspaper *Gardianul*, "the news" created a media event, if not national hysteria. Various television channels replayed and dissected the video, commenting on the significance of "what happened" and bringing in specialists to assess whether the video was a hoax or whether the footage showed Basescu "hitting with his fist" or merely pushing the child. On YouTube, numerous videos about the incident were uploaded and discussed at great length.

Cronica Cârcotaşilor responded to the scandal with a sketch in which actors reenacted the event with three alternative scenarios that isolated gestural performance. In the first one, a fidgety Basescu tells people that "together with our allies, the liberals still allied, I promise you an astonishing thing: you will live well, hah, hah, hah." When the woman shouts at him that she wants to give him something, he replies, laughing at his own joke, "Yes, as long as it is plum-made (brandy)!" When "the child" exclaims "Long live Patriciu" (Dinu Patriciu, the richest man in Romania and prominent member of the National Liberal Party), the president slaps him almost by instinct. In the second version of the scene, Basescu this time says that 2009 will bring a new economic crisis and "you won't live well, hah, hah, hah." When the woman predicts a bad year for him, he again responds with a joke, "Impossible! Winter is not like summer!" (Romanian expression). This time, the child makes slow-motion gestures with his hands, warning "Bee-waaare off Paa-Triiii-ciu." Finally, in the third version, the president's speech is reduced to short phrases, "Dear Voters, blah blah blah. The mafiots and the moguls, blah blah blah. You will live

---

[1] One can read these blogs at http://Găinuşă.wordpress.com/, http://www.şerbanhuidu.ro/, http://www.mistretzu.ro/, http://cronica.primatv.ro/forum/, and http://www.gogaie.ro/.

well!" When the woman calls his name, he appears befuddled, playfully imitating the lyrics of a popular Romanian song, "Who is calling me in the ni-ight, ha-ha-ha?" In the end, when he tries to hit the child, the latter punches him back, asking a friend nearby, "Have you caught everything on tape?"[2]

The primary conceit of this reenactment, as with *The Daily Show*, is not so much to change the news (to offer the "true" version) but rather to expose how media strive to divert people's attention away from real political debate toward the *performative* dimension of political life. Whether Basescu hit the child or not becomes irrelevant in the three reenactments. The show does not focus on exposing false intentions or uncovering hidden motifs, but rather aims to convert iterations into symptoms as gestural or linguistic performances characterized by repetition rather than signification (Bennett, 2009, p. 211). Basescu's speech ("You will live well" or "You will have a tough year, blah blah blah") thus seems ventriloquized, spoken in solidified chunks ("the mafiots and the moguls"), reduced to mimicry. The show thus addresses, as Jill Bennett would put it, a politics in which belief can no longer be tied to empirical truth in a simple or demonstrable way.

What remains in the three reenactments is a series of corporeal signs, "bodies performing actions that exceed the banal self-descriptions of performers and witnesses" (Bennett, 2009, p. 203). One could interpret this segment in the way Brian Massumi (2002) analyzed Reagan's speeches and their mime effect of interruption, mime being understood here as decomposing movement. Reagan, Massumi suggests, contracted into his person "operations that might be argued to be endemic to late-capitalist, image and information-based economies. Think of the image/expression—events in which we bathe. Think interruption [. . .] Think of the distractedness of television viewing" (p. 42). Thus, whether Băsescu anticipates a good or bad year or whether he hits the child or not and is "seen" by witnesses or the camera filming the event loses relevance. In restaging the media event of Băsescu purportedly hitting a child, *Cronica Cârcotaşilor* highlights in the president his characteristic mode of laughter, his confidence, and the timbre of his voice.

FAKE NEWS AND ALTERNATIVE POLITICAL CRITIQUES

Commenting on the role of his show on Romanian politics, Găinuşă once remarked with regret that despite his relentless efforts to expose media newscasts and pundits, nothing has changed in the ten years since the show first aired. Writing about Italian satire shows such as *Striscia la Notizia*, Franca Roncarolo (2004) is similarly skeptical about their potential to play a significant role in Italian politics. Arguing that ambushing politicians has become a trend and that Berlusconi (a populist at heart and a defender of his right to be informal in formal situations) has adapted quickly to the fake news style of coverage, she warns that in playing the game of catching politicians red-handed and embarrassing them, the media not only risk desensitizing the public but also feed the silent majority's opportunity to identify with populist leaders. Along similar lines, Jonathan Gray (2009) argues that fake news shows may help public figures author

---

[2]The reenactments can be seen on YouTube at http://www.youtube.com/watch?v=pvywQviVg.

their image, cautioning that satiric attack "risks perpetuating a notion of politics as being peopled and controlled by individuals, not institutions per se" (p. 164).

Examining the function of fake news shows, in what follows I argue that we need to understand them as performing a mode of critique which is not merely oppositional, but also operates "from within" or, as Jacques Rancière puts it, as aesthetics, simultaneously producing an understandable form of political signification and creating an experience that resists signification (Boyer & Yurchak, 2010, p. 212). Drawing on critics such as Massumi and Bennett, I wish to challenge the argument that the targeting of politicians on fake news shows merely creates opportunities for the masses to identify with them. As these critics underscore, politicians such as Bush and Reagan were "not successful in spite of their stumbles, malapropisms, and misadventures with language but almost because of them" (Bennett, 2009, p. 200). Such leaders understood and exploited the appeal of plain talking, yet "there is more at stake here than identification with the home-spun persona" (p. 200). For Massumi (2002), Reagan's mode of communication was affective, as opposed to emotional; it had nothing to do with empathy, emotive identification, "or any form of identification for that matter" (p. 40).

Under late socialism, when state-sponsored political discourse became oversaturated with dry, repetitive formulations (which distanced the authoritative discourse of the party from its desired intimate connection with the language of its citizen subjects), the question of whether any form of satire could affect *change* was similarly posed, and reality demonstrated how impossible such a task could be. In order to be politically correct, one had to adhere to *form*, so newspapers and other media invested considerable energy in negotiating a perfected language of political communication, the wooden language of propaganda. This entailed phraseological formulations rehashed ad nauseam, sentences with complex structures, and an adherence to precise objective norms in which the individual voice and subjective interpretation were minimized. Boyer and Yurchak (2010) persuasively argue that such conditions led to the creation of a particular parodic genre, which they call "stiob." Unlike sarcasm or cynicism, *stiob* irony implies a process of overidentification with what one criticizes (be it a person, an idea, or an object) to such a degree that it becomes impossible to tell whether the speaker is engaging in a sincere report or subtly ridiculing the target.

As Boyer and Yurchak astutely assert, in the context of such strict control over language, new constraints on the production of discourse emerged that were not necessarily planned by a centralized authority (p. 181). Rather, the conditions of oversaturated discourse mobilized a "performative shift" in communication, "away from constative (literal and semantic meaning) toward performative meaning" (p. 181). In other words, the practice of *stiob* or identification, had a *greater* potential to signal critical opposition (articulated in the language of *form* itself) than any direct ironic attack.

Boyer and Yurchak suggest that political discourse in contemporary US media reveals tendencies which are comparable to late-socialist normalization and are frequently exposed by comedians such as Jon Stewart and Stephen Colbert. Constantly drawing attention to recursive, citational, and performative tendencies in US political discourse, a satirist such as Stewart does not parody real news but rather provides a complex commentary on how media organize their coverage of politics. One of the ways of doing this is to expose how media tend to use a language dominated by repeated scripts and predictable rhetoric, for instance the obsessive focus on formal devices of representation that obscures understanding of the political process (p. 192). Colbert goes a step further than Stewart and literally inhabits formulaic political rhetoric through a process of overidentification with the language and performative style of populist news commentary.

The point, therefore, is not so much to "challenge" or "embarrass" political figures or celebrities in satire shows but rather to seek critical scrutiny through overidentification, as Tina Fey did in her famous imitation of Sarah Palin by inhabiting the language of her target. Critics such as Boyer and Yurchak argue against a politics of opposition by speaking "truth to power" in an effort of resistance and critique. However valuable, mere opposition for them ultimately is "unable to get critical traction on the discursive formalization that is part of political expertise itself. To expose hypernormalization, then, a different kind of critical intervention may be necessary, one that focuses on breaking the frame of perception and on causing a sensorial rupture, making that which is invisible and unthinkable suddenly recognized and apprehended" (p. 212).

The way in which fake news shows reiterate and accentuate sequences from news reports, therefore, can be analyzed in terms of how they produce an awareness of intensifications of affect produced by media. Bennett (2009) discusses the significance of gesture as a component of linguistic performance and the critical strategy of reducing a performance to its gestural elements through a process of extraction and recombination. Drawing on Judith Butler's 1997 *Excitable Speech*, she directs attention to a discussion of the experience of speaking belief, of doing something with language—not in the sense of creating an effect with it but of being *within* it, language that confers a speaking position upon us but which must be interiorized and spoken. "The critical function of media," Bennett points out, "arises from the capacity to capture gesture" (p. 200). To capture gesture, she explains, means to capture a face or body sustaining a feeling of insincerity, with feeling here understood not as "emotion," but the moment of awareness of affect through which the self is experienced as a deformation of itself. This feeling, she explains, does not precede its exhibition in media. It is not a characteristic of an individual which the media reveals but rather "a function of being in a medium," a gesture exposed in its mediality.

Doing this special type of critique, as is often the case with the fake news shows, means investigating the body to find out, not so much what language willfully covers up or denies, but "the point at which language fails." Put differently, Bennett argues for a criticism that "reduces expression to gesture," one that captures the condition of not being able to figure something out in language, as a moment *within* language rather than its breakdown or malfunction. Such a critique is particularly significant in our contemporary context, when images of politicians can function effectively by registering a struggle with language.

LINGUISTIC NATIONAL INTIMACY AND DOUBLE SPECTATORSHIP IN ROMANIA

To account for the popularity of *Cronica Cârcotaşilor* in Romania, one has to take into account the way in which the show situates itself in the context of Romanian literature, mobilizing the sketches and comedies of Ion Luca Caragiale, in particular. Born in a family deeply involved in the emancipation of Romanian theatre, Caragiale was an active promoter of satire and wrote plays which became part of the Romanian canon. A perceptive analyst of the ways in which reality is relayed by the media, he was among the first to destroy the myth of objective journalism in Romania. Targeting especially the rumor makers and the newsmongers who manipulated and confused reality in the 19th century newspapers, the writer exposed journalists much in the way *Cronica Cârcotaşilor* tries to do today.

If his world was that of the Romanian Francophile bourgeoisie of the 19th century, who tended to use French socio-political barbarisms, the world exposed in the fake news show is one impacted by the English language, technology, and various processes of coinage, borrowing, compounding, blending, derivation, suffixation, prefixes, and infixes. In one of Caragiale's plays, for instance, Rica Venturiano's use of French socio-political barbarisms in his writing for a pompously titled newspaper leads to inaccurate interpretations by his half-learned readers who confuse "sufragiu" (vote) with "sufragerie" (living room, also derived from French) and "suffrage" (elections). In another instance, the word "mânca" is interpreted as deriving from "manger" (to eat) instead of "manquer" (to miss) the elections. *Cronica Cârcotaşilor* relentlessly exposes similar unfortunate misinterpretations occurring in contemporary Romanian media, especially when the news is announced by unprofessional journalists.[3]

In his article on the artistic sophistication of Ion Luca Caragiale's sketches and grotesque farces, Cristian Stamatoiu (2006) argues that they anticipated the impact of the new media revolution and its forms as an imitation of "pathological situations" of public discourse and communication. Stamatoiu situates Caragiale within the aesthetic environment created by Titu Maiurescu's "Junimea" ("The Youth") literary circle (founded in 1863), whose writers became the founders of Romanian literature. As party leader, minister, prime minister, and political journalist, Maiorescu drew attention to the malfunctions of modern Romanian institutions and was determined to modernize Romania through a systematic assimilation of European values while maintaining the national traditions of the country.

Much like the nationalistic writers of "Junimea," who sought to discover their cultural identity by imitating national elements of literature rather than let themselves be integrated into foreign literary movements, Huidu and Găinuşă tap into the resources of the Romanian canon, reusing the flavor of comedic and satirical literature to facilitate what I call a *linguistic national intimacy*. The two hosts have often expressed unease with the recent impact of various global factors on the linguistic evolution of Romanian (the influence of English and of communication by electronic media for instance). Showing an excessive sensitivity to the esthetic component of the language, they situate themselves as defenders against the contamination of public discourse.

In addition, they stage their show as a reaction to the post-1989 invasion of global information and communication technologies on fresh Eastern European markets. Positioning himself as a member of a particular generation born in the mid-1970s, "too late to be classical and too early to be 'technologized,'" Huidu has asserted that he is suffocated by technology and the rapidly changing cell phone market that does not allow one get used to a certain product (Dutu, 2010). In this respect, Aniko Imre (2009b) has pointed out that although the various changes in communication technologies were reported as a success story for Eastern Europe, the consequences for the public sphere, civic society, and citizen identities and relations are in fact hard to theorize. Drawing on Svetlana Boym's defense of postcommunist nostalgia in Eastern Europe as a necessary exercise to reestablish a sense of posttraumatic cultural identity, Imre acknowledges the need

---

[3] For example, when a French TV station announced a "burr" (blunder) of the NATO air forces during the 1999 war in Kosovo, the news was broadcast by an editor at a Romanian private TV station as a new "bravură" (bravery) of the NATO air forces. In another instance, a television broadcaster whose task was to present a concert on Saint-Saëns adapted the name according to her intelligence by saying "Sans-Sense" (Non-Sense) (Stamatoiu, 2006, p. 6).

to build coherent narratives from the ruins of collective historical memory left after communism (p. 228). Reminding us that the small nations of Eastern Europe for centuries have cultivated an intimacy that goes beyond the bonds of citizenship, Imre defends the often derided backward-looking cultural intimacy created by the return to the familial memory of anti-communism. From this perspective, tracing the links among intimacy, national literature, and practices developed during communism yields multilayered social realities which may help one understand how a fake news show such as *Cronica Cârcotaşilor* attempts to re-establish a sense of posttraumatic cultural identity.

Cronica Cârcotaşilor, I contend, provides an important outlet for the emotional and ideological affiliation with a national culture threatened by rapid change. In a country such as Romania marked by a widespread sense of disappointment with local corruption scandals as well as by a profound sense of skepticism towards the unfulfilled promises of the postsocialist transition and the EU accession, the show's ability to curb Romanians' disaffection from politics is indeed remarkable. The backward look, in this case, is towards Romanian literature and the pleasures it offered under communism for a nation that actively cultivated reading and going to the theater as an alternative to watching propaganda on television. Like many other fake news shows, *Cronica Cârcotaşilor* engages in "political sabotage" (Harold, 2004, p. 190) and acts as a "political culture jammer" (Warner, 2007, p. 21). But what distinguishes it from other glocalized versions of the fake news format is the relentless enticement of people to embrace the cohesive emotional logic of national intimacy. Thus, rather than destabilizing the boundaries of the nation through its critique of media, the show strives to naturalize the affective ties with the national community by attempting to renew a particular Romanian fascination with language use and double-speak. Even as they relentlessly critique Romanian media, Huidu and Găinuşă seek to rebuild a "national family," stressing how the show's team itself has remained unchanged for many years. Quite intriguingly, they even bring their children on the show, proudly displaying them and the fact that they are all part of happy families.

In what follows, I consider the way in which language use takes center stage in the Romanian show more prominently than in other national adaptations. First, the show places great emphasis on exposing grammatical mistakes made on television, demanding that its viewers remain vigilant regarding the presence of illiteracy on television. For example, on the "Carcomunitate" forum one viewer expressed her frustrations for the fact that a news reporter incorrectly said that "luckily, people were *previzibili*" (which translates as "predictable," "avertable," or "foreseeable"—from the French *previsible*) instead of using the correct adjective *prevăzători* (i.e., "wary" or "cautious"). Further, Huidu and Găinuşă's creative use of language manages to shore up the (damaged) identity of an "in-group" that shares a similar context and is able to decode specific references to characters and situations from Romanian literature.

The trauma of being constantly criticized or derided has led Romanians to internalize the Western negative accounts of their country, making them belittle themselves to the point of "self-racism" (Aslama & Pantti, 2007, p. 57). At the same time, however, Romanians also position themselves as having a special status in Eastern Europe and Europe in general. This is because they are the only ones in the region who speak a Romance language and they maintain affinities with Europe, a line of compatibility reinforced even by communists (Drace-Francis, 2003).

In addition, Romanians perceive themselves as having a high level of literacy, a sense of cosmopolitanism, and a deep awareness of foreign languages and cultures. In this respect, they have always taken pride in the fact that they are one of the very few countries in Europe to use subtitles for foreign media instead of dubbing. As dubbing was considered a blasphemous butchering of a text even during communism, the attempts to introduce professional dubbing after 1989 were met with criticism and remained unsuccessful. Dwyer and Uricaru (2009) highlight that Romanian spectators developed a special fondness for the practice of double spectatorship, as they enjoy performing simultaneous comparisons between the "original" soundtrack and the subtitles. Such deep concern with linguistic accuracy has led cinema and television fans to develop Titrari.ro (titrări means "subtitles"), a noncommercial website for translations of foreign media. The serious way in which the problem of translation is discussed on the website reflects the average Romanian's fastidious concern for the flavor of language and accurate language rendition. Last but not least, Romanians also see themselves particularly predisposed to sarcasm, having a tendency to poke fun at everything (they have, after all, a Merry Cemetery!).[4] Huidu attributes the show's success to this understanding, admitting nonetheless that although his team tries to be subtle, the topics tackled by the show are often "grobian" (Dutu, 2010).[5]

The pleasures of watching *Cronica Cârcotaşilor* are thus inextricably tied to the pleasures of discursive contestation and scrutiny of power. Yet these pleasures are also connected to the process of taking comfort in the play of simultaneously decoding and encoding references along with the show's hosts, nostalgically revisiting the haunting familiarity of a linguistic world in which one may sometimes only guess the precise meaning of particular expressions. What stands out for me as I read the average Romanian's online response to the show is how much they relish using exaggerations, linguistic innovations, folk language, dialect, slang, rhetorical devices such as anacoluthon (change of syntax within a sentence), idiomatic syntactic constructions, verbal irony, paronimy, and regionalisms, which ultimately seems to give them an empowering sense of agency.

By practicing double spectatorship, that is, by recognizing and imitating this linguistic world, Romanians ultimately use the platform offered by the show to recreate the sense of national intimacy very much lost in the postsocialist world. As they became increasingly disengaged from a political process they believe largely ignores them and their interests, the Romanian people have gradually lost interest in their sense of national identity. Moreover, the international media's dark vision of Romania, verbalized in a rhetoric of corruption and nationalism, "has entered the national psyche" (Jäckel, 2001, p. 1), producing a crisis of credibility in the individual's power to affect any meaningful change.

Over the past 11 years, *Cronica Cârcotaşilor* has managed to build up a sense of solidarity and intimacy among citizens that, to a certain extent, replaced the prevailing sense of media saturation and indifference to politics. The show's success rests on its ability to engage Romanians by valuing their input while providing a context that encourages witty criticism and language play. Moreover, unlike other shows that aim to restore a sense of national dignity and pride, such

---

[4]In an article about the satiric spirit of Romanians, American scholar Robert Cochran (1989) describes his 1985 trip to the communist country as follows: "Romanians express themselves most characteristically and most profoundly in their joking. In the ironies, obliquities, and covert aggressions natural to the genre they find a vehicle perfectly suited to their situation, their history, and perhaps their temperament. Living in secular purgatory that at times must seem infernal, they inhabit a joker's paradise [. . .] Generically the joke is Janus-faced – at once assertion of defiance and admission of defeat, it disparages itself even in its telling, proclaims its own limits, and is always at least partly told on its teller" (pp. 260, 272).

[5]"Grobian" is a widely used word in Romanian. It refers to Saint Grobian, the fictional patron of coarse people conceived by the satirist Sebastian Brant (1457–1521).

as *Miss Country Girl* (which uses the competition between country girls to emphasize the splendor of the Romanian landscape and "authentic" Romanian traditions), the fake news show also displays an orientation towards the future, which some critics deem an essential element in the formation of national identity.

Huidu and Găinușă actively seek to instill a sense of hope in Romania's future, even as they relentlessly expose what is wrong with it. After they had spread a rumor that Găinușă had won the visa lottery and intended to leave for the United States, they subsequently highlighted how easily rumors can travel, and used the opportunity to reprove those "gullible enough" to believe that the television host would ever consider leaving his country. "I would never send my children to study abroad," Huidu stressed in an interview. "I specifically named my children Rareș and Mircea, Romanian names which are difficult to pronounce abroad [. . .] I want to instill in them a desire for change that our generation lacks, because our generation is a product of communism. My objective with the show is to encourage Romanians to break away from the old and dare to wish for a better future" (Craus, 2009). Such close interrelatedness between an active promotion of national identity and a fake news format that seeks to disrupt government officials' cultivated images of assurance further demonstrates how *Cronica Cârcotașilor* should be understood in relation to specific geopolitical contingencies.

REFERENCES

Aslama, M., & Pantti, M. (2007). Flagging Finnishness: Reproducing national identity in reality television. *Television and New Media, 8*(1), 49–67.

Baym, G. (2005). *The Daily Show*: Discursive integration and the reinvention of political journalism. *Political Communication, 22*, 259–276.

Baym, G. (2009). *From Cronkite to Colbert: The evolution of broadcast news*. Boulder, CO: Paradigm.

Bennett, J. (2009). A feeling of insincerity: Politics, ventriloquy, and the dialectics of gesture. In E. van Alphen, M. Bal, & C. Smith (Eds.), *The rhetoric of sincerity* (pp. 195–213). Stanford, CA: Stanford University Press.

Bonsaver, G. (2007). *Censorship and literature in Fascist Italy*. Toronto, Canada: University of Toronto Press.

Boyer, D., & Yurchak, A. (2010). American stiob: Or, what late–socialist aesthetics of parody reveal about contemporary political culture in the West. *Cultural Anthropology, 25*(2), 179–221.

Bujenita, A. (2005). Cronica Cârcotașilor: o cacofonie de care Românica avea nevoie. [The tattle's tattle: A cacophony "little" Romania needed]. Retrieved from http://www.cariereonline.ro/articol/cronica-Cârcotașilor-o-cacofonie-de-care-romanica-avea-nevoie

Cochran, R. (1989). What courage! Romanian 'our leader' jokes. *Journal of American Folklore, 102*(405), 259–274.

Craus, S. (2009). Interviu cu Serban Huidu. [Interview with Serban Huidu]. *CuzaNet* Retrieved from http://www.cuzanet.ro/index.php?option=com_content&task=view&id=4523&Itemid=67

Drace-Francis, A. (2003). Paradoxes of occidentalism: On travel literature in Ceaușescu's Romania. In A. Hammond (Ed.), *The Balkans and the West: Constructing the European other, 1945–2003* (pp. 68–80). Burlington, VT: Ashgate Publishing.

Dutu, T. (2010, April 08). Serban Huidu si Mihai Găinușă: 10 ani de umor pe subiecte grobiene." [Șerban Huidu and Mihai Găinușă: Ten years of Humor on Grobian Topics]. *Romania Libera*. Retrieved from http://www.romanialibera.ro/cultura/vedete/10-ani-de-umor-fin-pe-subiecte-grobiene-182497.html

Dwyer, T., & Uricaru, I. (2009). Slashing and subtitles: Romanian media piracy, censorship and translation. *Velvet Light Trap, 63*, 45–57.

Gilbert, A., Greenberg, J., Helms, E., & Jansen, S. (2008). Reconsidering postsocialism from the margins of Europe: Hope, time and normalcy in post-Yugoslav societies. *Anthropology News, 49*(8), 9–10.

Gray, J. (2009). Throwing out the welcome mat: Public figures as guests and victims in TV satire. In J. Gray, J. P. Jones, & E. Thompson (Eds.), *Satire TV: Politics and comedy in the post-network era* (pp. 147–165). New York, NY: New York University Press.

Harold, C. (2004). Pranking rhetoric: "Culture jamming" as political activism. *Critical Studies in Media Communication*, *21*(3), 189–211.

Imre, A. (2009a). Gender and quality television: A transcultural feminist project. *Feminist Media Studies*, *9*(4), 391–407.

Imre, A. (2009b). National intimacy and post-socialist networking. *Cultural Studies*, *12*(2), 219–233.

Istodor, E. (2003). 'Sîntem instrumentele rîcii populare': O convorbire cu Şerban Huidu si mihai găinuşă [We are the outlet for popular spite]. *Dilema*, *521*(20).

Jäckel, A. (2001). Romania: From tele-revolution to public service broadcasting, national images, and international image. *Canadian Journal of Communication*, *26*(1), 1–10.

Jenkins, H. (2006). *Convergence culture: When old and new media collide*. New York, NY: New York University Press.

Lemon, A. (2008). Writing against the new "Cold War." *Anthropology News*, *49*(8), 11–12.

Massumi, B. (2002). *Parables of the virtual: Movement, affect, sensation*. Durham, NC: Duke University Press.

McKain, A. (2005). Not necessarily not the news: Gatekeeping, remediation, and *The Daily Show*. *The Journal of American Culture*, *28*(4), 415–430.

Nip, J. M. (2006). Exploring the second phase of public journalism. *Journalism Studies*, *7*(2), 212–236.

Paleanu, G. (2010, September 17). Huidu si Găinuşă, dati in judecata de 'Cronica Cârcotaşilor' din Italia. [Huidu and Găinuşă sued by the Italian Cronica Cârcotaşilor]. *Cotidianul*. Retrieved from http://www.cotidianul.ro/huidu_si_Găinuşă_dati_in_judecata_de_cronica_Cârcotaşilor_din_italia-124640/

Roncarolo, F. (2004). Mediation of Italian politics and the marketing of leaders' private lives. *Parliamentary Affairs*, *57*(1), 108–117.

Stamatoiu, C. (2006). Media, communication, and the relevance of Caragiale's work today. *Comparative Literature and Culture*, *8*(4), 1–8.

Warner, J. (2007). Political culture jamming: The dissident humor on *The Daily Show with John Stewart*. *Popular Communication*, *5*(1), 17–36.

Political Satire in Danish Television:
Reinventing a Tradition

Hanne Bruun

This article highlights political satire as part of a long tradition of satirical sketch comedy in Danish public service television. Since the late 1990s, however, there have been major changes to this entertainment tradition. Taking these developments as a point of departure, this article argues that political satire has been trying to reinvent itself under these new conditions. By focusing more and more on the media themselves as the target for satirical ridicule, political satire is reshaping the ideological ambiguity typical of this entertainment tradition. In spite of these current efforts, political satire is presently a struggling branch of the satirical sketch comedy tradition in Danish public service television.

Actually, in my opinion, because of the speed of news production and the distribution of news on the Internet, ordinary news production is integrating humor nowadays. The producers of news have developed an eye for comedy, and it is very difficult to match this kind of political satire produced in the news in a satirical program.

> —Mikael Bertelsen, television producer and spoof news anchor on
> *Bertelsen–De Uaktuelle Nyheder* [*Bertelsen–News of No Current Interest*][1]

The Danish television producer Mikael Bertelsen made this short diagnosis of a possible trend in television news reporting. Bertelsen is also a former commissioning editor of satire at the Danish public service broadcaster, DR, from 2003 to 2006. In my interview with Bertelsen, he reflects on what he sees as a growing awareness among television news producers of the many spontaneous moments of absurd comedy with satirical potential provided by television's 24/7 news coverage. In Bertelsen's opinion, this possible trend questions both the need for political satire as a specific entertainment genre as well as the creative scope of political satire in this new media environment. The diagnosis was made as part of his answer to my question of why political satire no longer dominated the long tradition of *satirical sketch comedy* in Danish public service television, as it did from 1968 until the late 1990s. Satirical sketch comedy still is an important part of the entertainment profile these broadcasters offer the audience, but *political* satire is

---

[1] Interview with author, April 23, 2009.

struggling to survive. As this article will show, the way the Danish public service broadcasters use satirical sketch comedy has changed profoundly since the late 1990s under the influence of growing competition for specific audiences in the Danish media market. Political satire is trying to reinvent itself under these new conditions both within the tradition of sketch comedy and outside in different kinds of experimental factual programming.

Political satire traditionally directed its sting at the behavior of politically and economically powerful individuals and institutions. Since the late 1990s, however, the ridicule has to a greater extent focused on critiquing "the media" as powerful institutions in societies. In order to meet the satirical intentions, combinations of what I call *genre parody* and *genre pastiche* of key factual genres of television programming have become a more prominent tool over the past decade. The distinction between genre parody and genre pastiche is not easy to make, according to Richard Dyer (2007). Both tools imitate another aesthetic style or a specific artifact. But pastiche imitates aesthetics and conventional narrative logic, without offering negative or positive evaluations (pp. 3–5). In comparison, parody spells out its evaluation to the audience by exaggerations and blatant distortions that leave no doubt about its intentions.

This article argues that political satire is trying to reshape itself by using combinations of these two aesthetic tools. As a result, the satirical sting has become a bit subtler and more dependent on the media literacy of its viewers. Furthermore, the ideological ambiguity that has traditionally characterized satirical sketch comedy in Danish public service television itself is being reshaped. Even if this strategy marks a way to continue political satirical sketch comedy on Danish public service television, one also finds the ambition to do political satire outside the format of sketch comedy. Since the late 1990s, political satire has been a detectable *communicative intention* in experiments with current affairs programming and serial documentaries. This article will present these changes in Danish entertainment and discuss the consequences for Danish public service television and for satire as a communicative intent. It begins with a short outline of the tradition of entertainment, and its transformations in close interplay with both increased competition in the Danish media market and the growing importance of new media platforms.

THE HISTORY OF SATIRE IN DANISH PUBLIC SERVICE BROADCASTING

Like other European public service broadcasters, Danish public service television has a strong tradition of entertainment with an edge: the satirical sketch comedy. Currently, programs in this tradition are playing an important role in the growing competition for viewers, especially for young audiences. The development of this entertainment genre has brought about important innovations and experimentation involving the internet (Bruun, 2007, 2011). The genre is in many ways thriving in public service television and adds diversity to an entertainment profile otherwise dominated by reality shows and lifestyle television, as well as quiz, game, and talk show formats (Bruun, 2005). Unlike in the United States, only since the late 1980s has Danish television been a dual market of commercial and public service broadcasters. The country's two public service broadcasters, The Danish Radio and Television Corporation (DR) and TV 2, still dominate the market with a combined audience share of around 65%. DR is entirely supported by license fees; TV 2 is financed by a combination of commercials and subscription. Both broadcasters offer a mix of programming mandated by the nation's broadcasting laws as well as by more detailed broadcasting licenses and agreements that express an explicit obligation to produce and broadcast entertainment.

Television satire itself started as a specific entertainment genre on Danish television in 1968. The entertainment department at DR produced a number of satirical series, along with other kinds of entertainment programs such as variety and quiz shows (Bruun, 2005). This was during the period from 1925 to 1988 when DR had a monopoly on radio broadcasting and, after 1951, on television as well. The inspiration for television satire was taken from an already established tradition of radio satire on DR. The satirical sketch comedy series *Søndagsjournalen* ("The Sunday Journal": DR, 1966) and *Holdningsløse Tidende* ("The Spineless Daily": DR, 1967–1975) had provided DR with experience in producing programming that ridiculed politicians and political issues that had been part of the news of the week. Inspiration also came from the BBC series *That Was The Week That Was* (Wagg, 2002) and from programs produced by the Norwegian public service broadcaster NRK and the Swedish SVT. Last but not least, inspiration for satirical television came from a long history in Denmark of revue theater shows as well as political cabaret, which flourished in the 1960s.

It is important to note that from the beginning, television satire in Denmark was framed as entertainment and as a special kind of sketch comedy with the critical edge produced through reference to real events and people. Understanding television satire as entertainment, and in particular as sketch comedy, was by no means given, but in the Danish context has been the dominant approach. From 1968 until 1999, that meant satirical sketch comedy was part of primetime entertainment on the Saturday night schedule and aimed at a mainstream audience. There are no statistics on ratings available before 1988 in Denmark, but given the monopoly status of DR's one television channel, which left no other choice for Danish viewers, DR presumed that the programs were watched by a large audience and considered an important part of its entertainment profile.

At DR and in the entertainment department in particular, satire was considered to counterbalance the kind of entertainment normally produced such as quiz and game shows, talk shows, and variety shows (Bruun, forthcoming). To the cultural elite engaged in intense public debates over the cultural obligations of DR during the monopoly period, such entertainment was considered to be shallow, offering nothing of cultural value and wasting the viewers' time (Bruun, 2011). Satirical sketch comedy, however, was considered to contain high cultural value because of its combination of comedy with a critical attitude toward and reference to political issues on the weekly news agenda. The appreciation from this otherwise extremely critical cultural elite with many supporters among the employees at DR was important to the status of the genre. It meant that at DR and in the entertainment department, satirical sketch comedy became a flagship. It was a kind of entertainment that its producers were proud of, and when the second public service broadcaster TV 2 was launched in 1988, it too began producing satirical sketch comedy.

Sketch comedy was the primary satirical format, and each episode of the series consisted of a large number of different sketches. At the beginning these sketches were typically presented as a spoof newscast, with an anchor or just a voice-over presenting the context of the sketches to the viewer. Since then, other kinds of factual television genres, such as the current affairs program, the talk show, and recently the lifestyle program, have also been used as settings. The programs were characterized by the blending of two satirical modes: egalitarian and elitist satire. According to Larsen (2001), *egalitarian* satire is aimed at a society's political, economic, and cultural powers, including the media. Egalitarian satire attacks inequalities, and the injustices created by those inequalities. The mockery produced by egalitarian satire is directed at the establishment and is supposed to join the powerless, offering laughter as their weapon. Such satire presumes that its viewers identify with the powerless in a given satirical treatment of a case and gain self-affirmation by doing so. *Elitist* satire, in contrast, is aimed at those criticizing political and social changes in society or at those with lifestyles that can be ridiculed. The target groups there become everyday citizens, as well as specific social groups. Elitist satire facilitates self-criticism and self-affirmation by encouraging the audience to *not* identify with the target groups. Both satirical modes involve an appeal to the viewer's experience of his or her social status and psychological place in the hierarchy of society by these inclusion-exclusion dynamics.

This blend of the two modes meant that many of the sketches and the satirical programs as a whole were marked by ideological ambiguity. On the one hand, they offered viewers a critical perspective on the lifestyles and self-delusions of ordinary Danes from different socio-economic groups. On the other hand, the programs were critical towards the political, economic, and cultural establishment. Such ideological ambiguity became a part of the satirical tradition in Danish television. Because of this legacy, Danish television satire could be criticized for being anything but dangerous, while it could also be seen as disturbing because no political viewpoints and no groups in society have been safe from satirical treatment. From this perspective, the blending of egalitarian and elitist satirical modes emphasizes critical political and social self-reflection. Furthermore, it emphasizes an anti-authoritarian, ironic, and perhaps misanthropic attitude beyond political points of view—with laughter as its weapon (Schwind, 1988).

As noted, during the monopoly period, satirical entertainment satisfied the dual needs of the public service broadcaster. First, it satisfied the need for entertainment that was able to attract a mainstream audience in order to secure the *political* legitimacy of public service television. Second, it satisfied the need for entertainment that had *cultural* legitimacy in the eyes of the cultural elite both inside and outside the public service broadcasting corporation (Bruun, forthcoming). As a result of this dual need, satire continued to be an important part of the public service entertainment profile as the competition for viewers between the two public service stations, DR and TV 2, and the new commercial stations grew more intense during the 1990s. That increased competition was due to a combination of national and EU deregulation, satellite distribution across national borders, and digital technology. Furthermore, the daily ratings that had become available in 1988 showed that the satirical sketch show comedy series did not deliver the kind of ratings other entertainment genres were able to generate among a mainstream audience on the Saturday night schedule. For example a talk show broadcasted in 1998 generated ratings of 30%, while the satirical sketch comedy series *Tv-Ansjosen* ("The Television Anchovy": DR, 1995–1998) had ratings of 12%. All in all, during the 1990s, the competition for audiences became more and more important to the public service broadcasters. DR especially had to struggle to meet enough of the population to support the political legitimacy of its license fee.

By the end of the 1990s, these important developments began to affect the genre and push further developments within it. In 1996, DR launched a second channel, DR2, which was aimed at the well-educated segments of the Danish audience. In 1999 satire was among the programming with relatively low ratings that was moved to this new channel. This was done for two connected reasons: first, to trim the schedule and tailor DR1's content for a mainstream audience and, second, because they were considered of importance to DR's political and cultural legitimacy as a public service broadcaster in a much more commercialized and competitive television environment. The programs for the schedule of this new niche channel had to be financed within the fixed budget of DR, and new ways of producing on very low budgets became the norm. This meant that producing the familiar kind of satirical sketch comedy was no longer affordable—economic conditions that would pave the way for a new generation of comedians and new ways of producing satire. From 2000 to 2009, the number of series DR scheduled in primetime grew from one series with a maximum of 12 episodes a year to around five series with 10 or more episodes a year, all scheduled on DR2. In many ways satire was very important in branding the new niche channel for well-educated young adults. But as a consequence, DR no longer produced satirical sketch comedy for the mainstream audience as it had for the past 30 years. TV 2 largely followed the same strategy, producing satirical sketch comedy from the early 2000s until 2009 only for TV 2/Zulu, a niche channel that is part of the purely commercial arm of the TV 2 company and targeted at teenagers and young adults (Bruun, 2011).

Because of these new production conditions, the nature of satirical television changed, developing into two different branches. For the sake of distinction, the first branch will be called *political satire*, which continued to reflect the current news flow of the media and was oriented towards specific political issues, social problems, and people on the national agenda—the kinds of content traditionally addressed by the daily news flow and governed by topicality. Furthermore, such political satire was at the same time largely egalitarian. The second branch will be referred to as *social satire*, which cultivated an interest in the lives of ordinary Danes. The focus of social satire was on different lifestyles and mentalities, and the way cultural and political trends and new social demands affected individuals' behaviors, norms, and self-image. An elitist satirical mode characterized these programs, which cultivated loss of face as their driving comedic force. In this manner, social satire moved beyond current political issues and broadened the range of areas in life that could be the objects of television satire. Furthermore, social satire took aim at new factual entertainment genres such as docu-soaps, lifestyle television, talk shows, and reality shows. In this manner, emphasis was given to the audiences' knowledge of different lifestyles and mentalities, as well as their media literacy. In short, social satire benefited enormously from the growing interest in the private sphere of everyday life evinced by public service television since the early 1990s.

Currently, social satire is the dominant satirical form on Danish public service television. This approach to satire is far more independent of the topicality of the news flow and the audience's knowledge and memory of its issues than is political satire. As a consequence, its content has a longer lifespan than political satire, which mirrors the news flow of the week. In this way, social satire is better suited to the long-term recirculation of content through new media platforms used by the public service content providers, especially DR. In a very small media economy like Denmark's, content with a long lifespan is desirable. However, even if social satire is the leading form of satire, the political branch of satirical sketch comedy has been striving to reshape itself under these new conditions. Below I will elaborate on the ways this is being done.

PARODY, PASTICHE, AND IDEOLOGICAL AMBIGUITY

From the beginning of the 2000s, the political branch of satirical sketch comedy has put more emphasis on critiquing television's political and cultural power, and it has been the key factual genre through which it performs politics. This was done in series that combined the aesthetic tools of parody and pastiche to achieve the satirical intention. As mentioned above, the difference between parody and pastiche is a question of whether an evaluation can be found directed at the genre or specific artifact being imitated. As the Norwegian comedian Harald Eia (2006) argues on the basis of his own experiences producing satirical comedy in Norwegian public service television, enacting a genre pastiche is an effective comic tool in combination with genre parody. According to Eia, it is important for the program or specific sketches to stick to the constitutive features of the genre used for a satirical purpose (e.g., the docu-soap or the television newscast). By sticking to the constitutive features, it is possible to confront the audience's expectations for the genre with undermining discrepancies, distortions, and exaggerations that foreground the constitutive features of the particular factual television genre. In this way genre pastiche paves the way for genre parody (p. 185). This combination produces much of the entertainment value in the programs, as Eia puts it, because "our feelings believe in it" (p. 194).

In Danish television the combination of the two aesthetic tools in the political branch of the satirical sketch comedy tradition meant that the satire thus produced became more dependent on the media literacy and interpretive abilities of the audience. The audience had to master the constitutive features of a whole range of television genres and to detect the deviations from the expected conventions that gave way to parody. The new series also marked a change in political satire by putting emphasis on recruiting multifunctional comedians in small ensembles (Bruun, forthcoming). Traditionally, television satire had been written by a crew of professional writers and performed by professional actors with known comic talent. In the new types of low-budget political satire, however, the comedians themselves were expected to produce the programs, write the material, and act in the shows. In effect, satirical comedy has become much more personalized and tied to the performers comic abilities to "playing themselves" on screen. Finally, and in line with the specific factual genres being parodied, the new series used real news footage as well as real-life politicians, celebrities, and ordinary citizens as participants in the shows. This confrontation in the series between a comedy show with satirical intentions and real people resulted in an ambiguity between the scripted and non-scripted parts of the programs.

As the following example shows, the satirical sting produced by the political branch of the satirical sketch comedy has become subtler. Furthermore, the egalitarian satirical mode that dominates the political branch has resulted in programs more open to interpretations. This trend has certainly not been only a Danish phenomenon. It can be seen in what is referred to as the "reality comedy" trend, particularly in British television from the same period, with series such as *Brass Eye* (discussed by Meikle in this special issue) and *The Mark Thomas Comedy Product* (Hall, 2006).

THE NEWS AS THE TARGET

One of the first examples of these new trends is the show *Bertelsen—De Uaktuelle Nyheder*, produced by DR2 in 2002. The title consists of the surname of the show's spoof news anchor, Mikael Bertelsen, who was quoted at the beginning of this article. Bertelsen co-authored the series with two well-known satirical comedians, Jens Korse and Oliver Zahle, the latter also playing the role of a spoof news reporter in the series. The title of the show is also an oxymoron, which in English translates into *Bertelsen—News of No Current Interest*. As mentioned, the new style of political satire directed its satirical sting at television's key factual genres, and *Bertelsen–De Uaktuelle Nyheder* enacted a newscast. In keeping, the satire was aimed at the current agenda of the real news media, while representatives of the government and different political parties in parliament were the preferred interviewees.

To produce its satirical sting, the constitutive features of the newscast were imitated in great detail. The setting of the series was a state-of-the-art news studio with the traditional desk and a busy newsroom in the background. It also contained the kind of musical fanfare and aesthetic screen layout common to television news worldwide.[2] The program also contained all the expected features and narrative elements of television news: headlines and different news stories, live reports from reporters in the field of action, and the studio interviews. Furthermore, it contained news footage taken from real newscasts and built into the spoof newscast. The appearance and mannerisms of the anchor also corresponded to the genre expectations. The anchor, dressed in suit and tie, looked seriously and calmly into the camera and greeted the viewers while moving his papers around and holding a pen in his hand. Again according to the television news genre, the anchor was staged as the authority of the program, not just representing himself as a television personality but also "the news" as a societal institution with all the positive political values associated with this institution: objectivity and facts independent of economic and political affiliations, importance for democracy and citizenship, and so on.

All in all, the genre markers and conventions signaling "the news" were imitated, but such pastiche was combined with undermining discrepancies. Above all, the series was dominated by very *strange news criteria*. An example of this is a story under the headline "We are all going to die." The story is introduced by the anchor imitating the kind of rhetoric typical of "breaking news":

> I have just received a telegram saying that everybody has to die. According to the information available right now, this will affect everybody in Denmark . . . and in the USA. The USA is also affected. It has been revealed that everybody has to die . . . everybody in the whole world except Sweden . . . I am being informed right now that Sweden is also affected.[3]

Bertelsen goes on performing this pastiche of breaking-news rhetoric associated with major catastrophes, such as epidemics, and then interviews a (real) chief physician Henrik Kehlet who appears live from a hospital. Professor Kehlet confirms the fact: We are all going to die, and he explains that there is no vaccine against it as suggested by the anchor. In spite of the information given to him by the expert interviewee, the anchor sticks to framing the information from another semantic taxonomy (the biological facts of life) as news important to the survival of the population of the whole world here and now. Here he invokes one of the most potent genres of news reporting, the live coverage of such crises as epidemics, disasters, and terror attacks—and as something the media can help to prevent. At the end of the interview, the anchor asks Professor Kehlet if he would recommend that the viewers stay indoors and listen to DR in order to get information on how the catastrophe develops. Instead Kehlet recommends the opposite, suggesting the viewers go out and enjoy life.

By using the clash between the expected conventional characteristics of television news in a breaking-news situation associated with a major catastrophe and the issue (the mortality of all humans), the sketch relies on the audience's ability to deduce the underlying criticism. The clash could be understood, first of all, as criticism directed at the sensationalism of the news discourse

---

[2] Segments from the series and the interviews can be seen on DR's homepage: http://www.dr.dk/satire/uaktuelle/.

[3] Translation by author.

with limited or absolutely no relevance to the issues reported. Second, the incongruence could be understood as backfiring on the news itself. Its need for audiences in spite of all normal journalistic news criteria paints its view of the world and what is going on in specific ways. Thirdly, the incongruence could be seen as an important part of the general comedy style of the series very much in debt to the kind of absurd and black comedy typical of *Monty Python's Flying Circus* and still typical of much British comedy that has long been popular on Danish television.

In addition to its strange news criteria, the series was characterized by a very *odd interview style* in sketches focusing on real political issues and their presentation in the media. An infamous interview demonstrating this approach features the young politician Morten Messerschmidt. In 2002, Messerschmidt was the deputy chairman of the youth organization of the right-wing Danish People's Party and a candidate for the Danish Parliament. He was a rising political star and would become a Member of Parliament from 2005 to 2009, before being elected to the European Parliament with the second highest number of personal votes. The Danish People's Party supports the ruling coalition government in the Danish Parliament between the Liberals and the Conservatives, in power since 2001. Having secured the majority of votes for the government, the People's Party maintains a strong influence. The context of Bertelsen's interview with Messerschmidt is that in 2002, Messerschmidt had formed *The Association of Critical License-Fee Payers* with the declared purpose to act as a watchdog over the alleged left-wing bias of DR. This alleged bias of DR has been part of the agenda of right-wing parties in Denmark since the 1970s, but has had a strong revival since 2002, influencing the cultural politics of the government.

The interview starts off with Bertelsen asking Messerschmidt to object if he feels that the anchor is politically biased at any point during the interview. If so, he is asked to slap the anchor across his fingers with a ruler placed on the desk. Long ago this was a popular type of punishment used by schoolteachers in Denmark. Of course, Messerschmidt refuses to do so, but by using the ruler Bertelsen has already positioned Messerschmidt as a powerful law-and-order-authority interested in editorial control and punishment. Then Bertelsen asks his first question: "What is the purpose of 'The association of critical license-fee payers,' *you right-wing bastard*?" Messerschmidt hesitates and then he politely asks Bertelsen to repeat the question, which he does. Again Messerschmidt hesitates, but then he calmly answers. The purpose is to stop the journalists at DR from promoting left-wing politics, values, and points of views and to prevent them from giving left-wing politicians more positive treatment. Bertelsen then asks him: "Could you give an example, you right-wing bastard?" Again Messerschmidt shows signs of insecurity, but he answers the question with a little smile on his face: "You just gave a good one yourself."

Bertelsen asks why Messerschmidt did not use the ruler, and he again refuses. He is now offered to punish the anchor by giving him an electric shock from a device now attached to the anchor's forehead. Messerschmidt refuses once more, and the anchor assures him that from now on he will "stick to the subject in a completely objective way." For the third time, Messerschmidt is asked to answer the same question, but he is stopped after just two seconds by the anchor telling him that his speaking time is up. Messerschmidt objects to the unfair terms he is given to present the political aim of the association, but Bertelsen argues that these are the terms given to all of his guests. To prove it, Messerschmidt is shown a clip from an earlier interview with Keld Albrechtsen, a well-known politician from the left-wing party *The Red-Green Alliance*. The "questions" put to Albrechtsen are a summary of the party's political program reformulated as questions by means of phrases such as "is it true that . . ." or "can you confirm that . . ." placed in front of the sentences. Not surprisingly, Albrechtsen is able to confirm that this is indeed the political aim of the socialist party by a simple yes.

Back in the studio, Messerschmidt objects, but again he is asked why he did not punish the anchor. Messerschmidt refuses to use physical punishment and is now offered to behead Bertelsen. An executioner enters the studio and Bertelsen's head is placed on a small wooden block while Messerschmidt, with an uneasy laugh, finally gets the chance to answer the question: the association fights for objective, impartial news, he says, instead of the kind of socialist propaganda promoted by DR. Finally, Messerschmidt says that instead of beheading Bertelsen he prefers to ask the responsible manager at DR to fire him, and after a few more absurd comments from the anchor, the interview ends.

The satirical sting produced in this interview is ambiguous. Combined with the persistent denial of DR's bias by means of the methods of punishment offered to Messerschmidt, the absurd and exaggerated bias of the interview could be said to demonstrate that value-free news coverage is an illusion constructed by the media. Furthermore, the interview could be said to demonstrate that value-free news coverage is itself a ridiculous political issue for the politicians to pursue, and in fact that pursuit prevents proper political journalism from being produced for the benefit of citizens and politicians alike. Instead of telling the viewers this in a straightforward way, however, the viewer is asked to make the deductions herself. It could be argued that the interview becomes too grotesque, making the sympathy of the audience turn towards Messerschmidt, regardless of his political opinions. He stands out as the only sane and polite person in the studio. Even though he is the guest, he is treated impolitely; yet he is able to keep calm, demonstrating that he can keep a cool head and has a sense of humor, too. In short, the satirical sting is by no means clear-cut but is also open to the interpretations of the audience.

The indirect criticism produced by the interview style in the series was used in different ways to ridicule politicians' political views and behaviors as well as to ridicule the hypocritical strategies of the news. Even the prime minister at the time, Anders Fogh Rasmussen, appeared in the series.[4] Like Messerschmidt, he also managed to stay calm, sticking to his role as an interviewee throughout an interview in which the anchor accused him of delivering subliminal messages to the viewers. The "proof" presented to the prime minister was excerpts from real television speeches and interviews played and then played backwards. This gimmick produced sound bites that were subtitled to fit the accusations. The accusations claimed to reveal the aggressive maniac hidden behind the super-ego controlled personality of Anders Fogh Rasmussen. One of the sound bites "revealed" that instead of talking about the liberal government's plan to close down an allegedly large number of surplus state committees and institutions, he in fact said: "I want to kill someone at breakfast television." Second, the accusations were said to reveal that Anders Fogh Rasmussen at heart was an aggressive anti-state right-wing liberalist with the political goal of dismantling the welfare state—a goal publicly refuted by the prime minister and his government. One of the sound bites thus "revealed" that instead of following the government's plan to use retirements as the way to cut back the number of employees in the public sector, the hidden message actually was: "All of you employed in the public sector should be shot."

During the interview the prime minister objected to the accusations and stated that *he* was the victim of media manipulation and not the Danish viewers. But after the interview concluded the

---

[4] Available, in Danish, at http://www.dr.dk/satire/uaktuelle/?i=4111.

PM said something backwards. After the interview the anchor then played the excerpt forward and the hidden message was "Vote for *Venstre* [The Liberals] and win one million." As all of the interviews in the series this one also ended up in a kind of absurdity questioning the target of the ridicule: The prime minister and his government, the media as powerful institutions getting more and more influenced by ratings and commercial logics instead of the ideals journalism, both or none of the above?

The new trend in political satire exemplified by *Bertelsen–De Uaktuelle Nyheder* also gave high priority to the comedy talent of the comedians, adding to the satire directed at the media in the series. As the "we are all going to die" story demonstrates, the anchor is trying to adapt to the conventions and rhetorical style of "breaking news" journalism. But he is in fact trying so hard that the exaggerated and compulsive behavior of the news anchor is detached, and it turns into canny mania. As a comedian, Mikael Bertelsen was on the one hand able perform the authoritative rhetoric, mode of address and mannerisms of the news anchor, making a deadpan attitude collide with the absurd news stories, the news criteria, and the interview style in the show. On the other hand, Bertelsen was also able to perform the host's inability to adapt to the role of news anchor and this was also a tool to ridicule the conventions of television news. Finally, the uncertain boundaries between the staged and the nonstaged, the scripted and the nonscripted, were an important tool in the series. Were the interviewees from the various political parties, political organizations, and big businesses informed of what was going to happen to them in the program, or were they not? And how would they react confronted with the interview style and the staging of the host? Would they be able to keep face or would they lose it? For example, by having no sense of humor? In fact, they were given a rough outline of the interview so that they would participate but no details.

This way of using real people from different realms of society became a tactic in the strategy to renew the political branch of the entertainment tradition. Other series added to the attempts by merging with stand-up comedy in a variety of ways.[5] A very successful example of this merger was the series made by a stand-up comedian named Jan Gintberg. His series *Gintberg Show Off* (DR2, 2000–2001) and *Vindhætterne* ("The Wind Caps": DR2, 2002) were characterized by an interest in portraying the political views of the common Danes. Using vox pops is a popular technique in Danish television news production, and, among other things, Gintberg cultivated the spoof vox pop interview, with real people giving their opinions on current political issues in the news. As a prompt he often used a spoof "ordinary Dane" played by Carsten Bang, a stand-up comedian who was fairly unknown at the time. Bang's character interrupted the short vox pop interviews on the streets by misunderstanding the questions asked in horrible ways, making the ordinary Danes appear a bit more informed and sensible on camera. Nevertheless, these vox pops also displayed ordinary Danes who were neither politically correct nor well informed.[6] In this manner, Gintberg was able to hold on to the combination of elitist and egalitarian satirical modes typical of the Danish tradition and add media satire directed at the news to the menu.

More recently, both DR and TV 2's commercial youth channel Zulu tried to use these aesthetic strategies to reshape political satire in the series *Tjenesten* ("The Service": DR2, 2007–2008) and *Mørck & Jul* (TV 2/Zulu, 2009). But these series did not add anything new, and in many ways they also demonstrated how difficult it is to produce political satire reflecting the issues on the

---

[5]The stand-up comedy scene in Denmark has existed for less than 20 years.

[6]Examples can been seen in Danish on YouTube: http://www.youtube.com/watch?v=MRXWqmLk_vE.

NEWS PARODY AND POLITICAL SATIRE ACROSS THE GLOBE

news agenda on very low production budgets. It is safe to say that the political branch of the satirical sketch comedy tradition did not benefit in the same way as social satire did from the move to
niche channels and the low-budget production culture dominating these channels. Furthermore,
the move to niche channels like DR2 and Zulu directed at specific segments of the audience
meant that the ratings for satirical sketch comedy became extremely small. The series typically
had ratings around 2% compared to around 13% in the period when such satirical programming
was still produced for a mainstream audience. Even if there is a tradition to build on, segmentation of the audience is of limited value when producing television in a country with a population
of only 5.5 million.

POLITICAL SATIRE OUT OF THE BOX?

The aesthetic strategies used in reshaping political satire during the 2000s also characterized
experiments with current affairs programming and serial documentaries in the same period. But
the experiments produced were typically neither announced as satire nor as entertainment by
the broadcasters, even though many of them were in fact both. An overall tactic in these series,
all broadcast on DR2, was to imitate traditional journalistic genres of television like the current affairs program and political reportage. An example was the current affairs program *Indefra*
("From the Inside": DR2, 1998–2003). The constitutive features of the genre was undermined by
two horribly naïve journalists broadcasting from the corridors of the Danish Parliament. By having politicians take part in face-threatening experiments and interviews on current issues, the
series tried to capture the backstage behavior of the politicians. The disarming attitude of the
journalists as well as politicians eager to show themselves off as individuals with a sense of
humor resulted in highly embarrassing situations in many episodes. On the one hand, the series
portrayed the politicians as human beings; on the other, they were portrayed as idiots eager to
please the media and the voters. By deliberately going for the backstage of the political system, the series was able to tell stories not possible to tell in conventional political current affairs
programs, and this made these conventions distinct.

The clash between the staged and the un-staged was taken to new extremes by the journalist
and television producer Mads Brügger. Brügger produced, among other shows, two series using
the form of political reportage and serial documentary. The first series was called *Danes for
Bush* (DR2, 2004), featuring two young Danes (Brügger himself and Jakob Boeskov) traveling
the United States to convince Americans to vote for George W. Bush in the 2004 election. The
two Danes passed themselves off as great admirers of Bush and as true Republicans to a degree
that embarrassed even the real-life Republicans they met. Another of Brügger's series, *Det Røde
Kapel* ("The Red Orchestra": DR2, 2006), used the same clash, though at the opposite end of the
political spectrum. In the series, three young Danes (Brügger, Simon Jul, and Jacob Nossel)—
two of them in fact adopted from Korea and one of them handicapped—pretended to be a small
communist theatre ensemble doing a comic variety show as part of a cultural exchange program
with North Korea. On the one hand, the series showed the authoritarian regime in action, as well
as the very negative attitude towards handicapped people in North Korea. On the other hand, the
prank presented the North Koreans as extremely tolerant towards the horrible show the Danish
ensemble produced. As a consequence, the criticism intended also pointed to the North Koreans
as human beings and not just loyal soldiers of the regime. The series was later edited into a

documentary film entitled *The Red Chapel*, which won a documentary prize at the Sundance Festival in 2010.

By using these aesthetic strategies across genres, political satire is still a part of Danish public service television. First, it occasionally can be found as part of the entertainment tradition, even if today social satire dwarfs political satire. Second, however, political satire as a communicative modality permeates other kinds of factual television genres that form the political agenda and our understanding of the world around us through specific aesthetic practices. Across different factual genres these aesthetic strategies produce comedy as well as critical commentary on political issues and on the ways they are presented by the media. Political satire as a modality has also been on the increase in public service television in other Scandinavian countries since the late 1990s (Kjus, 2005). Furthermore, British series such as *Bass Eye, Little Britain, The Smell of Reeves and Mortimer, The Ali G. Show,* and *The Office* have also had considerable influence on the development in Danish television, while *The Daily Show with Jon Stewart* has been shown on DR since 2009. This series and other international inspirations for domestic television satire might once again pave the way for political satire in Danish public service television and with the mainstream audience as its target group. In 2009, for example, TV 2 introduced a live comedy show called *Live fra Bremen,* "Live from Bremen," a Danish adaptation of *Saturday Night Live* that contains political satire as a small part of the show. Furthermore, the show is produced for a mainstream audience and scheduled on the main channel of TV 2 on Friday nights. For four seasons it has generated ratings of 13%. This new initiative might be an indication of a coming change to the present state of the television satire tradition in Denmark in the coming years.

REFERENCES

Bruun, H. (Forthcoming). Changing production cultures in entertainment: A case study of television satire. *Northern lights: Film and media studies yearbook: Rethinking film and media production: Creativity, convergence and participation, 10*(1).

Bruun, H. (2011). *Dansk tv-satire. Underholdning med kant.* København, Denmark: Books on Demand GmbH.

Bruun, H. (2007). Satire as cross-media entertainment for public service media. In G. F. Lowe & J. Bardoel (Eds.), *From public service broadcasting to public service media* (pp. 187–199). Göteborg, Sweden: Nordicom.

Bruun, H. (2005). Public service and entertainment: A case study of Danish television 1951–2003. In G. F. Lowe & Per Jauert (Eds.), *Cultural dilemmas in public service broadcasting* (pp. 143–163). Göteborg, Sweden: Nordicom.

Eia, H. (2006). Fra parodi til pastiche. In Y. Kjus & B. Hertzberg Kaare (Eds.), *Humor i medierne* (pp. 183–198). Oslo, Norway: Cappelens Forlag.

Dyer, R. (2007). *Pastiche.* London, England: Routledge.

Hall, J. (2006). *The rough guide to British cult comedy.* London, England: RoughGuides.

Kjus, Y. (2005). Kanevalets formspråk i humor-TV. *Norsk Medietidsskrift, 3,* 214–231.

Larsen, L. O. (2001). Respektløs moro? Satire og Parodi i 1960-årenes tv-komedie. *Norsk Medietidsskrift, 1,* 5–25.

Schwind, K. (1988). *Satire in funktionalen Kontexten.* Tübingen, Germany: Gunter Narr Verlag.

Wagg, S. (2002). Comedy, politics and permissiveness: The "satire boom" and its inheritance. *Contemporary Politics, 8*(4), 319–334.

Live From New York, It's the Fake News! *Saturday Night Live* and the (Non)Politics of Parody

Amber Day

Ethan Thompson

Though *Saturday Night Live*'s "Weekend Update" has become one of the most iconic of fake news programs, it is remarkably unfocused on either satiric critique or parody of particular news conventions. Instead, the segment has been shaped by a series of hosts who made a name for themselves by developing distinctive comic personalities. In contrast to more politically invested contemporary programs, the genre of fake news on *Saturday Night Live* has been largely emptied to serve the needs of the larger show, maintaining its status as just topical, hip, and unthreatening enough to attract celebrities and politicians, as well as a mass audience.

If one were to measure the success of any given news parody program by traditional industry parameters such as numbers of viewers or seasons on the air, *Saturday Night Live*'s "Weekend Update" stands without peer. True, "Update" may make up fewer than 10 minutes of a 90-minute program. But given its history dating back to 1975, the subsequent careers of its various anchors, and the superior ratings of network programming, even late at night, even on the weekend, and even in the "postnetwork" era, "Weekend Update" still enjoys a privileged spot among the "fake news."

As "Update" has maintained its presence on *Saturday Night Live* (*SNL*) for so long, it has also borne witness to profound transformations from the height of the network news in the 1970s to the rise of cable in the 1990s and the convergent 2000s. However, transformations in what the news looks and sounds like (and indeed, what constitutes "news") have not necessarily been the predominant influences on *SNL*'s news parodies. Neither has *SNL*'s longevity been the byproduct of cutting-edge political satire. Despite *SNL*'s posturing as countercultural, rebellious, or at least impolite television, any number of commercial imperatives have taken precedence over the qualities we would highlight as key to "real" satire. As we will explore, the show has certainly included a good deal of political humor over the years, but far less satire. While the former is simply humor about politics and politicians, the latter, though often light-hearted, includes aggression and critique, focusing not just on personalities but also on institutionalized policies, norms, and beliefs. As Gray, Jones, and Thompson (2009) explain, "it is the ability to attack power and pass judgment on the powerful while doing so in playful and entertaining ways that makes satire a particularly potent form of political communication" (p. 12). "Weekend Update" has doubtless had moments of satiric bite, but we argue that the segment has developed primarily as a vehicle for comic personalities rather than as a platform for political critique or parody of news conventions. "Update" has been central to creating and maintaining the *SNL* brand as "hip" or relevant TV, a site for topical humor and new comic voices, as well as a relatively nonthreatening space where "real" celebrities and public figures can play comic versions of themselves. But, in order to be these things, the fake news on *SNL* has historically been emptied of real satire.

Nevertheless, *SNL*'s continued notoriety and its subsequent impact on the "face" of news parody, as well as its ability to grab headlines with successful caricature, from Chevy Chase's Gerald Ford in 1975 to Tina Fey's Sarah Palin in 2008, suggests the importance of understanding what molds the content and tone of its "fake news." The evolutions of *SNL*'s news parody have been greatly shaped by the specific creative and industrial context of the program. We look to developmental and transformative moments in the history of *SNL* to better understand how creative shifts and executive decisions have resulted in limitations upon the satiric and political content of the program, and how "Update" has parodied changes in news programming in the network and postnetwork eras. We also briefly touch on several of the most successful news parody programs that have subsequently developed in the contemporary moment of niche programming (e.g., *The Daily Show*, *The Colbert Report*, and the *Onion News Network*), tracing their divergent approaches.

ORIGINS: THE PREHISTORY OF *SNL*'S FAKE NEWS

News parody was, of course, not invented by *SNL*. In broadcast history, comic commentary on the news dates back to radio. On television, there were several examples of genre-blending satirical news programming in the 1960s that lived somewhere between real news reportage and satire by irreverently interpreting the news of the week, notably, *That Was The Week That Was* in Britain and later the United States and *This Hour Has Seven Days* in Canada. As Day (2011) has argued elsewhere, because of their hybridity these shows could all be considered closer relatives to more political contemporary programs such as *The Daily Show* and *The Colbert Report* than what came after them for several decades, but it was this slipperiness that also made them potentially dangerous during the more jittery network era. All three were cancelled amidst industry worries that they were pushing too far. After their demise, US parodic news found a less contentious home in the variety show, programming more clearly demarcated as light entertainment removed from the political world. Programs such as *Rowan and Martin's Laugh-In* and *The Flip Wilson Show* included news reports alongside other sketches, but the scenario became popular so that by the time *SNL* premiered, it was a well-established format—and a politically safe one at that.

While *SNL* did not invent fake news, its creators and cast did imagine themselves as *reinventing*—or at least tearing down and reconstructing—TV comedy for a new generation. *SNL* has become the standard-bearer (for better or worse) of sketch comedy and parody on television. At its creation, however, both the network and the show's producers conceived and marketed the program as a pronounced break from other television comedies, to the point of even distorting how "different" it really was. NBC was looking for some way to bring back baby boomers who had soured on television, and a space with relative freedom to try out different strategies to do so became available when Johnny Carson no longer wanted "Best of Carson" reruns in syndication on Saturday nights. NBC president Herb Schlosser, who eight years earlier had green-lit *Laugh In*, tasked late-night programming supervisor Dick Ebersol with doing this. Ebersol turned to the man who would become synonymous with *SNL*, a young veteran of Canadian and American television comedies named Lorne Michaels (Shales & Miller, 2002).

Michaels recognized the imperative to create a show that was self-conscious about seeming different from other television, even if its substance was not exactly revolutionary. In the program's first season he explained, "I wanted a show to and for and by the TV generation. 30-year-olds are left out of television. Our reference points, our humor, reflect a life-style never aired on TV" (*Time*, 1976). The generational appeal of *NBC's Saturday Night* (the original title) relied less on innovative comic strategies than it did on articulating an us/them dichotomy based in cultural tastes rather than politics. *SNL* foregrounded the performers as the embodiment of breaks with the "square" connotations of television, claiming that its ragged and uneven nature gave access to authenticity, as opposed to the professionalization and compromise of typical network entertainment. In a 1976 *Rolling Stone* profile of the show, Michaels said:

> I envisioned this show in which all these individual styles were gotten across as purely as possible, with me clearing away the network and technological barricades. This is why *Saturday Night* must stay a *live* show, I've fought for that, to keep it *theater*, a pure communication between writers, players and audience. (Burke, 1976, p. 34)

Michaels conceptualized *SNL* as revolutionary not because it would break new satiric ground but because of this "pure communication"—the presentation of authentic selves, unfiltered, and uncensored. What seems exceptional in retrospect, is how that presentation of authenticity was achieved by opposition to TV artifice through parody. "The nonpareil achievement of 'Saturday Night'," wrote David Tipmore in *The Village Voice*, "is to be the first TV show which could not exist without the form of TV. Parody commercials and 'Weekend Updates' and references to products and soap operas and other TV shows compose its reflexive and conceptual comedy" (p. 21). But as the development of "Update" makes clear, the parody was aimed more at a diffuse "establishment" than at the substance of any particular conventions.

THE MOLD: CHEVY CHASE AND NOT CHEVY CHASE

While *SNL* took advantage of its fringe timeslot, executive thinking at NBC had always been that the show could function as a sort of workshop, spinning off performers and projects that could be moved to primetime (Hill & Weingrad, 1986). The first to leave for other projects was the first "Update" anchor, Chevy Chase. Chase needed no long-term historical perspective to recognize how important the role had been to launching his career. He explained his success in a 1977 *Playboy* article: "The fact that I said my name and said, 'I'm Chevy Chase and you're not' [. . .] That, more than anything, made me stand out. [. . .] I had a showcase—Weekend Update—and you heard my name every week and I got to play to the camera" (p. 220).

One way in which Chase embodied Michaels' rhetoric about unfiltered authenticity was that he had been hired as a writer, and in fact never had a contract as a performer on the show. Once given the "Update" chair, Chase set the tone for the recurring sketch. Rather than focusing on trenchant political commentary, it became more of a vehicle for developing comic personalities, while taking the self-seriousness of public figures down a notch. In this template, the anchor quickly jumped from story to story, creating a rapid-fire succession of one-liner jokes, most of which began with a true-to-life premise or picture but were followed by a comically fictional twist. So, for instance, in the opening joke of the first "Update," Chase announced that "dedication ceremonies for the new Teamsters Union building headquarters took place today in Detroit," a real headline of the day, but he continued, "where union president Fitzsimmons is reported to have said that former president Jimmy Hoffa will always be a cornerstone in the organization" (October 11, 1975). Subsequent jokes in that episode jumped from the Emperor of Japan's visit to Disneyworld, to president Gerald Ford's supposed ineptness, to a new stamp commemorating prostitution (costing 10 cents, but 25 if you want to lick it). As Geoffrey Baym has pointed out, this is a version of what Neil Postman called the "now this" format of news, "in which no topic is placed in wider context or receives elaboration" (2005, p. 263). On the straight news, Baym argues, this reduces the importance of political information to fodder for trivia games with seemingly little real-world importance, while the comic version "further reduces any sense of engagement with or connection to the political public sphere" (p. 263). Indeed, the emphasis on Chase's "Update" was certainly not in-depth political analysis. But its rapid-fire style also effectively parodied the "now this" real news which was itself far from thorough.

As "Update" developed, jokes about politicians and celebrities began to fall into repeated motifs. Most famously, Chase took regular aim at then-President Gerald Ford, creating a vision of Ford as both stupid and hopelessly clumsy, needing the Secret Service to protect him from everyday objects and activities. Each episode would invariably include at least one such joke, usually ending with "alert Secret Service agents" seizing Ford's car/handkerchief/thumb, etc., and "wrestling it to the ground." The appeal of these jokes was intertextually reinforced in other segments as Chase developed a regular routine of impersonating Ford, always ending with a spectacular pratfall. It was a vision of the President that ended up sticking, becoming an indelible piece of Ford's legacy. Following that success, *SNL* has continued to rely on caricature for the bulk of its political humor—but as Jeffrey P. Jones argues, typically these are toothless impersonations with "an emphasis on physical or phonetic resemblance that focuses on the politician's representation of self" (2009, p. 43). Rather than critiquing substantive policy issues, then, these impersonations have tended to focus on personality quirks and physical flaws.

Beyond impersonations, however, part of the appeal of news parody in particular is the pleasure of witnessing the self-seriousness and importance of a newscast deflated and of glimpsing the fallibility of the "reporters." Chase played the part of a newscaster with conviction, rarely if ever breaking to giggle at his own jokes or otherwise acknowledge that he was not really a newscaster. In that sense, he conveyed full belief in his own status and importance as a journalist. However, his character (like those of the correspondents) was often comically unprofessional. On Chase's "Update," the audience got the pleasure of glimpsing a news team's personal secrets and bad behavior. Beginning on the second episode of the program and continuing throughout his tenure at *SNL*, Chase would start the segment while chatting on the phone, seemingly unaware that the cameras were rolling while he indulged in intimate sexual conversation before noticing he was on air. In addition, Chase as anchor could not abide another cast member having something serious to say. When one would appear to deliver a serious response to an "Update" editorial, Chase would make silly faces at the camera as he or she spoke, undercutting whatever the speaker was saying.

Chase's comic lack of professionalism stood in stark contrast to the posturing of network news anchors at the time. Baym (2010) describes the 1970s as the "high-modern" era of television news, which was predicated on a clear distinction between journalism and entertainment and the notion that journalists relayed information in an unbiased manner. He describes how that distinction led to institutionalized strategies that codified disinterested journalism, such as written guidelines at CBS that instructed journalists to appear "in a restrained and disciplined manner" (p. 32). Chase's authentic/parodic voice subverted the high-modern distinction between journalism and entertainment, symbolically striking a generational blow against the establishment as he stumbled through the news or across the stage.

In the 1977 *Playboy* profile, Chase managed to both flippantly downplay the significance of the program's satire ("These folks are the best writers and performers around, but remember that this is just showbiz—so who gives a shit how great we are?" [p. 65]) and take credit for Carter's defeat of Ford ("It's the most heinously egotistical thing to say I had anything to do with it, but I think I must have had some influence" [p. 76]). While Chase seems to contradict himself here, his statements are consistent with *SNL*'s emphasis on the articulation of comic personality and individual perspective as the defining characteristics of comedy freed from old-style television constraints. *SNL* was conceived as TV by and for the TV generation, but without bothering to tether that generational perspective to a particular political ideology. Chase's anchor effectively parodied the "high-modern" news anchor, but "Update" made no explicit critical statements about the media or the political landscape as a whole. Instead, it created a platform for the talents of the cast, raising Chase's profile, and also launching well-remembered characters like Gilda Radner's constantly mistaken Emily Litella.

It would be many seasons before another cast member successfully established "Update" as his or her comic springboard. Jane Curtin, who immediately followed Chase in 1976, was a talented performer adept at delivering punch lines with feigned professionalism and seriousness. However, she did not write her own jokes, was hampered by the mildly sexist material often written for her, and was often teamed with Dan Aykroyd or Bill Murray. "Update" no longer showcased a charismatic writer/performer as it became a spot for recurring characters who were not otherwise written into skits. Despite Chase's early departure, the first five years of *SNL* continued to be a success, and fans and critics consider those years to be the program's golden era.

TRANSITIONS: MILLER, MACDONALD, AND NOT AL FRANKEN

When Michaels left *SNL* at the end of his five-year contract, most of the remaining writers, producers, and cast left with him, and the popularity and critical reputation of *SNL* suffered greatly. Still, fake news continued to play a key role on the show via "Update" and other parodies. Anchor Charles Rocket did a recurring segment titled "The Rocket Report," which parodied soft news segments and "man on the street" interviews. In contrast to Chase's insouciance, Rocket, who worked professionally as a newscaster prior to getting the *SNL* gig, played news anchor straight. Unfortunately, he also said "fuck" on the air and was fired before the 1980–1981 season ended.

The final episode of that disastrous season was hosted by a returning Chase, who assumed the role of anchor again (April 7, 1981). Most notable about that particular "Update," however, was a monologue from Al Franken, who was one of the first writers hired by Michaels, and was thought of by many as the logical choice to replace him as producer. Franken used the opportunity to vociferously complain that he had been passed over yet again in favor of another non-comedian replacing Michaels. This time it was for Dick Ebersol, the executive who had hired Michaels to develop the show. Ebersol did not have a background in comedy, and according to cast and crew, would routinely ask whether a bit was funny.

Ebersol did, however, successfully turn around *SNL*'s fortunes, although the anchor of "Update" was more or less a revolving gig during his years in charge. Brian-Doyle Murray, Mary Gross, Christine Ebersol, Brad Hall, and assorted cast members and even hosts took turns at the desk. Ebersol's final season in 1984–1985 (featuring one-year stints from Billy Crystal, Martin Short, and Christopher Guest) is considered a series high mark, but not because of a renewed sense of social relevance. At the time, an article in *Newsday* noted that "the new 'Saturday Night Live' angles for well-crafted professionalism rather than inspired (or insipid) amateurism" (Robins, 1984). Indeed, it was with the polished characters they created (Crystal's Fernando) or brought with them (Short's Ed Grimley, from *SCTV*) and filmed segments (a Guest-directed film starring Short and Harry Shearer as synchronized swimmers) that the show regained its footing, not through biting satire. As Jones (2009) has noted, *SNL* was surprisingly "hands off" during the Reagan years, and remained so even when Michaels returned in 1985 (p. 42).

The 1985–1986 season, with Michaels back at the helm, proved so disappointing that the following year's premiere began with Madonna reading a formal apology for it. On the bright side, however, two future standouts were hired: Dennis Miller and Jon Lovitz. Miller would prove to be the first "Update" anchor post-Chase to leverage that position into a successful post-*SNL* career. Miller veered further away from news parody than any of the other news anchors, using his time on "Update" to develop a comic persona known for rants and obscure references, not insights on political life or media critique, even relative to Chase's subtle subversion of the network anchor. Indeed, Miller's anchor was a rock star: Each week his "Update" started and ended not with the sound of teletype or a generic instrumental like the real news but with a different rock song. Miller developed a trademark smart-ass style that was the core of the segment. Making no pretensions about being a serious news host, he instead regularly commented on his own delivery and chided or congratulated the audience on their reactions to the jokes. While other "Update" anchors parodied news anchors, Miller himself became an object of parody. Cast member Dana Carvey, host Tom Hanks, and future anchorman Jimmy Fallon all have imitated Miller's characteristic facial ticks, head shaking, and sarcasm-drenched rants and references.

Miller was most famous for that delivery, not for any particular devastating critiques. Nor was there anything populist about Miller's approach. On the contrary, he was known for his misanthropy, often turned against nonurban, nonupwardly mobile America. Wrote Stephen Holden, "Mr. Miller can be scathingly contemptuous of rural and working class people. 'If you make it to age 38 and your job still requires that you wear a name tag, you probably made a serious vocational error'" (1988). He was, however, the star of "Update," and the segment would make him a successful comic and pundit. His HBO program *Dennis Miller Live* lasted nine years, and in addition to appearing on various cable news shows to voice increasingly conservative viewpoints, Miller has had his own daily talk radio show since 2007.

Al Franken, on the other hand, was never given the chance to helm *SNL*'s parodic news. Though he returned to *SNL* in 1985 and continued there for ten years, he never served as "Update" anchor. Franken's failure to take the reins, despite his seniority at *SNL* and many years writing and performing commentary on the segment, is an important piece of the puzzle for under-standing the nature of *SNL* news parody. Franken would achieve greater success post-*SNL* as he became more explicitly political, with best-selling books such as *Rush Limbaugh is a Big Fat Idiot* and *Lies and the Lying Liars Who Tell Them*, and as host of a political talk show on the "liberal" talk radio network, Air America. Franken ended his final radio show with the announcement of his candidacy for the US Senate in 2008, which he won following a bitterly contested recount. Such explicit politics, however, were never part of the *SNL* equation. Miller's and Franken's career trajectories suggest a diffuse politics might have been below the surface of their performances at *SNL* but never fully articulated. Also, while Miller's and Franken's personas/performances became more political, they did so in niche media environs (e.g., talk radio, cable television) which in the 1990s and 2000s increasingly turned to explicit politics to attract audiences.

Franken left *SNL* in protest after Norm MacDonald was chosen in 1994 to follow Kevin Nealon's lackluster run as anchor. Michaels blamed the choice on NBC West Coast head Don Ohlmeyer, who he said believed Franken was too associated with the "old" show (Shales & Miller, 2002, p. 411). NBC's decision could very well have been based on perceptions of gener-ational appeal (MacDonald's youth to Franken's "oldness"), but it also resulted in a less political tone for "Update." MacDonald relished being apolitical. He was uninterested in the "real" news, claimed only to read the sports page, and relied upon writer-producer Jim Downey to stay current about politics, which he said he "had no interest in at all" (Shales & Miller, p. 413). Instead, he had his own favored topics, such as the ongoing saga of OJ Simpson's murder trial, and a long-running fixation with jokes about anal rape in prison and how much the Germans love David Hasselhoff. Like Miller, he pointed to the fact that he was not a real newscaster, frequently using the opening tag-line "I'm Norm Macdonald, and now the fake news" and also happily touting his own lack of knowledge or even interest in what he reported. After a story about the stock market rallying past 4,000 points, for instance, he quipped "I have no idea what that means" (February 25, 1995). While he made no particular critique about the genre of television news, he was, like Chase, playing with the pleasure of taking the news down several pegs. Unlike Chase, he was doing so in the multichannel 1990s, when the self-importance of news was already sig-nificantly deflated. His flippant attitude toward current events was not so much a critique of the news as it was an analogue to the transformation of news content. After all, the "real news" was as obsessed with the OJ Simpson trial as was MacDonald. In that environment, why not just see "Update" as another chance to tell jokes?

NBC executive Ohlmeyer objected. Although he had chosen MacDonald for the anchor chair, he would soon target "Update" as the source of *SNL*'s mid-1990s woes. Ohlmeyer had a clear sense of what he believed the function of the segment should be:

> "Weekend Update" is what gets you to midnight. You tune in and there'll be a couple of weak sketches, and there might be a sketch that works and then a couple that don't work, and that's the nature of the show. But you grew up knowing that "Weekend Update" was coming. [. . .] That's part of the brilliance of Lorne's construction of the show—that you have this thing at midnight that would hold people there for the first half hour even if some of the sketches in the first half hour weren't that strong. (Shales & Miller, 2002, p. 443)

MacDonald, on the other hand, regarded "Update" as a stand-alone arena for what he (and Downey) thought was funny, explaining "we figured it wasn't that important to the show, you know, and we could just do whatever and they'd leave us alone. I didn't even want to go to dress rehearsal because I didn't care about the audience reaction at all" (Shales & Miller, 2002, p. 430). Ohlmeyer argued that rather than serving to pull the audience through the rest of *SNL*, people were starting to tune out during "Update" (p. 432). MacDonald was sacked before the 1997–1998 season was done, and cast member Colin Quinn took over, initiating another uninspired "Update" run.

MacDonald's crime was not his approach toward politics; rather, it was his proprietary attitude toward "Update" and his failure to see the segment's centrality to the overall show. "Update" provides continuity as the one continual, recognizable segment amongst a changing cast of players and sketches, sometimes even driving home the theme used to open the episode. Within a single episode, it can provide variety through its topical humor based on "reality" versus the fictions of the surrounding sketches. Still, it can serve as a zone to develop characters that do not otherwise fit in sketches, as well as a place where "real" people such as celebrities and politicians can make comic appearances. Thus, the primary function of the fake news of "Update" has never been to provide satire or political comment, but to act as a familiar segment and episode linchpin. While critics balked at the notion that firing MacDonald would cure the show's ills, the centrality of "Update" does suggest that changing the anchor can have a powerful impact on the *SNL* brand.

RENEWAL: FINDING A VOICE IN THE 2000S

When "Weekend Update" received a makeover in 2000, Michaels turned to a young cast member who did not even want the job (Jimmy Fallon) and the show's head writer who had seldom appeared in front of the camera (Tina Fey). According to Fallon, Michaels told him, "Tina's going to be the smart, brainy girl, and you're going to be the kind of goofy guy that doesn't do his homework and asks her for answers and stuff" (Shales & Miller, 2002, p. 441). The instructions from Michaels were to foreground performance, again with an emphasis on perspective, not parody, and certainly not politics. Fey and Fallon both affected a vaguely professional demeanor, but like Miller and Macdonald, they would acknowledge the artifice of the sketch, regularly commenting on their own and each other's jokes or the audience's reactions. True to Michaels' instructions, each played up a particular version of themselves. Throughout his tenure on "Update," Fallon came off as an amiable, goofy guy who was thoroughly enjoying himself on the set, but who was neither political nor knowledgeable about current events. This was set up on their first episode together when a number of the night's jokes were focused on the recent 2000 presidential debates. Fey attempts to engage Fallon in a conversation about the debate, but he reveals, to Fey's feigned annoyance, that he found it too boring to sit through so he ended up watching *Dark Angel* instead (October 7, 2000). For her part, Fey portrayed herself as slightly nerdy and awkward and as more politically invested. As with the other hosts, while these are crafted personas, they are rooted in their real personalities rather than in parody.

For her part, as head writer, Tina Fey gave herself more barbed zingers, visibly taking pleasure in landing a particularly good one. Says Fey:

> I wanted to make sure I felt that the point of view of the jokes was in keeping with [. . .] my own point of view of the story. And Lorne said to not worry about it as a parody of the news so much

anymore. We use that when it helps us and not worry about it when it doesn't. Because there've been so many parodies and satires of TV newscasts over the years. (Shales & Miller, 2002, p. 442)

Since most of her tenure on the show was during George W. Bush's presidency, many of her jokes were directed his way. For instance, in the midst of the scandal over Valerie Plame's blown cover, Fey announced:

> As of yesterday, the Bush administration said that they still hadn't found the source of the White House leak that outed a woman as a CIA operative. So, just to recap, here are the things President Bush can't find: the White House leak, weapons of mass destruction in Iraq, Saddam Hussein, Osama bin Laden, a link between Saddam Hussein and Osama bin Laden, the guy who sent the anthrax though the mail, and his own butt with two hands and a flashlight. (October 4, 2003)

Though Fey also delivered plenty of fluffy one-liners, she was cuttingly direct when tackling an issue she cared about. For example, after a true-to-life headline about scientists working on producing genetically modified onions missing the enzyme that makes one cry, Fey cupped her hands to her mouth and shouted, "Hey guys, AIDS! There's still a lot of people dying of AIDS. Put the onion thing on the back burner and cure AIDS!" (October 19, 2002).

True to its well-established template, "Update" in the 2000s remained primarily a platform for jokes delivered by specific comic personalities; in this case, Fey's persona was a particularly critical one. Fey, more than any of the other "Update" anchors, periodically spoke her mind about larger political debate and public life, similar to the more politically invested *Daily Show* and *Colbert Report*. For Fey, though, this would only be one joke among many, whereas Stewart or Colbert frequently engage in ten-minute explorations of political issues. Fallon later left *SNL* and was replaced by Amy Poehler, who cultivated something of a quirky, upbeat persona, frequently hinting that she was an enthusiastic pot-smoker and party animal. Like Fey, though, she also became linked with more political material, particularly during the 2008 election season.

In what is probably the most explicitly political moment on *SNL* ever, Fey and Poehler endorsed Hillary Clinton as Democratic candidate on the February 23 show, arguing that primary voters should elect her because "bitches get things done." Poehler's and Fey's profiles would increase even more due to their impressions of candidates—Poehler's Clinton and Fey's Sarah Palin. Though these impersonations occurred almost exclusively in other parts of the program (with the exception of one "Update" installment briefly visited by the real Sarah Palin), they were intertextually reinforced by "Update" jokes, and created a buzz that stoked audience interest in political humor.

The skit that first caught popular attention opened the program in September 2008. Fey, who had by then left the program for her own show, *30 Rock*, returned to impersonate Sarah Palin alongside Poehler as Clinton, the two of whom were supposedly collaborating for a joint statement on sexism in the election. Poehler portrayed Clinton as quietly seething over the fact that Palin was still in the race when she was not, as Fey's Palin vamped for the camera and made obtuse policy statements such as her idea that global warming "is just God hugging us closer" (September 13, 2008). While Clinton came off at worst as a sore loser, Palin was depicted as absurdly unqualified for office. The skit became an immediate internet sensation and was rebroadcast and discussed on "real" news shows. The impression of Palin in particular resonated with audiences and Fey was pressed into service several more times, while the show's election-focused skits moved to the forefront of popular cultural attention. As Gray et al. (2009,

March 20) have argued, "Fey's sketches bristled with judgment and aggression. This wasn't just mocking Gerald Ford for being clumsy or Hillary Clinton for wearing pantsuits; something important was being said." Fey largely used Palin's own words and embellished them to highlight their naivety and nonsense, ultimately creating a vision of the politician as hopelessly vapid and uninformed. It was, in fact, more satiric than the vast majority of *SNL*'s material, including "Update."

TRANSFERENCE: OTHER SEGMENTS, OTHER SHOWS

Oddly enough, the delivery of the news on "Weekend Update" in the 2000s bears closer resemblance to network news of the 1970s than contemporary "real news." Profound changes have been brought about by changing ideas about the economic role of news amidst the greater competition for viewers in the multichannel era. In contrast to the "high-modern" news of the 1970s with its assumptions of a clear distinction between journalism and entertainment, Baym (2010) describes the postmodern "turn toward infotainment, the hybridization of genres of broadcast journalism and televisual entertainment" (p. 41). While the "high-modern" news relied upon relaying information and long "actuality" clips, the truth of which were assumed to be self-apparent, postmodern news relies upon "packages" of visual imagery and sound bites to "narrativize" the real. "Update" rarely puts together such news packages, and instead continues the model of one or two anchors at a desk, going through the "top stories" in order to set up one joke after another. As such, they bear little resemblance to the carefully produced packages that now dominate TV news. As Fey mentioned, "Update" turns to news parody only when it helps them because there have been so many news parodies by now. In contrast, parody of the news package is a mainstay of *The Daily Show*, and several scholars (Baym, 2010; Day, 2011; Jones, 2010) have shown that that program deals largely in critical deconstruction of how TV news constructs the "true" and the "real." Most recently, the *Onion News Network* meticulously reproduces the postmodern aesthetic of cable news, taking aim at its excesses and extravagance.

However, as the popular response to Fey's Palin impersonation shows, "Update" is not the only place on *SNL* where it has been possible to experiment with parodic material. Because "Update" has avoided extended news parody or political critique, *SNL* has produced other one-time segments created for this purpose. In the early seasons, Jane Curtin played host on a roster of fake programs even as she was hosting "Update," perfecting her air of authority while interviewing absurd guests. Many of these were faux talk show programs, but over the years, fake news reports of varying types have also increased. Mentioned earlier, "The Rocket Report" amounted to a "soft news" parody that was featured in eight of the 11 episodes Charles Rocket appeared on before he was fired. A number of others have been parodies of particular programs; for example, spoof versions of the *Charlie Rose Show* or *Meet the Press*. One particular parodic target repeatedly used to open the show in the 2000s was *Hardball with Chris Matthews*. In it, Darrell Hammond, a cast member particularly gifted at impersonations, plays real life newsman Chris Matthews as a constantly shouting, cantankerous host who takes pleasure in the craziness of his guests, asking them serious questions, but then reveling in the absurd extremes of their positions. For example, in an episode aired in the early stages of the "War on Terror" in Afghanistan, then-Attorney General John Ashcroft (played by Senator John McCain who hosted *SNL* that evening) is portrayed as rabidly anti-libertarian, announcing that "as Americans, we will never truly be free until each and every one of us is afraid of being thrown into jail," and boasting that he has been able to "detain tens of thousands of potential American terrorists for months at a time for little or no reason, just like the founding fathers dreamed" (October 19, 2002). His counterpart, a faux representative from the ACLU, argues that detained terrorists should be given guns and badges and allowed to police the police as a system of checks and balances. Thus, the segment achieves its own political "balance," and the fact that the Republican "hawk" McCain could caricature Ashcroft suggests the critique that US policies were seriously encroaching upon civil liberties was by then familiar and comfortable.

Segments such as these become a platform for parody of a particular news program and a rotating slate of pundits. The typical formula begins with a public figure's perceived views and personality quirks and then exaggerates both to comical extremes. The humor can sometimes be stinging, certainly as far as the individual targets are concerned, but because these segments tend to be premised on the idea that all of the personalities are kooky and the positions absurd (none really more so than others), they rarely incorporate any clearly defined social critique. Rather, the take-away is that the public square is dominated by a crazy cast of characters. This would seem to support many of the recurrent criticisms of political humor, which charge that the genre encourages cynicism and retreat from political ideals. Indeed, much political humor, including much produced by *SNL*, could be described as the "equal opportunity offender" style of comedy which paints all players as flawed, sending the message that everyone is equally inept and immoral and that not much can be done about it—an arguably cynical view.

Since *The Daily Show* has gained prominence, this cynicism charge frequently has been lobbed its way. Hart and Hartelius (2007), for example, warn that Jon Stewart "saps the audience's sense of political possibility" (p. 263). We would argue, however (as have many others), that *The Daily Show* and *The Colbert Report* do precisely the opposite. Though these programs do take pot-shots at individuals, they also dissect policy, breaking down the agenda behind political talking points, and pointing out where media coverage of a particular issue is lacking, often very clearly taking a position on the issue. More importantly, they imply that there can and should be *alternatives* to the problems they highlight, gesturing toward desired-for solutions rather than simple withdrawal. The way in which the cynicism critique is marshaled, though, often unhelpfully lumps all political humor together, assuming that it all operates in the same way and is received similarly by audiences. It is likely even too simplistic to say that the parodic news on *SNL* is always of one type. "Update" has had moments of critical satire, while some of its other news parody skits have pointed to the particular (correctable) failings of the news media, such as a segment titled Action 8 Newswatch, which highlighted the tendency of news shows to rely on fear as a means of hooking their audience (Oct. 2, 1999). But, as we have argued, due to a number of executive and creative decisions, the show itself, and "Update" in particular, has *chosen* a path other than that of trenchant satire and political critique.

Of course, it is important to acknowledge that *The Daily Show* and *The Colbert Report* were created and continue to thrive during the post-network era of niche broadcasting, a different world from the one *SNL* originally entered, one in which there is far less worry about appealing to a mass audience or guarding against offense. These newer shows also are entirely devoted to news parody and critique, while "Update" fights for airtime amongst all manner of comic sketches and musical performances. It is unsurprising, then, that the fake news on *SNL* is often emptied of satiric critique, and instead generally serves to maintain the program's topical-but-not-political brand.

CONCLUSION

Of these successful American programs that have constituted a boom in news parody since the late 1990s, there has been a split in terms of their relative investment in genre parody, satiric critique, and comedic personalities. While the correspondents of *The Daily Show* are committed to the fiction of the newscast, anchor Jon Stewart is not, as his comedy is often built on his own personal reactions to the political hypocrisies of the day. Stephen Colbert exists somewhere in-between as he maintains the fiction that he is a pompous, conservative pundit, but provides sly winks to the audience to make his real opinions clear. The *Onion News Network*, on the other hand, is built almost entirely on its unblinking commitment to parody the cable news form. Its humor lies primarily in its note-for-note re-creations of the excesses of broadcasters such as CNN. The program is full of ridiculously overwrought graphics and music, weirdly boastful catch phrases, and absurdly high tech gizmos used to illustrate little. In that sense, *ONN* is closer to the occasional *SNL* parodies of shows such as *Hardball* than it is to "Weekend Update." However, its humor is far darker, and its critique dryer than the comedy derived from the wacky parade of characters on *SNL*.

Both *The Daily Show* and *The Colbert Report* have proven successful by cable industry standards of audience share, and they have already logged respectable numbers of seasons on air, and garnered considerable critical acclaim. *ONN* will have to prove that a strictly news parody program can be successful in the long-run without the comic personalities and non-news parody segments of *SNL,* or the biting critique of up-to-the-minute political developments that Stewart's and Colbert's audiences have grown to crave.

As noted, *SNL* was conceived as a program that could succeed as fringe programming, but also could spin off performers into primetime slots for more mainstream TV comedies. By those criteria, "Weekend Update" is more successful than ever. Fallon, Fey, and Poehler all left the anchor chair and ended up elsewhere on NBC television: Fallon as host of "Late Night" (Lorne Michaels, Executive Producer), Fey as creator and star of the sitcom *30 Rock* (Lorne Michaels, Executive Producer), and Amy Poehler as star of *Parks & Recreation.* While "Weekend Update" may fulfill the spin-off promise of *SNL* imagined at its creation, Colbert and Stewart succeed in a niche manner unavailable in 1975. That is, they enjoy a committed following that hungers for the satiric deconstruction of political debate, and tune in nightly in numbers large enough to satisfy cable television executives. But what also is not likely is that NBC or Michaels will start thinking of Stewart or Colbert as their competition in the near future. Michaels and crew may have started out with one hand "flipping the bird" at the establishment and mainstream society, but as Jones (2009) has noted, *SNL* has effectively ceded the audience for cutting-edge satire to cable. Says Michaels, "We're a big tent show. We bring a coalition of tastes. A cable show can do a 1 rating and be enormously popular. We're not that show" (p. 46). To borrow a metaphor from sports, it's not that the playing field for news parody has changed. It's that news parody shows like Colbert's, Stewart's, and *ONN* play on a different field, with different equipment, for fans looking for a different kind of game.

Having been a leader in its game for so long, *SNL* continues to benefit from being a popular cultural staple. It remains a show that celebrities are honored to host, and it is just topical and hip enough to make it attractive even for politicians to drop by to play comic versions of themselves. Such appearances, regardless of possible PR benefits or effects upon the electoral process, help maintain *SNL*'s status. Michaels, NBC, and his cast and crew have learned that the program will always be criticized as uneven, and that every few years there will be speculation of its imminent cancellation. Nevertheless, the *SNL* formula for "fake news" has proven resilient.

REFERENCES

Baym, G. (2005). *The Daily Show*: Discursive integration and the reinvention of political journalism. *Political Communication, 22*, 259–276.

Baym, G. (2010). *From Cronkite to Colbert: The evolution of broadcast news*. Boulder, CO: Paradigm.

Burke, T. (1976, July 15). Laughing, scratching, mocking, smirking, stumbling, bumbling and pratfalling into the twisted hearts and minds of America . . . live, from New York . . . it's NBC's . . . *Saturday Night! Rolling Stone, 217*, 32–39, 68, 70, 72, 75.

Day, A. (2011) *Satire and dissent: Interventions in contemporary political debate*. Bloomington, IN: Indiana University Press.

Gray, J., Jones, J., & Thompson, E. (2009). The state of satire, the satire of state. In J. Gray, J. Jones, & E. Thompson (Eds.), *Satire TV: Politics and comedy in the post-network era* (pp. 3–36). New York, NY: NYU Press.

Gray, J., Jones, J., & Thompson, E. (2009, March 20). Using one of its lifelines: Does politics save *Saturday Night Live* from oblivion? *Flow TV*. Retrieved from http://flowtv.org/2009/03/%E2%80%9Cusing-one-of-its-lifelines-does-politics-save-saturday-night-live-from-oblivion-jonathan-gray-fordham-university-jeffrey-p-jones-old-dominion-university-and-ethan-thompson-texas-a/

Hart, R., & Hartelius, J. (2007). The political sins of Jon Stewart. *Critical Studies in Media Communication, 24*(3), 263–272.

Hill, D., & Weingrad, J. (1986). *Saturday night: A backstage history of* Saturday Night Live. New York, NY: Beech Tree Books.

Holden, S. (1988, January 8). Comedy: Dennis Miller. *New York Times*. Retrieved from http://www.nytimes.com/1988/01/08/arts/comedy-dennis-miller.html?src=pm

Jones, J. (2009). With all due respect: Satirizing presidents from *Saturday Night Live* to *Lil' Bush*. In J. Gray, J. Jones, & E. Thompson (Eds.), *Satire TV: Politics and comedy in the post-network era* (pp. 37–63). New York, NY: NYU Press.

Jones, J. (2010). *Entertaining politics: Satiric television and political engagement* (2nd ed.). Lanham, MD: Rowman & Littlefield.

Playboy interview: NBC's *Saturday Night*. (1977, May). *Playboy, 24*(5), 63–66, 68, 70–72, 76, 78–82, 86, 88, 212–215, 220–222, 224, 228.

Robins, W. (1984, October 21). "Saturday Night's" new face. *Newsday*, section 2, p. 3.

Shales, T., & Miller, J. A. (2002). *Live from New York: An uncensored history of* Saturday Night Live. Boston, MA: Little, Brown and Company.

Time. (1976, February 2). Flakiest night of the week. Retrieved from http://www.time.com/time/magazine/article/0,9171,945531,00.html

Tipmore, D. (1975, November 24). NBC's "Saturday Night" milks America's sacred cows. *Village Voice*, pp. 20–21.

Young, D. G. (2008). *The Daily Show* as the new journalism: In their own words. In J. Baumgartner & J. Morris (Eds.), *Laughing matters: Humor and American politics in the media age* (pp. 241–259). New York, NY: Routledge.

Index

Media Accountability

Who Will Watch the Watchdog in the Twitter Age?

Edited by William Babcock

A small collection of well-honed tools has been employed for some time by media practitioners and the public to help maintain and improve the credibility of journalism and the mass media. These media accountability tools have included ethics codes, media critics, news councils, ombudsmen, journalism reviews and pubic/civic journalism initiatives. Now, in the 21st Century, the mass media are increasingly being buffeted by a perfect storm of declining subscribers and audience share, dwindling advertising revenue, changing corporate demands, unpredictable audiences and new-media competition. If journalism and the mass media are to stay afloat and be credible, the media accountability toolbox needs to contain suitable tools for the job, which begs the question: *Who will Watch the Watchdog in the Twitter Age?* This book contains answers to this question from the perspective of 17 media ethics experts from around the globe. Their answers will help shape and define for years to come the tools in the media ethics toolbox.

This book was originally published as a special issue of the *Journal of Mass Media Ethics*.

December 2011: 234 x 156: 176pp
Hb: 978-0-415-69839-9
£80 / $125